# The State of
# Graduate Education

## Brookings Dialogues on Public Policy

*The presentations and discussions at Brookings conferences and seminars often deserve wide circulation as contributions to public understanding of issues of national importance. The Brookings Dialogues on Public Policy series is intended to make such statements and commentary available to a broad and general audience, usually in summary form. The series supplements the Institution's research publications by reflecting the contrasting, often lively, and sometimes conflicting views of elected and appointed government officials, other leaders in public and private life, and scholars. In keeping with their origin and purpose, the Dialogues are not subjected to the formal review procedures established for the Institution's research publications. Brookings publishes them in the belief that they are worthy of public consideration but does not assume responsibility for their accuracy or objectivity. And, as in all Brookings publications, the judgments, conclusions, and recommendations presented in the Dialogues should not be ascribed to the trustees, officers, or other staff members of the Brookings Institution.*

# The State of Graduate Education

*Papers by* BRUCE L. R. SMITH

ROBERT G. SNYDER

MICHAEL S. MC PHERSON

F. KARL WILLENBROCK

JAMES W. JOHNSON

LINDA S. WILSON

JOHN C. VAUGHN

MICHAEL J. PELCZAR, JR.

HARVEY BROOKS

*presented at a conference at the Brookings Institution, November 15–16, 1984*

*Edited by* BRUCE L. R. SMITH

THE BROOKINGS INSTITUTION

*Washington, D.C.*

*Copyright © 1985 by*
*THE BROOKINGS INSTITUTION*
*1775 Massachusetts Avenue, N.W.,*
*Washington, D.C. 20036*

*Library of Congress Catalog Number 85-072214*
*ISBN 0-8157-7995-X*

9  8  7  6  5  4  3  2  1

# About Brookings

THE BROOKINGS INSTITUTION is a private nonprofit organization devoted to research, education, and publication in economics, government, foreign policy, and the social sciences generally. Its principal purpose is to bring knowledge to bear on the current and emerging public policy problems facing the American people. In its research, Brookings functions as an independent analyst and critic, committed to publishing its findings for the information of the public. In its conferences and other activities, it serves as a bridge between scholarship and public policy, bringing new knowledge to the attention of decisionmakers and affording scholars a better insight into policy issues. Its activities are carried out through three research programs (Economic Studies, Governmental Studies, Foreign Policy Studies), a Center for Public Policy Education, a Publications Program, and a Social Science Computation Center.

The Institution was incorporated in 1927 to merge the Institute for Government Research, founded in 1916 as the first private organization devoted to public policy issues at the national level; the Institute of Economics, established in 1922 to study economic problems; and the Robert Brookings Graduate School of Economics and Government, organized in 1924 as a pioneering experiment in training for public service. The consolidated institution was named in honor of Robert Somers Brookings (1850–1932), a St. Louis businessman whose leadership shaped the earlier organizations.

Brookings is financed largely by endowment and by the support of philanthropic foundations, corporations, and private individuals. Its funds are devoted to carrying out its own research and educational activities. It also undertakes some unclassified government contract studies, reserving the right to publish its findings.

A Board of Trustees is responsible for general supervision of the Institution, approval of fields of investigation, and safeguarding the independence of the Institution's work. The President is the chief administrative officer, responsible for formulating and coordinating policies, recommending projects, approving publications, and selecting the staff.

# Editor's Preface

THIS VOLUME is the result of a Brookings conference held on November 15–16, 1984, reviewing the efforts of the nation's universities to sustain the quality of graduate programs. The conference planners felt that even though advanced training faces challenges as great as those of elementary and secondary education, it has received little attention. Nine educators and scholars prepared papers for the conference which were then revised in the light of the conference discussion.

The National Science Foundation supported the project. I am particularly grateful to Carlos Kruytbosch of the NSF, who was a patient and understanding program officer and a valuable contributor to the whole effort. His NSF colleagues Penny Foster and Mary Golliday attended the conference and made many useful suggestions. Laurence Berlowitz, of the Massachusetts Biotechnology Research Institute, was an early proponent of this review of graduate education and helped give focus to the task.

Those who played important parts in shaping the project are so numerous that I cannot thank them all by name. But I must acknowledge the role of my fellow contributors, who acted as an informal steering committee throughout the effort and were generous, hardworking, and good-humored beyond any reasonable expectation. I deeply value their friendship and colleagueship. We in turn benefited from the informed and stimulating comments of the other conference participants. They were an outstanding group from government, the universities, and industry who took their responsibilities seriously, raised our sights, and brought an uncommon wisdom and experience to the discussion.

David Z. Robinson, executive vice-president, Carnegie Corporation of New York; Richard C. Atkinson, chancellor, University of California at San Diego; Robert Rosenzweig, president, Association of American Universities; Bernard V. Khoury, vice-president for academic affairs, University of Maryland; and Raymond H. Dawson, vice-president, University of North Carolina, did not attend the conference but contributed significantly to my thinking. Michael McPherson, of Brookings, kindly provided detailed comments on the introductory chapter, as did Harvey Brooks, of Harvard University. Sherman Beychok, of Columbia University, generously shared his knowledge of the life sciences and of the effect of the biological revolution on society.

The volume is dedicated to my late friend Leon Peres, of the University of Melbourne, who was a close observer of the American research system and who spent many hours discussing this project with me.

Deborah Styles edited the manuscript; Hedy E. Sladovich prepared an extensive bibliography for the authors and served as research associate. Timothy Bladek, Carol Graham, and Alex P. Orfinger assisted in the conference preparation and in editorial, proofreading, and research chores. Maxine R. Mennen smoothly coordinated conference arrangements.

BRUCE L. R. SMITH

*August 1985*
*Washington, D.C.*

# Contents

# Contents

# Graduate Education in the United States

BRUCE L. R. SMITH

THE QUALITY of the nation's educational system has recently become a matter of widespread concern. Major reports have focused public attention in particular on the elementary and secondary school systems, on undergraduate education, and, somewhat less, on the financial problems confronting students as they seek formal education beyond the B.A. and B.S. levels.[1] Despite the attention given to elementary and secondary education and to undergraduate education, the linkages among the different levels of the nation's educational system have not been fully explored, and the role of graduate education in the life of the nation has been neglected.[2] Yet some of the most far-reaching changes seem to be occurring here. Certain changes seem bound to affect graduate education in important ways: changes in student demographic trends, in the life-styles of faculty, in the rapid advance of knowledge and the proliferation of new fields, in the capital intensity of the research effort, in the transformation wrought by the new information technologies, in the traditional career expectations of advanced students, and in other areas. Consequently the Brookings Institution decided to convene a

1. See, for example, U.S. Secretary of Education, *Report of the National Commission on Excellence in Education* (Government Printing Office, 1982); National Commission on Student Financial Assistance, *Signs of Trouble and Erosion: A Report on Graduate Education in America,* A Report to Congress and the President (Washington, D.C.: The Commission, 1983); Twentieth Century Fund, *Task Force Report on Higher Education* (New York: The Fund, 1982); National Institute of Education, *Involvement in Learning: Realizing the Potential of American Higher Education* (Washington, D.C.: NIE, 1984). For a thoughtful critique, see Paul E. Peterson, "Did the Education Commissions Say Anything?" *The Brookings Review,* Winter 1983.

2. Compare, however, Robert M. Rosenzweig, *The Research Universities and Their Patrons* (Berkeley: University of California Press, 1982); John Brademas, "Graduate Education: Signs of Trouble and Erosion," *Change,* March 1984, special issue devoted to graduate education; Council on Graduate Schools, *Recent Developments in Graduate Programs* (Washington, D.C.: CGS, October 1982); Bruce L. R. Smith and Joseph J. Karlesky, *The State of Academic Science* (New Rochelle, N.Y.: Change Magazine Press, 1977); National Board on Graduate Education, *Federal Policy Alternatives toward Graduate Education* (Washington, D.C.: NBGE, 1974). For a review of earlier studies on graduate education, see Charles V. Kidd, "Graduate Education: The New Debate," *Change,* May 1974.

conference in November 1984, with the assistance of a grant from the National Science Foundation, to focus attention on the adequacy of the knowledge base, the problems, and the issues in this advanced level of the nation's educational system. In the system of elementary, secondary, undergraduate, graduate, and "lifelong" education, our focus was primarily on the graduate level, and in particular on the fields of science, social science, and engineering. We also found it necessary, however, to include the undergraduate context and the emerging patterns of mid-career education in many professions. This volume presents the papers prepared for the conference as revised by their authors to reflect the discussion among the conference participants.

*Some boundaries*

Graduate education is a broad concept whose boundaries are fuzzy. As of 1982 there were some 399,000 students enrolled in graduate programs in the science, social science, and engineering fields in the nation's universities (out of a total population of some 1,343,000 graduate students in all fields). As Robert Snyder's paper explains, the students are disproportionately clustered in the great research universities of the country, where a large part of the research effort is concentrated. The Ph.D. is most commonly thought of as the advanced degree, but there are forty-nine other types of doctoral programs listed in a current registry of graduate offerings.

Of the students enrolled in graduate programs in the physical, biological, and social sciences, and in engineering fields, some 56,000 received master's-level degrees and nearly 19,000 received doctoral degrees in 1982. The central themes of this inquiry are the growth of this system, the close linkage between the educational and the organized research effort, the strength and vitality of the system in the face of rapid changes within the scientific fields and in the external environment, and the contribution of university science and engineering programs to the achievement of wider social goals. The authors are aware that the humanities are a vital part of the university and of our culture, and some papers—most notably that of Michael McPherson—deal with selected aspects of the humanities. The primary focus, however, is on the science and engineering fields. Our conclusions about the larger problems facing the universities arise from a vantage point that emphasizes those fields.

The aim of these papers in general is more diagnostic than prescriptive. The papers seek to identify a baseline, including suggestions for new sources of data where these are needed, by which observers can begin to make assessments of the current state of graduate education. Blueprints for action, clarion calls to decisionmakers, and appeals for public support are not the primary thrust of the volume. The authors hope, nevertheless, that the following pages will at least help to focus public attention on the most important problems facing the universities and the nation in graduate education. Graduate education relates to the most cherished social goals—a strong national defense, enhanced international economic competitiveness, and the quality of life—and a broad base of support exists for a strong national effort.

Four-year liberal arts colleges, although they provide an important source of future scientists and engineers, are largely excluded from our attention, as are the galaxies of two- and four-year community colleges, trade and proprietary schools, and freestanding centers set up by individual faculty members outside of the formal university structure.

The institutional boundaries between the universities, as the traditional providers of graduate educational services, and other parts of society, as consumers of those services, have begun to blur at the edges, especially with respect to the role of industry in providing post-entry training to engineering and scientific professionals and with respect to the new technology networks that package knowledge for presentation at decentralized locations. This potential competition between universities and other institutions is a significant factor, especially the booming corporate educational efforts whose dimensions we have only recently begun to recognize.[3] The "industry" that remains our focus of inquiry here, however, consists of the nation's eighty research universities (both public and private) classed as Doctorate I and II by the Carnegie Council, the remaining doctorate-granting institutions (which number nearly two hundred), and the somewhat larger number of educational institutions providing only the first professional degree beyond their undergraduate programs.[4]

The graduate education system is highly competitive, decentralized, and dynamic. A select group of traditional elite institutions provides the center of gravity. Nonetheless, fortunes rise and fall, key people move, and rankings shift across the broad spectrum of the scientific disciplines. Unlike the practice in many other nations, the university is the "home of science" in the American context; that is, it performs much of the important basic research

3. Nell F. Eurich, *Corporate Classrooms: The Learning Business* (Princeton University Press, 1985).

4. Carnegie Council on Policy Studies in Higher Education, *A Classification of Institutions of Higher Education* (Berkeley: University of California Press, 1976).

in the nation (about half when measured in dollar terms, but such figures alone do not convey the full role that the university plays in setting the tone and direction of the nation's entire basic research effort).[5]

Within the universities, although there have always been large research centers, organized across traditional departmental lines, individual professors in collaboration with small groups of graduate students carry on most of the research. This close tie between the research effort and the educational process is another distinctive feature of the American system, as is the expectation that the graduate student will become an independent investigator at an early stage of his or her career.

A combination of federal, state, industrial, philanthropic, and institutional funding supports the system, and the individual scientist or engineer is expected to show entrepreneurial talents to gain support for chosen lines of inquiry. Faculty positions are typically allocated within the university according to formulas that emphasize undergraduate teaching needs. This system, with its complex fiscal and administrative relationships and with the delicate understandings among diverse actors that sustain it, forms the object of our inquiry.

*Enrollment trends and shifts in student career expectations*

Fears of sharply declining graduate enrollments have concerned educators for a decade since the late Allan Cartter first called attention to the implications of demographic changes. More recent reports have focused renewed attention on the problem.[6] Such studies have been based on broad demographic trends affecting the 18- to 24-year-old age cohort. The studies have projected potential future enrollments based on assumptions about the college participation ratio, the state of the economy, and other relevant variables. The conference participants addressed this problem as an initial concern and sought an accurate profile of aggregrate enrollment patterns (even while recognizing the limits of a purely macro-level analysis). Perhaps surprisingly, as detailed in Robert Snyder's paper, the sharp drops in overall graduate enrollments predicted in the earlier studies did not turn out to be the reality—at least up to 1982, the last year for which definitive

5. Dael Wolfle, *The Home of Science: The Role of the University* (McGraw-Hill, 1972). See also National Science Foundation, *Federal Support to Universities, Colleges, and Selected Non-profit Institutions, 1981–84* (GPO, 1984).

6. Allan M. Cartter, *Ph.D.'s and the Academic Labor Market,* Report prepared for the Carnegie Commission on Higher Education (McGraw-Hill, 1976); David W. Breneman, *Predicting the Response of Graduate Education to No Growth,* Reprint 310 (Brookings, 1976); William G. Bowen, *Report of the President, Princeton University, 1981* and *1984.*

figures are available. The reasons for this lie in the increase in foreign student enrollments and in the increasing enrollment of women in graduate education, most notably in the life sciences.

The increase in foreign students (and the decreasing numbers of qualified U.S. applicants) in many graduate engineering programs has become striking. Foreign students now constitute slightly more than half of all students enrolled in such programs. The mix of foreign students, moreover, seems to reflect disproportionate numbers from third world nations and from East Asia. Assessment of this trend has been difficult. Most conference participants agree on the importance of the free flow of ideas and peoples across national boundaries. The presence of many talented students from abroad has undoubtedly contributed to the dynamism of the U.S. system of advanced training and research. Almost no one seems willing for the moment to curb the flow of such talent by changes in the immigration laws (such as occurred in the late 1970s with respect to foreign medical school graduates employed in the nation's hospitals) or through the imposition of export controls on the universities (that is, allowing only American citizens to work at university laboratories). The effect of foreign students seems to vary considerably from institution to institution, the traditionally elite universities being much less dependent on foreign students for enrollment in their science and engineering programs. We need to explore this foreign student phenomenon carefully, to gather more accurate data on the numbers of such students, and to assess more fully the implications for the quality of undergraduate instruction. Furthermore, the benefits to the United States of training foreign scientists to rely on the use of American equipment, as well as other potential benefits and costs to the nation (and to other nations) of the students' acculturation, need to be assessed. Before we embrace the concept of serving as the world's science and engineering graduate school, we need more information on its benefits and its costs.

Another trend of great interest is the apparently dramatic shift by undergraduate students in their choices of majors and fields of concentration. As examined in Michael McPherson's paper, the rush to embrace more vocationally oriented fields of study presents a historic dilemma for many American universities—a greater challenge than the growth era of the 1960s. Then, the universities were faced with the need to expand rapidly, but the expansion took place more or less evenly across the traditional fields of specialization and professional study. The humanities, the social sciences, the sciences, and most professional disciplines grew in nearly equal proportions (though Ph.D. programs in engineering grew very rapidly). The universities were thus faced with the need for incremental expansion in all traditional functions. Growth without change characterized the higher education scene in the 1960s. Now this rapid growth, which smoothed over many internal conflicts within the universities and forged a community of interest between the universities and outside parties, is at an end. The shifts in student preferences have created boom or bust conditions across departments and divisions that stretch to the limit the universities' traditional management capacities.

The fallout from the undergraduate trends affects graduate programs because staffing at most institutions is closely related to undergraduate teaching needs. Deans have cushioned the effect of changing labor markets by reassigning teaching responsibilities to areas of heavy student demand. Of course changes have occurred before in the career preferences and most desired fields of study of undergraduates, but the current changes seem to be on an unprecedented scale. For the moment most universities have resisted fundamental change, hoping that the student interest in computer science, business, and other "practical" courses of study will crest. Since institutions of higher learning in the American system are competitive and are responsive to consumer demand, however, they seem to have adapted to student preferences. The adaptations manifest themselves in different ways in different universities: some universities seek to buffer themselves from change and others rush to ride the wave. *Numerus clausus* limits are extending beyond the traditional fields of medicine and law. Universities are adding computer science offerings to many different undergraduate majors, hiring part-time or temporary faculty, changing distribution requirements, and merging or consolidating departments. Market pressures have distorted salary scales in many universities. The same kind of differentials that used to exist only between the salaries of the faculties of the professional schools and those of the faculties of other schools now appear within the arts and sciences faculty as well. Salary compression between faculty recently hired and senior faculty hired before the period of peak demand presents some knotty management issues.

Science and engineering, at first glance, appear to be the beneficiaries of this shift in student interest, but the matter is more subtle than that. In fact, some technical fields, especially those perceived by students to have good job prospects and rapid career payoffs, are highly popular, while the "purer" aspects of mathematics, physics, and chemistry are less popular. Thus the pure sciences and the humanities, as McPherson demonstrates, reflect the reverse sides of the same problem. These departments may suffer from lack of new hires, loss of morale, and salary disadvantages relative to departments in high-demand subjects. Since graduate students in the arts and sciences originate in the pool of undergraduate majors, undergraduate enrollments may have a ripple effect on subsequent graduate enrollments. Hence, pressures have arisen to uncouple hiring from teaching needs. The idea is to provide the nucleus for a continued strong department and research effort in those fields suffering or about to suffer a decline in the number of graduate students.

While the number of nonteaching workers in the university setting has swelled in the past decade, no major university to date has been willing to abandon the policy of the traditional close link between the teaching and research function in graduate education. To do so would invite fundamental changes in the American idea of a university. The nation would be propelled toward the practices of some European nations. With American science and learning still broadly preeminent, few educators will depart from the system that has brought the United States a leading role in the world's intellectual and cultural life. Yet changes are taking place that seem to be working slowly toward a transformation of the system, and merely clinging to the past is not a recipe for sustaining the vitality and dynamism of our institutions of higher learning.

*New patterns of university-industry relations*

Enrollment trends and the shifting career expectations of students are linked to a broad realignment in the relationship between the research universities and private industry. The engineering schools, as analyzed in Karl Willenbrock's paper, most dramatically manifest the changing relationships. Undergraduate engineering programs typically reflect "boom" conditions, while graduate programs seem in danger of atrophy in many institutions. The problems are complex and varied, making generalization difficult, but a common driving force is the explosive growth of new technologies in private industry. University engineering laboratories lag behind the industrial state of the art in key areas. Several decades ago, for example, the universities played an important supporting role in the origins of the computer revolution; some of the most advanced computers were located on campuses. Universities have now generally fallen behind. Only a handful of the nation's universities currently have outstanding computer science departments with strong research programs (and even these, though still playing important roles in such areas as expert systems and computational logic, do not have the access to the most powerful facilities that colleagues in the computer industry or in leading industrial laboratories may regularly enjoy).

In the biological sciences, too, though discoveries in university laboratories made possible the new industries built around genetic engineering, the pace of developments outside the universities has quickened, and the future university role is less clear. One hopes that academic biology and bioengineering will continue to support the growth of the biotechnology industry as, say, chemical engineering supports the chemical industry, geology supports the petroleum industry, electrical and solid state physics support electronics. But this kind of function weakens if the academic community falls so far behind that it is no longer effectively in the picture.

The growth of research capacity in any sector is, of course, good for the country. The dynamic growth of the information, bioengineering, and other new technologies strengthens the nation's economy and justifies its investment in a strong graduate education system. The problem for the universities stems from their need to preserve distinctive characteristics while striving to achieve closer working relations with industry. The new relationships cover a broad front, ranging from simply information exchange, to research support, to licensing arrangements, to sharing of facilities and a wide variety of other arrangements. The universities, however, are not equipped to play the same role as industry in the scale-up of a new technology toward production and commercialization.

While welcoming the strengthened ties with industry, the conference participants devoted attention to several issues posed by the new university-industry relations. One is the need to define the boundaries of public versus proprietary knowledge in such a way as to preserve a common core of knowledge accessible to all. The point is not that proprietary knowledge is unjustified; rather, the object is to devise mechanisms to protect the free movement of ideas, of people, and of techniques across the fields of scholarship within the university and between the academic community and the wider society at a time when commercial and other pressures work against the free traffic of ideas. University involvement in patentable discoveries, user charges for access to data bases, exclusive licenses, temporary publication delays, cataloguing of knowledge in forms that restrict access, national security restrictions on foreign visitations, and a host of other developments pose potential dangers to scientific communication. Each step needs to be measured against the standards of broad access and the free flow of ideas. As intellectual property rights play a larger role in the mushrooming information revolution, it is especially important that we avoid the splintering of knowledge into proprietary fiefdoms.

Another issue is "lifelong learning." Professional workers, and especially those in rapidly developing fields, need to have their professional skills upgraded at various times throughout their careers. Indeed, the society whose sources of employment growth can shift rapidly requires an adaptive underlying skill base; many individuals will pursue several careers in the course of a lifetime. How will such trends affect graduate education? At present universities seem unsure whether education for the initial professional degree should be tailored closely to the initial entry of students into the employment market or whether the kinds of graduate programs offered should aim at maximizing the individual's ability to cope with change over the course of an entire professional career.

Philosophical questions also arise as to the nature of graduate education: is it, like undergraduate education, designed to discipline one's thought, enhance the enjoyment of life, and broaden understanding—only at a higher level? Or is its purpose to provide research skills, specialized knowledge, and training designed to "fit" the manpower needs of an increasingly specialized economy and social order? If the creep of specialism has altered the content of undergraduate programs, can graduate education provide the broader cultural exposure once considered the aim of the undergraduate liberal arts degree? Can the university serve effectively the persons who seek to enhance or to refresh their professional skills at the mid-career level, or is an entirely new set of social institutions necessary for such nontraditional educational programs?

Arrangements between industry and the universities paralleling the clinical training of the teaching hospital are interesting in the context of engineering education, but no proven model of this sort seems to exist. What is certain is that universities across the country have begun to rethink the goals of their graduate programs, including those at the master's level that are the point of entry into various professions and the traditional doctoral programs emphasizing research, and to experiment with their own approaches to the challenge of lifelong learning.

Even traditional doctoral programs have not been immune from change because the rapid advance of knowledge has expanded the range of what can be taught and has forced attention to the essential aspects of the field. Should a student be allowed to spend his or her entire academic career in a single laboratory learning one specialized line of inquiry or technique at the expense of breadth in the traditional discipline? Is there a common body of knowledge, research techniques, or applications that every student should learn in a fast-moving field? Research undertaken for the thesis should normally advance the frontier of knowledge, but is this a realistic aspiration for fields where the university sector has fallen behind industry or the national laboratories? Faculties are beginning to devote increasing attention to the goals of their graduate programs and to have less confidence that there is some unidimensional attribute of quality by which to judge the research-based doctoral program—a debate reminiscent of the efforts at some leading institutions to define a "core" curriculum for the undergraduates.

Academic science and engineering can no longer proceed with only casual attention to the supporting infrastructure for research. No industrial firm would imagine hiring a scientist or an engineer and then turning the individual loose to struggle for the resources and the wherewithal to do the job. A commitment to hire is typically a commitment to back up the individual with the necessary resources to accomplish the initial research objectives (at least until large development costs force hard choices on management). Yet all too often for the university the hiring decision does little more than give the individual a license to hunt for support. The entrepreneurial pressures on faculty members, both senior and junior faculty members, are enormous. This factor, combined with inadequate facilities, creates an unattractive working environment that may deter the incipient young investigator from seeking an academic career. Heavy undergraduate teaching loads, inadequate support, and constant pressure to seek new extramural research funds are the way of life of young academic engineers. The unfavorable contrast with industry often leads the engineer to leave the university setting to join industry immediately after completing the B.S. degree. The universities' difficulties in maintaining modern facilities across all of the engineering fields increase the disincentives to an academic career.

*A shift in the ratio of capital to labor in academic work?*

Research in the American university, as noted above, has typically been carried on by individual professors in collaboration with small groups of graduate students. This quintessential "little science" mode of operation has meant that much of a university's budget has gone to cover the cost of labor inputs. What would happen if the historic ratio of labor to capital were to shift drastically? If university research were to become a more capital-intensive operation? A gradual shift of this sort is exactly what seems to be taking place in field after field (organic chemistry, solid state physics, molecular biology) and in universities across the country. At any rate, university administrators have begun to grasp the true costs of doing business, and they have been led to a more sophisticated understanding of the nonlabor inputs. Like private industry, universities now see that plant and equipment must be modernized, replaced, and paid for in the normal course of business. The value of such investments must be weighed against other factors of production. Donald Kennedy, president of Stanford University, summarizes this shift in outlook:

> In the 1960's, the main problem for department heads in making appointments had to do with billets: that is, with persuading the dean and the provost that the growth potential of our discipline justified the retention of an additional faculty position. A decade later, an interesting transition occurred. Although we still worried about the billets, the main problem became whether we could commit the equipment and space renovations necessary for the new appointee to do the work. The capital cost of the equipment and special facilities, in short, had become larger than the capital value of the endowment necessary to yield the faculty member's salary.[7]

The recognition that there has been a massive capital deficit confronting the universities is part of the new awareness. Since World War II, when the universities first entered into their compact with society as research performers, the issue of capital costs has been left ambiguous. The federal government was buying research from the universities, but normally it did not consider that paying for the capital facilities in which the research activity took place was part of its responsibility. Various forms of institutional support did provide capital funding, as Linda Wilson's paper documents, until 1969. In that year the federal government phased out the last of its major support programs for capital facilities. Since federal support then provided about one-third of the universities' capital costs, this policy shift contributed to the deferred maintenance and the postponed investment in the intervening years.

The universities have attempted to recoup their capital costs to some degree through the indirect costs included in federal research grants. The costs of buildings and maintenance are the fastest growing aspects of indirect costs. The disputes over increasing indirect costs in the past decade reflect the continuing debate over

---

7. Donald Kennedy, "Government Policies and the Cost of Doing Research," *Science*, vol. 227 (February 1, 1985), pp. 480–81.

federal responsibilities for the institutional support of universities. The intensity of these disputes is likely to increase.

Small-scale instrumentation and laboratory equipment, in contrast to physical plant and large facilities, have long been considered integral parts of a research proposal, and hence have been less a matter of contention. Instrumentation requests, however, were often left out or negotiated out of research proposals in the lean years of federal research support (beginning in 1967 and lasting for nearly a decade). Many of the nation's universities thus need to catch up in the area of laboratory instrumentation as well as in space and physical plant. The full implications of the transformation from little science to a more heavily instrumented, costly, and large-scale mode of operation remain to be thought through by university scientists, administrators, and state and federal government officials.

The special concerns stemming from the computer revolution are a complicated part of the larger problem. The computer is a tool increasingly used across virtually all scientific fields. Computer science is itself a discipline linked to electrical engineering, logic, mathematics, philosophy, and cognate fields. It is a discipline that requires both theoretical and experimental inquiry. Knowledge of the techniques—of processing, retrieving, and storing information—becomes indispensable to and somewhat indistinguishable from the progress of science in many disciplines. Computers, including data bases and networks, are thus an urgent concern for research and instructional purposes. As shown in James Johnson's paper, the entire system of academic science and engineering has problems regarding its access to the most powerful computing machines. In addition, the individual campuses must decide what general and special-purpose computing facilities they need and who should pay for them. Overriding issues of intellectual property rights, incompatibility of the different information systems, and cost allocation influence the general debate and the decisions taken at each university. Conference participants generally expressed the view that the universities have fallen behind relative to their position at an earlier stage in the computer revolution and relative to computer use in other sectors of society. Special steps are now needed to ensure that universities participate fully in this major revolution of our times. Graduate education will probably require an environment even richer in computers than the environment of undergraduate studies.

The humanities share in the gradual extension of computer uses into some of their fields as developments push the research libraries into the thick of the information revolution.

A strong minority at the conference expressed the view that, by singling out the computer as a special class of scientific instrument needing favored treatment, we may skew the progress of science too far in the direction of manipulating large quantities of numeric data as against accurate initial measurement of phenomena and hard conceptual thought about physical laws. This group urged balancing the choice of instruments available to the investigator—in effect, providing a market in the choice of instruments for various purposes—instead of treating the computer as a kind of infant industry requiring special attention. Professor Rustum Roy of Pennsylvania State University summed up this view:

> I believe the role of the computer, which is but one tool in the total armamentarium available to the scholar, should not be exaggerated.
>
> Speaking for the applied sciences and engineering, an institution needs a balanced set of synthesis and analytical tools. The potential of the computer in this set of tools varies from discipline to discipline; but to take one example in my own field of materials science and engineering, special computing tools would be far behind the many different tools for synthesis of materials, another set for processing, another set for characterization of composition and structure, still another for the determination of the useful property. Virtually all analytical instrumentation has already incorporated the computer inside the "black box." Only if the practitioners are allowed to choose among different sets of instruments will we give the "market" its rightful place in allocating research resources.[8]

The other side argues that computers are general purpose; that is, they can be used in a much wider variety of projects than most measuring instruments. Reflections on the effect of computers on scientific inquiry need to balance software development and hardware acquisition.

**Academic "pork barrel": episode or trend?**  The capital facilities problem has driven a number of universities to seek and to obtain special appropriations for research facilities on their campuses by engaging the services of lobbyists with close ties to the congressional leadership. Spokesmen for the scientific community, some congressional committee chairmen, executive branch officials, and others who fear the encroachment of logrolling tactics on the peer review process for research grants have sharply condemned these practices.[9] The critics fear, in the extreme

8. Correspondence with Professor Rustum Roy, December 1984.
9. Barbara J. Culliton, "News and Comment: Press Calls for End of Special Lobbying," *Science,* vol. 227 (January 11, 1985), p. 153.

case, a breakdown of the tacit postwar bargain between universities and society. The bargain provides government support for research useful to society, but according to terms that largely protect the autonomy of the scientific community. The peer review systems used by the federal granting agencies have left most critical choices on the progress of the scientific fields, once funds have been voted, to the scientists themselves. Faculty members, of course, have the burden of writing and evaluating specific proposals, and administrators have the responsibility of accounting strictly for the expenditure of public funds.

The conference participants in the main, while troubled by the pork-barrel tactics, did not see the likelihood of political decisions on buildings and other large facilities intruding on the federal grant-making programs. They noted that large undertakings have always involved politics and politicians. Peer review works best when individual proposals are evaluated in a well-understood and defined discipline, less well across a broad and ill-defined field. It works poorly in evaluating the relative merits of wholly different fields, in assessing the institutional capacities of entire universities, or in appraising the merits of different regions as the site for a major facility. Though pressure for academic pork-barrel appropriations will probably continue as long as capital needs are so great and so underfunded, equilibrating forces may prevent the process from gathering momentum. In the game of pork-barrel politics, the universities are not the most powerful claimants—indeed, they could easily be squashed by more potent constituencies. This recognition can moderate the temptation to adopt a public works mentality or to spend money freely on lobbying campaigns.

Earlier federal programs of capital assistance were launched in an era of growth—a time, in fact, when the expansion of the whole system meant that facilities for research could blend together with capital projects needed for a growing student population. Now we have a mature enterprise in which the issues of new facilities versus renovation, instructional needs versus research needs, and other trade-offs are more sharply drawn. What sort of strategy for coping with the capital needs of the nation's universities is called for under these circumstances? What options are available? Indeed, what combination of roles and responsibilities is appropriate for the universities themselves, for the federal government, for the states, for private industry, and for philanthropy on the whole range of issues that graduate education faces? Is it fruitful to talk of a national strategy for graduate education?

*Elements of a national strategy for graduate education*

The idea of a national strategy, if not a commitment, has considerable appeal for many conference participants and for other observers from the universities, industry, and government. The report of the National Board on Graduate Education, *Federal Policy Alternatives toward Graduate Education,* was a model effort of this kind a decade ago.[10] Many others, however, do not see such an effort as a feasible goal at this time. The idea that the federal government might outline a comprehensive policy toward graduate education seems too grandiose and reflects too great a focus on the federal role alone. Industry, the states, philanthropy, and the universities themselves are all critical actors. Yet all observers seem to agree on the importance of an overall sense of purpose and on the need to strengthen the quality of the nation's graduate education effort (or at least to prevent an erosion in the national capacity). The difficulty of assigning practical responsibility to the different actors in the process shows that the choices are unclear, fraught with uncertainty, and contingent on wider currents in the nation's economy and political life. Nonetheless the conference participants believed it would be useful to define some broad elements of a national policy, not as any formal set of proposals or concrete plans but as a stimulus to thought. These policy recommendations are intended as first steps, not the end result, of a wider public debate about the aims, accomplishments, and requirements of graduate education.

### Student Financial Assistance

One element of an effective strategy for graduate education is clearly the need to assure a continued supply of highly talented students in graduate programs. Although there is as yet no sharp overall decline in student numbers, certain fields have shown declines, and further declines may be experienced later. Moreover, while there is as yet little firm evidence, the professional schools may be luring the more gifted students away from traditional doctoral programs. Public policy should thus strive, through an appropriate mix of financial assistance measures, to provide incentives for a share of the nation's talented youth to pursue graduate education. Government should provide these incentives even though some of the students receiving such public support would pursue studies in fields with a high market demand and could convert their education into financially lucrative careers in the private sector.

10. National Board on Graduate Education, *Federal Policy Alternatives toward Graduate Education,* especially chaps. 1, 4–6.

The most conspicuous trends in financial assistance are those noted by the National Board on Graduate Education a decade ago: decreases in the number of fellowships and traineeships and increasing reliance on teaching and research assistantships, loans, and student self-support. This mix now perhaps lacks the proper balance among the various components of a total plan for graduate student support, insofar as the competitive fellowship and traineeship awards have shrunk to small numbers. The nation would benefit from more merit stipends given to talented students and to strong departments for subsequent award to individuals.

The shift to student self-support is by no means an unwelcome development. Loans should remain a significant component of a total plan for graduate student support. But, as the National Board on Graduate Education noted, "There are limits to the utility of loans. In individual cases, loans should not be so large that highly capable students are discouraged from undertaking graduate work."[11] The burden of heavy undergraduate indebtedness has become a public concern, and it may already be discouraging students from graduate study in the arts and sciences.

Teaching assistantships and research assistantships are also desirable and should be important continuing sources of support. They need, however, to be supplemented by a small number of competitive grants that would enable some of the most promising students to move ahead rapidly with their own work. The National Research Council recently cited the difficulties caused by lack of support to enable students to concentrate on research as a major problem in U.S. mathematics study: "There must be much wider availability of graduate student support other than teaching assistantships, so that a period of intense concentration on dissertations is possible."[12] The traineeships of the National Institutes of Health, the merit fellowships of the National Science Foundation, and some programs of the defense agencies embody this concept of allowing uninterrupted time for student research. These programs need expansion beyond their present limited numbers. Stipends for engineers are too low to be competitive and must be raised.

Special programs targeted for minority students must also be part of the strategy on financial assistance. At present various small programs exist in several agencies. Title IX of the Higher

11. Ibid., p. 7.

12. National Research Council, *Renewing U.S. Mathematics: Critical Resource for the Future,* Report of the Ad Hoc Committee on Resources for the Mathematical Sciences, Commission on Physical Sciences, Mathematics, and Resources (Washington, D.C.: National Academy Press, 1984), p. 58.

Education Act provides a program for minority students and women: the Graduate and Professional Opportunities Program (GPOP). The National Science Foundation and the National Institutes of Health also have fellowship programs for minority students. These programs all have modest appropriations and could reasonably be expanded in future years, serving the wider social goal of increasing opportunities for disadvantaged students in programs of advanced study.

The access of minority students to programs of advanced study has been an intractable problem. The record of failure to attract minority students to graduate education is clear enough, as described in John Vaughn's paper, but it is difficult to explain why the record has been so poor and what strategy would cope effectively with the problem. Fresh efforts are clearly needed, not only on the sufficient moral grounds that the nation must improve its record here; the practical reason is that minority youths will constitute a growing share of the undergraduate student population in coming years. The time seems right for renewed efforts to cope with the problem, but what form should these efforts take?

A federal responsibility to help broaden minority access to graduate education is clear, but will the present policies succeed? The pattern of a small number of special fellowship programs combined with modest recruitment efforts at the university level does not seem to produce noticeable results. An alternative approach might target access to graduate education as a general problem and redefine financial aid policies broadly to emphasize need. Such an approach might have some appeal to institutions that emphasize master's-level programs for entry into certain professions (for example, social work, nursing, public adminis- tration, city planning, allied health). But it would do little to deal with the fundamental problems blocking entry or interfering with the success of minorities in the arts and science programs, in engineering, and in medicine. The roots of the problem can be traced to inadequate elementary and secondary school preparation for many minority students (for example, failure to learn enough mathematics in high school may effectively block the minority student from a scientific career). Minority students with good educational backgrounds are under pressure to seek early career payoffs. Financial assistance alone would not enable the less prepared to succeed in graduate studies and would not provide sufficient incentives to lure the well-prepared minority student away from a lucrative career in law, business, or government service.

Since the problem relates so deeply to institutional practices at different levels, the solutions will emerge only through a combination of efforts at many levels—improvements in elementary and secondary education, redoubled efforts by the universities in recruitment and retention, corporate and foundation support, federal and state government assistance, and other efforts. Successful programs have usually reflected sustained efforts over a long period.

To summarize, a sensible strategy for providing student financial assistance suggests a strong federal role in a few areas of high national priority. These areas include assuring the flow of some of the nation's brightest youth into graduate programs and creating additional opportunities for minority students. A better mix in the financial support system can meet the goal of assuring the flow of highly talented youth into graduate programs; additional merit fellowships are the first priority, and an increase in traineeships is the second priority. Loans, research assistantships, and teaching assistantships would remain important elements in the total support system but would not carry the whole burden. The goal of improved minority access will come with steady and consistent efforts at many levels; targeted federal programs, combined with state, university, and corporate initiatives, will play a part. Foundations can play a role in assisting minority students, but universities must view the problem as an ongoing responsibility for which they must provide the necessary continuing budget and staff support, not merely as something to be undertaken when external funds are available on a special basis.

### Faculty Development

The recent shifts in academic labor markets have created problems for the nation's universities that resist easy definition or pat resolution. High demand for certain skills—notably computer science and electrical engineering—has created shortages and unfilled faculty positions, while in other fields faculty members have been underemployed because of shifts in student interests. Universities have the choice, broadly, of adapting to the market forces and even accelerating change, or moderating the effect of the changes. In practice, universities have usually tried to do both, seeking a mix of responding to and of cushioning the effects of market forces, depending on how they have defined their educational missions. This process of institutional self-appraisal will remain an important element of a national strategy for graduate education. Certainly the universities themselves must play the major role in coping with an academic labor force in transition.

Each university must choose for itself a strategy that fits its unique tradition, faculty resources, and character. The best national strategy is the sum of the individual choices made by deans, department chairmen, and faculty members throughout the system.

This loose-jointed system provides no mechanism for central planning and leaves the universities free to respond with fundamental changes or to improvise temporary solutions. Since the engineering fields, where the shortages are currently most in evidence, are also traditionally the most volatile, this flexibility is highly desirable. A logical corollary is that graduate education in the United States is likely to evolve away from any uniform pattern and toward even greater differentiation as the many actors pursue strategies tailored to their diverse strengths and circumstances.

Yet a few general guidelines for the behavior of the universities, the federal government, the states, and industry seem worth noting. The federal government can play a useful role in a number of ways. Support for a limited number of young scientists and engineers at the beginning of their academic careers is a logical extension of policies providing for a small number of competitive fellowships for the most able graduate students. The National Science Foundation has embodied this principle in the Presidential Young Investigator Program, which will provide 200 new awards in fiscal year 1985 and a total appropriation of $24 million. Industry provides matching funds for laboratory equipment for the young investigator. The program provides for new funding for additional fellowships each year while supporting the current recipients for up to five years, a significant commitment by government and by private industry.

Financial assistance policies for graduate students also help smooth the flow of talented graduate engineers into teaching and research positions. But beyond the fellowships for the young, the general policies of the federal granting agencies can play an important role in shaping the climate that will attract students into teaching and research careers. For example, the length of grant award periods for established faculty investigators, which began to decrease in the 1970s in response to calls for greater accountability, has contributed to the harried life style and entrepreneurism that dim the appeal of an academic career. Adequate facilities, supporting research infrastructure, and the ability to work for a time as part of a larger team before embarking on the proposal-writing treadmill could make an academic career more attractive. The shortages of faculty are real, as identified in the work of national study commissions, but financial assistance for graduate students is only one part of the larger problem.[13]

Industry can play an important role in this broader context. Other fields, like medicine, have drawn their clinical faculty from among practitioners, a model that might in some form be appropriate for the engineering schools. Other nations have typically turned to industry to recruit distinguished senior faculty in engineering, and the United States could develop this practice among the new patterns in industry-university relations. Wider career opportunities for faculty members should not be viewed as contrary to the interests of the universities.

For the universities, the challenge is to recognize that the growth, the enhancement, and the productive effort of faculty members, in both the current surplus and shortage areas, is a central task of administrative leadership. Administrators have only begun to consider seriously a whole panoply of management tools—early retirement plans, "refresher" leaves, salary incentives, released time, and many others that can make sense in a particular setting. Universities have frequently been undermanaged and underled. Personnel decisions other than tenure and promotion have received scant attention. Rigid rules and terms of appointment are common. It is time for imaginative programs and ideas, some of which will be natural candidates for support from foundations and industry. The list of foundations playing creative roles in assisting universities to implement faculty development programs includes the Alfred P. Sloan Foundation, the Northwest Area Foundation, and the Andrew W. Mellon Foundation. The skill of the universities in nurturing their faculty assets remains the most critical variable in determining whether the pressures of the changing academic marketplace will tear the universities apart or will stimulate a creative adaptation.

### Capital Facilities

The need to modernize, to upgrade, or to replace aging capital facilities is a key aspect of a national strategy for graduate education. That much can be said with assurance. Definition of the problem of the policy options, as Linda Wilson's paper makes clear, remains

---

13. National Research Council, Commission on Human Resources, *Research Excellence through the Year 2000: The Implications of Maintaining a Flow of New Faculty into Research* (Washington, D.C.: National Academy Press, 1979); Margaret S. Gordon, "Smoothing Out the Flow of Young Scientists into Universities," supplement J to *Final Report of the Carnegie Council on Policy Studies in Higher Education* (San Francisco: Jossey-Bass, 1980).

a most difficult challenge. The first step is to discard the notion of a single, integrated, overall plan, presumably funded by the federal government. Instead of such a comprehensive package, the solution seems to require a more decentralized and market-driven approach. A modest federal program of construction or renovation grants would relieve some of the pressures behind the academic pork-barrel tactics that arose in the Ninety-eighth Congress. But such a program would probably be difficult to achieve in the present budgetary circumstances. Furthermore, the overall capital needs vastly exceed the capabilities of such a program alone.

The earlier federal programs for physical facilities were geared to the expansion of the higher educational enterprise. Now the universities need an ongoing system focused on replacement and modernization more than on growth, and driven by the needs of research and advanced training more than by the needs of under-graduate teaching. That is, the federal government would provide a stable base of research support covering direct costs and helping to amortize the costs of capital facilities through indirect cost recovery. The universities would then pursue additional sources of support for their capital needs.

For private universities, planning for capital needs means looking to traditional philanthropic sources, borrowing, research undertaken in collaboration with private industry, and a range of esoteric financing mechanisms involving tax-free bonds. In all research support, accounting and operating costs should more accurately reflect capital costs.

For public universities, the situation is perhaps even more complicated. General obligation bond issues have been floated in a number of states to strengthen the state's science and technology base, with funds earmarked for public (and private) universities. In some cases bonds have even financed the purchase of large research facilities (for example, a computer at Colorado State University). Revenue bonds have also been issued, primarily for buildings but also for student loans. In some instances, the Board of Regents of the state university has been designated as the state agency empowered to issue bonds; other states have created a special authority for this purpose. Counties have also acted as the public agency arranging for the issuance of tax-exempt bonds in some states. In the absence of an explicit statutory base providing for borrowing by colleges and universities, higher education institutions in some states have used industrial development bonds to gain access to the tax-free bond market for capital purposes.

State practices vary so greatly that a tidy summary is impossible. The growth of tax-exempt financing in recent years is notable; it amounted to more than $3 billion in 1984.

Budgetary practices also vary greatly. Many states do not allow universities the flexibility to shift funds between capital budgets and expense budgets. While public universities naturally look first to the states for their capital needs, efforts to enhance fund-raising and to forge new ties with industry are also part of their strategies. As with the federal government, any long-term strategy involving the states will require that the states assume some share of the maintenance and operating costs of capital facilities. Appropriate understandings will have to be worked out in each of the states, as well as between the state and federal governments as to their roles.

The universities are venturing into an uncertain and risky world in their investment decisions. Obviously, they do not have the same capacity to generate earnings, to depreciate assets, or to cut costs as does the private firm. Unwise investments in plant may merely add to maintenance costs, to pressures for expansion of staff, or to the hoarding of space. Universities are likely to embark on new capital ventures cautiously and only after careful scrutiny of existing space use. Moreover, they will invest only where there is a strong prospect of attracting operating support for a new program area—which is exactly the way the system should work. The individual decisions are generally based on an assessment of the unique strengths of a university, the special needs of a local or regional economy, and the long-range goals that the institution sets for itself.

Both public and private universities need to develop more realistic accounting policies and to plan for the repair, the maintenance, and the replacement of plant and equipment as a normal cost of doing business. The understanding and support of federal and state officials will be necessary to help the universities to achieve a realistic and sustainable system for capital replacement. The universities must have this broad base of support or they may find themselves acquiring huge new debts based on optimistic assumptions. The sale–lease-back scheme that so angered the U.S. Congress and caused a change in the tax code is an illustration of the type of arrangement that goes beyond acceptable limits.

Industry's role is twofold: one avenue is traditional corporate philanthropy; the second emerges from the new pattern of industry-university research relationship. The new industy-university relationship is smaller in dollar amount than traditional philanthropy, but it is growing rapidly in importance. The business community as a whole in 1983 contributed more than $1.2 billion in charitable giving to American higher education in the form of research grants, capital grants, fellowship support, gifts of equipment, and grants for other special purposes.[14] In 1984 corporations spent an estimated $425 million on university research; a portion of that total was for the new collaborative research ventures of universities and industry or for targeted research projects.[15] Corporate funds for university research often include the cost of facilities.

The growth of industry-university joint research activity has undoubtedly been stimulated to some undetermined degree by passage of the University and Small Business Patent Act, Public Law 96-517, in 1980 (and the amendments adopted in 1984 when Congress extended the life of the original act) and by passage of the Small Business Innovation Development Act of 1982, Public Law 97-219. The Patent Act and its amendments extended the principles of the Institutional Patent Agreements to all government-sponsored research, enabling universities to freely patent and license discoveries made in their laboratories with the aid of public funds. Thus the mingling of public and private funds in the same laboratory is no longer a problem. The universities have also been empowered to grant exclusive licenses. The Small Business Act provided that federal research and development agencies designate a portion of their grant funds (up to 1.25 percent) for research in small businesses, and specified that up to 30 percent of those funds be directed to joint research ventures of universities and small businesses. The universities initially fought the small business proposal, but they have benefited from the new linkages stimulated by the act.

The resulting relationships have taken many forms, including single-company-to-single-university, industry-consortium-to-single-university, and single-company-to-university-consortium ventures. This loose framework, which has permitted many different types of arrangements to develop, seems to be all that is needed for the moment—at least until more experience is gained and more is known about recent trends. Several general observations can be made at this point: first, the new relationships with industry have grown rapidly since 1980 and have become an

14. *Corporate Support for Education, 1983,* Joint Survey (Conference Board and Council on Financial Aid to Education, December 1984), p. 1.

15. Unpublished data, National Science Foundation, Science Resources Studies, January 1985.

increasingly important factor in the support of university research (though still small in comparison with federal research support). From 1980 to 1984, industry support of total university R&D grew to 4.9 percent from 3.9 percent, and from 1982 to 1983, industrial support grew 12.2 percent (as compared with a total university research and development growth rate of 6.7 percent). Second, there have been few new one-to-one agreements like those that flourished briefly in the 1980–81 period (such as Hoescht–Harvard Medical School, Monsanto–Washington University). Instead, the cooperative mode has blossomed and seems to be the emerging pattern of industry-university relations. Joint industry consortia with a university (or with two or three universities) seem to be a common pattern. Another interesting development is the growth of state R&D initiatives for economic development purposes, often involving bond issues, efforts to create technology parks, and cooperative industry-university relations. Limited R&D partnerships have not attracted much university interest and seem unlikely to be a favored mode of university cooperation with industry.

Traditional philanthropy plays a smaller role in capital support than it did when the scale of expenditures was smaller. Private philanthropy funded most early medical research in the United States. The Rockefeller Foundation, for example, supported with its own funds efforts to wipe out yellow fever in the American South. It also played a major role in promoting the "green revolution" in the third world through its support for agricultural research. Efforts on this scale and such effective support by a single foundation are now rare. Yet the role of philanthropy remains critically important for many innovative projects in universities and for projects that industry is unwilling to support. The Whitehead Institute at MIT, the gift of a $75 million optical telescope to be operated by the California Institute of Technology, and the vast new assets to the Hughes Medical Institute for the support of biomedical research are recent examples of the continuing relevance of philanthropy for academic science.

### Computers and Research Libraries

Computers and research libraries are special areas of concern. As James Johnson argues in his paper, there is a case for a federal commitment to promote university access to the most advanced computational tools and to provide research support for computer science as a discipline. Foundations have played a valuable role in assisting research libraries in such areas as computer cataloguing for new acquisitions, the problem of "brittle books" (books that are printed on paper whose rag content is low and thus are subject to flaking and disintegration), and research on library services and information systems. The Council on Library Resources, the Exxon Educational Foundation, and others have been particularly active in several of these areas in recent years. Much remains to be done in many discrete problem areas that are well suited to a creative foundation role.

The opportunities for market incentives to play a role in the "wiring" of the campus are considerable, including price reductions for student purchase of computers, the use of universities as testing grounds for advanced computer applications, collaborative research, and software development. Some form of market in the pricing of information services seems bound to emerge for both research and instructional purposes. A student, for instance, might be expected to pay a certain fee, which would entitle him or her to run a specified number of computer searches of the literature in a field. Use beyond that level would entail additional fees. Use of these services raises problems of deciding who pays for what, whether big users or little users are served, which costs are classified as direct and which as indirect, how user and access fees are precisely calculated, and so on. The revolution in telecommunications policy that has brought the pricing of information services more in line with actual costs across the entire economy will surely have an effect on the university environment as well.

### Tax Issues

Tax issues will significantly affect the universities' efforts to upgrade facilities and graduate education generally. Uncertainties cloud the picture, however. The debate over the federal deficit and the various tax reform proposals complicates the analysis of trends and forecasts of the macroeconomic context for university planning purposes. These are matters of the greatest importance to universities, but the resolution of the issues will emerge from a broad and complex political process whose outcomes the universities will have only a limited capacity to shape.

The university role in the tax and budget debate should reflect the best efforts of analysts in the academic community to seek creative solutions to the nation's problems. A narrow interest group approach by the universities would not serve their own or the country's long-term interests. In turn, the higher education community can reasonably ask of its representatives in Congress and of executive branch officials that they do not unknowingly

harm the interests of higher education in their efforts to balance
the budget and to achieve tax reform. The various proposed tax
changes now under discussion could have a significant potential
effect on the research universities, since they rely heavily on
charitable gifts (voluntary support totaled $5.1 billion for all of
higher education in 1982–83, and individual gifts apart from
bequests composed 47 percent of that, or $2.4 billion). The
greatest effect on the overall level of individual giving would
result from the reduction of the maximum tax rate from 50 to 35
percent. Apart from the rate reduction, the effects on gifts of
appreciated property and on tax-exempt financing would perhaps
be the most significant. Traditionally, some 40 percent of all
individual gifts to universities, and a significantly higher percentage
of larger gifts, have taken the form of securities, real estate, and
other appreciated assets. The growth of tax-exempt financing in
recent years reflects the belief of many educators that this approach
may be a partial answer to the capital deficit problem facing the
research universities.

While there is no fully satisfactory way at the moment to assess
the effect of the various proposed reforms, preliminary analyses
by the Association of American Universities and by Independent
Sector suggest that a marked reduction in giving would result
from the U.S. Treasury Department's plan and other proposed
changes.[16] These analyses do not, of course, settle the issue.
Proponents of tax reform argue that the wider benefits to the
nation are the overriding goals—in particular, the sustained economic growth that tax reform could help to achieve. Exempting
some groups from the proposed reforms might cause the whole
package to unravel. Moreover, some estimates suggest that the
rate reduction might constitute as much as 80 percent of the effect
on giving, which would potentially put the universities in the
untenable position of arguing against a rate reduction.

There is no fully satisfactory model to explain how deductibility
affects charitable giving or what the elasticities of the effects are.
Certainly, the broad macroeconomic problems confronting the
nation must be addressed, and a strong economy provides the
best assurance of a secure future for the nation's universities, as
it does for Americans generally. One can accept the philosophy
of tax reform proposals that different categories of income and
expenditures should be treated equally but still argue that a category

16. See Derek C. Bok, William G. Bowen, and Robert M. Rosenzweig, cover
memorandum to *Impact of Treasury Tax Proposal on Charitable Giving to Universities*
(Washington, D.C.: Association of American Universities, 1984), p. 1; Charles T.
Clotfelter, *Tax Reform and Charitable Giving in 1985* (Washington, D.C.: Independent
Sector, 1984).

of "charity" exists that is different in kind. A more restrictive definition of the public purposes that charity serves is also possible and is an alternative worth considering, as is the idea that the federal government might match gifts to universities instead of helping them through the tax structure. However, the historic national policy of encouraging the transfer of wealth by classifying some activities as "charitable" should not be lightly abandoned. As Albert Rees, president of the Alfred P. Sloan Foundation, observed in this context:

> Let me emphasize . . . that I do not regard the charitable tax deduction as another special tax privilege. First, it is one of the oldest deductions in the tax code, going back to 1917. Second, it promotes the support of educational, cultural, and welfare activities that would have to be supported by government if there were not private voluntary support for them. The new and expanded government that would be needed to replace private philanthropy would probably be less efficient than the private ones they replaced and certainly would be far less diverse. This diversity of voluntary activity is a precious asset of our pluralistic society.[17]

Tax issues have emerged as a major university concern for the foreseeable future. Even in the absence of a comprehensive tax reform such as the Treasury plan, the Bradley-Gephardt proposal, or the Kemp-Kasten proposal, there is a cluster of tax concerns pending or soon to be debated.

The 1984 Tax Reform Act, Public Law 98-369, formalized in statute a number of "nonstatutory fringe benefits" but left other related matters in a state of uncertainty. Provisions regarding the tax treatment of research and teaching assistants, for example, will expire after one year and must be resolved for future years. The language of the nondiscrimination clauses (for example, benefits available equally to all individuals within the category of "student") will require clarification in a number of contexts. The R&D tax credit available to industry in the 1981 Economic Recovery Tax Act is due to expire in December 1985 unless reauthorized. This complex legislation, allowing a partial tax credit only for research and development expenditures beyond a previous year's base, applies to research that is contracted out to universities as well as to internal expenditures. There is little indication that the legislation, as drawn up, has resulted in a significant increase in university contract research.

A related pending issue concerns corporate gifts of computers to universities. Senator Lloyd Bentsen, with the cosponsorship of

---

17. Quoted in Bok, Bowen, and Rosenzweig, *Impact of Treasury Tax Proposal*, p. 2.

Senators John C. Danforth, George J. Mitchell, John H. Chafee, Steve Symms, and David Durenberger, has introduced Senate bill 58, The High Technology Research and Scientific Education Act of 1985, to establish a framework for such gifts. Tax-free financing for capital projects and for student financial assistance is also subject to close scrutiny and is under intensive study by congressional staff agencies. The 1984 tax act greatly reduced the incentives for the sale–lease-back practice for universities and placed limits on the use of industrial development bonds by the states or their agencies to assist universities. The states henceforth may not exceed $200 million, or $150 per capita, whichever is greater, in the issuance of such bonds. Congress and the IRS will scrutinize closely the novel financing schemes that the universities devise, and they will respond with restrictive legislation or regulations when such arrangements provide unusual tax advantages to industrial partners or to individual donors.

The academic community has not been able to develop any broad strategy on tax issues because of the uncertainties. The universities must be prepared for their share of sacrifices to achieve important national objectives, but they are entitled to make their voices heard in the public debate. While the central lines of the budget and tax debate are being resolved, the universities can begin to develop the knowledge base to help clarify the many remaining tax issues affecting them. Reasoned analysis and debate on the merits of using the tax code or alternative instruments of public policy to accomplish purposes vital to teaching and research can take place only with reference to concrete issues.

*Change and leadership in the universities*

The prospect of change is one of the recurring themes in all of the papers in this volume; and it was echoed throughout the conference discussions. Change is occurring on many fronts—in the rapid advance of scientific knowledge, in the global economy, and in the university's role in society. Yet, as Harvey Brooks notes in his concluding chapter, we have hardly begun to assimilate the meaning of these changes for graduate education. Universities are accustomed to "surprise-free" projections, but he produces a list of developments that could dramatically alter the assumptions underlying current policies and practices. How are university officials to plan for the future with the ground rapidly shifting under their feet? One conclusion, as Brooks suggests, is that universities should experiment on a small scale with curricula, pedagogical techniques, shared facilities, and the like, and should make the results of well-conceived experiments broadly available.

A related conclusion is that the universities need more and better data on internal developments as the basis for informed policy judgments. Data compiled by the universities themselves, tracing their own graduates or assessing pertinent trends, constitute a logical source little used at present in the broad public debate. Each of the authors shares the view that the data base on graduate education is inadequate, and each proposes corrective steps within his or her area. All authors stressed the need for a more disaggregated information base. Aggregate trends for all classes of institutions, data on a large and undifferentiated cluster of disciplines, and other measures currently available are too crude and unrefined to be of maximum assistance as tools of policymaking.

A standard definition of graduate education has never been possible, given the variety of professionally oriented, interdisciplinary, and special-purpose programs coexisting with the research doctorate programs in many universities. But joint ventures with industry, cooperation between universities, nontraditional midcareer training, and greater specialization within established disciplines all seem to be propelling the universities into a new world of diversity, of experiment, and of uncertainty. There is a great need for quality in this vast enterprise, but quality is not a simple matter, as "product differentiation" occurs even within the traditional Ph.D. programs. Many of the established verities with respect to faculty-student ratios, the roles of course work and of independent research, and technique versus substance no longer seem to apply. Basic philosophical questions about the purposes of graduate education arise with urgency and insistency.

In light of the forces working to fracture the community of learning, the role of central and unifying leadership grows in importance for the period ahead. No central authority within a university, any more than a planner for the whole system, can know enough to make rational decisions for the entire enterprise. Let the universities respond, as America's higher education system has always done, to the economic, demographic, and political trends affecting the rest of society. Within the university, let the strong flourish and the weaker programs atrophy as this process of adaptation gradually transforms the academic landscape. None of the conference participants accepts this simple view, however. Certain of the pure sciences, generic applied science and engineering, and many other areas of knowledge evidently could not flourish under such pure market conditions. Latent tensions would erupt into open conflict. Basic research, indeed, is almost a classic case of the public good requiring broad social support and a certain degree of insulation from the pressures of the marketplace. As Harvey Brooks notes, however, research and graduate education may not be as closely linked as in the past; indeed, universities may not be the major performers of basic research in all areas.

In the past, when the higher education system was expanding, shortages and manpower needs were the rationales for society's investment in graduate education. Now many graduate programs beyond those granting the initial professional degrees needed for entry into various careers would have a hard time justifying themselves by a short-run market test alone. But if a market test is inadequate, what is the rationale for graduate education? As educators and policymakers ponder these issues, most will share the feeling that society surely benefits from a broad and deep supply of talented men and women to be found at the many way stations along the path of learning and scholarship. Yet there is a need to define some common destination and to invest the journey with moral as well as practical meaning. The critical challenge of academic leadership will be to articulate a new vision of graduate education's service to society—and of the common values underlying the scholarly enterprise.

# Some Indicators of the Condition of Graduate Education in the Sciences

ROBERT G. SNYDER

FOR GRADUATE education in science and engineering, the last decade has overall been one of steady state. In stark contrast to the spectacular growth of the late 1950s and of most of the 1960s, and in contrast to the abrupt contractions of the early 1970s, the period since 1974 has been one of modest overall growth. However, one is impelled to ask how the parts are performing below the apparent calm of the whole. Are certain fields increasing in size while others are not? Are private institutions faring less well than their public counterparts? How have patterns of financial support changed in recent years, especially the use of personal resources? And finally, there are questions of quality. How are our best research doctorate departments faring in enrollments, in Ph.D. production, and in support? Are our graduate programs attracting their share of the finest talent in the nation?

*Dimensions of the system*

In 1981 there were 3,231 institutions of higher education in the United States. The graduate science and engineering system comprises 654 institutions, of which 361 award the master's as the highest degree and 293 award the doctorate as the highest degree.[1] Most graduate education, however, takes place in doctorate-granting institutions, which account for 85 percent of graduate science and engineering departments and 87 percent of total graduate enrollments.[2]

As one would expect, the number of institutions awarding masters' and doctoral degrees rose dramatically in the 1960s—from 180 institutions awarding the master's as highest degree in 1960 to 287 in 1971 (+59 percent), and from 141 doctorate institutions (which also award masters' degrees) in 1960 to 229 in 1971 (+62 percent). Even in the 1970s, however, the number of graduate institutions continued to rise, though at a lower rate.

---

1. National Science Board, *Science Indicators, 1982* (Government Printing Office, 1983), p. 298.

2. National Science Foundation, *Academic Science/Engineering: Graduate Enrollment and Support, Fall 1982* (GPO, 1984), p. 2.

The number of master's-highest institutions rose to 361 in 1981 (+26 percent), and the number of doctorate institutions rose to 293 (+28 percent). Apparently, then, even the downturns in financial support and in the labor market of the 1970s did not dissuade increasing numbers of institutions from seeking the patina of prestige afforded by the presence of graduate education on campus.

Because the use of the master's degree varies both within and among fields and institutions—in some instances, it is a terminal degree, in others it is routinely awarded as part of a doctoral program, while in other cases it is not awarded at all in a doctoral program—it is impossible to differentiate precisely masters' from doctorate enrollments. Degree production is known, however, and there is considerable variation among fields. Engineering and computer science are heavily master's-oriented fields, with seven times as many masters' as doctorates awarded. In contrast, the physical and environmental, life, and social and psychological sciences are more doctorate-oriented, with only roughly twice as many masters' as doctorates awarded.[3]

It is also worth noting the role of private institutions in graduate science and engineering. Although enrollments of private institutions compose roughly 22 percent of total higher education enrollments, they compose 36 percent of total enrollments in doctorate science and engineering departments.[4] This illustrates the disproportionately larger share of graduate education in private institutions.

***Overall trends in enrollments and degree production***　Graduate science and engineering enrollments have undergone radical shifts since the late 1950s, when Sputnik first generated an outcry about the state of American graduate education. In the 1960s, total enrollments in the sciences and engineering more than doubled (114 percent), rising at an average annual rate of about 8 percent.[5] Largest increases were in the social and psychological sciences and in the biological sciences, with smaller, but still substantial, increases in engineering, in mathematics, and in the physical sciences.

Beginning in the late 1960s—1968 or 1969—the outlook for graduate education turned precipitously downward because of a

3. National Science Board, *Science Indicators*, pp. 271–72.

4. National Center for Education Statistics, *Digest of Education Statistics, 1982* (GPO, 1982), p. 91; Robert G. Snyder, "Graduate Science and Engineering Student Enrollment and Support by Department Quality, 1974–1982," paper prepared for the National Science Foundation, Science Indicators Unit, Washington, D.C., 1984.

5. National Center for Education Statistics, *Digest of Education Statistics*, p. 101.

declining labor market, a change in political climate, and budgetary problems that led to cutbacks in federal support. Enrollments were markedly affected. Overall enrollments declined only slightly from 1970 to 1974; but while the biological and social and psychological sciences had significant increases, engineering, mathematics, and the physical sciences had significant declines.[6]

In marked contrast to the sharp perturbations noted above, the period from 1975 to 1982 was one of relative quiescence. Total enrollments (1975–82) rose from 337,526 to 399,682, an average annual increase of 2.4 percent.[7] In contrast to the period of contraction, the largest increases were in engineering, especially electrical engineering and computer science, while the other fields remained relatively level in their enrollments during this period.

Graduate enrollment trends give no evidence that private institutions fared less well than public institutions in the 1975–82 period.[8] Differences among fields were slight, except in the field of computer science, where private full-time enrollments increased at higher rates (16 percent a year) than enrollments in public institutions (9 percent).

Graduate science and engineering enrollments would not have increased were it not for the marked increases in female and foreign enrollments. Full-time enrollments of women in doctoral institutions rose 53 percent in the 1975–82 period, while enrollments of men remained level.[9] Although engineering and environmental and computer sciences experienced sharp percentage increases in enrollments of women, these increases were built on a meager base. As of 1982, women composed only 11 percent of full-time engineering students, 20 percent of physical and environmental sciences students, and 25 percent of mathematics and computer science students.[10] The greatest impact of female enrollment increases has been in the biological sciences (40 percent women) and the social and psychological sciences (46 percent women). In fact, male full-time enrollments in the 1975–82 period declined 14 percent in the biological sciences and 17 percent in the social and psychological sciences, compared with female enrollment increases of 38 and 35 percent, respectively, in the same period. Female enrollments were thus wholly responsible for positive enrollment trends in these two broad fields.

6. Ibid.
7. National Science Foundation, *Academic Science/Engineering*, p. 60.
8. Ibid., p. 271.
9. Ibid., pp. 106–07.
10. Ibid., pp. 101, 107.

In engineering, physical and environmental sciences, and mathematics and computer science, enrollments of foreign students have significantly increased.[11] In engineering, foreign full-time enrollments rose at an average annual rate of 8.4 percent from 1975 to 1982, reaching almost 21,000 students, or 43 percent of total full-time students in this broad field. This compares with an annual increase of only 1.6 percent among U.S. students. Mathematics and computer science showed an even larger discrepancy. Here, foreign enrollments increased at a rate of 12.7 percent per year, to a 36 percent share of full-time enrollments, compared with a 0.5 percent per year increase for U.S. citizens. In 1981–82, the most recent year for which data are available, U.S. enrollments in both these broad fields rose at much higher rates than in the years preceding.

Minority participation in graduate science and engineering education does not present an encouraging picture in recent years. Extended trend data are not available, but recent National Science Foundation (NSF) data show very low rates of minority participation.[12] For all fields, blacks represented only 2.5 percent and Hispanics 2.1 percent of full-time science and engineering enrollments in 1982. In engineering and the natural sciences, these percentages were even lower—less than 2 percent—while in the social and psychological sciences these percentages were somewhat higher—4.8 percent for blacks and 3.5 percent for Hispanics— but still much lower than these groups' share of the population.

Considerable speculation has taken place in recent years over the extent to which nontraditional, namely part-time and older, students are participating in graduate education. Concern has focused on accommodating individuals whose circumstances (family or work responsibilities) necessitate part-time attendance or retraining for new careers and has also focused on the problem of obsolescing skills and knowledge and the consequent need to view education as a lifelong process.[13] Unfortunately, data in this area are insufficient to explore these issues adequately. NSF data for both masters' and doctorate institutions indicate little upsurge in part-time *degree-credit* graduate enrollment in science and engineering in the 1975–82 period.[14] Part-time engineering enrollments rose more slowly than full-time enrollments. Only in

11. Ibid., pp. 101, 139–40.

12. Ibid., pp. 99–100.

13. See, for example, Massachusetts Institute of Technology, Department of Electrical Engineering and Computer Science, *Lifelong Cooperative Education* (MIT Press, 1982).

14. National Science Foundation, *Academic Science/Engineering*, p. 63.

computer science have part-time enrollments risen rapidly, from 4,000 students in 1975 to 11,000 students in 1982, an average increase of 16 percent per year.

Information on adult learners at the graduate level who are employees in the private or government sector is important because many of these students are trying either to gain career promotions or to combat knowledge obsolescence in their fields. Census data provide a general overall figure for this population, but little else is known about employer-paid training at institutions of higher education or employer-provided training in-house at the graduate level. The fact that many of these students are part-time and nonmatriculated contributes to their invisibility to traditional surveys and to policymakers. This lack of knowledge is additionally regrettable given the heightened concern for closer industry-university relations. Data from the 1978 Current Population Survey (CPS) indicate that 872,000 private sector employees with four or more years of college were attending higher education institutions at employer expense. The comparable figure for government employees was 222,000.[15] Data from the 1981 CPS show that an extensive amount of employer-provided training is also available. In 1981, 1.2 million private sector employees with four or more years of education and 0.6 million government employees were undertaking such training.[16]

The principal product of graduate education is degree production, whether at the master's or doctoral level. As noted in the introduction, some fields—engineering and computer science—produce primarily masters' degrees and are oriented toward private sector employment. Other fields—physical and environmental, biological, and social sciences—produce higher proportions of doctorates and are more oriented to academic employment.

Master's degree output in science and engineering increased rapidly in the 1960s, from 20,000 to almost 50,000, fluctuated around the 54,000 level in the 1970s, and increased to 57,000 in 1982.[17] All fields shared in the rapid increases of the 1960s. After that, however, patterns of growth differ dramatically. Masters' degrees in the physical and environmental sciences diminished by almost 20 percent in the 1970s. Degree output in the master's-

15. Michael Tierney, "Trends in Employer-Sponsored Education and Training, 1969–1978" (University of Pennsylvania, Higher Education Finance Research Institute, September 1982), p. 35.

16. Michael Tierney, "Employer-Provided Education and Training in 1981" (University of Pennsylvania, Higher Education Finance Research Institute, June 1983), p. 15.

17. National Science Board, *Science Indicators*, p. 271.

oriented fields of engineering and computer science remained approximately level during the 1970s, then increased sharply from 1980 to 1982. On the other hand, the life and social and psychological sciences continued to increase their masters' output slowly through most of the 1970s, thereafter declining.

Doctorate production in science and engineering followed a somewhat similar course to that of masters' production. Overall doctorate output rose dramatically in the 1960s, nearly tripling from 6,300 in 1960 to 19,700 in 1971, the peak year.[18] Thereafter, output fell 10 percent in the 1970s (to 17,000 in 1979), then rebounded to 18,800 in 1983. Among the various fields, the EMP fields (engineering, mathematical, and physical sciences) experienced significant reductions (25–30 percent) in doctorate production in the 1970s, although they rebounded in the 1980s. In the life sciences, doctorate production remained constant throughout the 1970s and 1980s. In contrast, in the social and psychological sciences doctorate output continued to increase another 20 percent through 1976, after which it remained stable.

The decline in doctorate production in the 1970s was accompanied by a decline in the rate at which bachelor's degree recipients continued on to doctorate degrees in their fields (table 1). Thus not only did the absolute number of persons completing doctorates decline in the 1970s, but the undergraduate portion of the pool choosing to continue declined as well. It is also worth noting that the downward trend in the rate of doctoral study was arrested in the 1980s, the same point at which doctorate production rose. Because it takes roughly six years to produce a doctorate, students must have begun to perceive a change to a more favorable climate in the late 1970s.

Trends in doctorate output, like trends in enrollments, have been fundamentally affected by the heightened participation of women and foreign nationals in graduate science and engineering education. The effect of women has been felt primarily in the life and social and psychological sciences. In the life sciences, male doctorate output has remained level since 1974 at approximately 4,000 per year, while female doctorates have almost doubled, rising from 900 in 1974 to 1,700 in 1983 (30 percent of the total).[19] In the social and psychological sciences, the trends are even more striking, with male doctorates declining 20 percent from 1973 to 1983, while female doctorates doubled in the same period to

18. Ibid., p. 272; National Research Council, *Summary Report, 1981* and *1983: Survey of Doctorate Recipients from United States Universities* (Washington, D.C.: National Academy Press, 1982, 1984).

19. National Research Council, *Summary Report, 1983,* p. 7.

Table 1. *Number of Doctoral Degrees in Science and Engineering per 100 Bachelors' Degrees Awarded Six Years Earlier*

| Year of doctorate | All fields | Engineering | Mathematics and computer science | Social and psychological sciences | Life sciences | Psychological and social sciences |
|---|---|---|---|---|---|---|
| 1970 | 11.9 | 9.7 | 6.5 | 25.0 | 14.9 | 9.1 |
| 1975 | 7.8 | 7.2 | 4.1 | 16.7 | 10.3 | 5.8 |
| 1980 | 5.9 | 5.7 | 3.6 | 14.8 | 8.0 | 4.0 |
| 1983 | 6.5 | 6.7 | 4.8 | 15.2 | 7.1 | 4.8 |

Sources: National Science Board, *Science Indicators, 1982* (Government Printing Office, 1983), pp. 270–72; National Research Council, *Summary Report, 1983: Survey of Doctorate Recipients from United States Universities* (Washington, D.C.: National Academy Press, 1983).

compose 40 percent of the total. In the EMP sciences, female doctorates rose rapidly in the 1970s and 1980s, but they still compose only 10 percent of doctorates in these fields.

Foreign citizens, on the other hand, have had a significant effect on the EMP science fields.[20] In the extreme case of engineering, foreign citizens received 26 percent of doctorates awarded in 1970. This figure rose to 46 percent in 1980 and to 54 percent in 1983. The absolute number of U.S. citizens receiving engineering doctorates declined in the 1980s. Increases in the number of foreign citizens receiving doctorates more than offset this decline. In the small field of computer science, two-thirds of the growth since 1980 has resulted from increases in the number of foreign citizens.

The minorities' share of doctorate output, however, remains almost negligible in science and engineering.[21] In 1983 black U.S. citizens received only 1.6 percent of total science and engineering doctorates awarded that year, and U.S. Hispanics received only 1.3 percent. Their portions of EMP doctorate output were each less than 1 percent; their highest participation was in the social and psychological sciences, which were 3.1 percent black and 2.2 percent Hispanic in 1983. These figures point out clearly the virtual absence of participation by minorities in doctoral-level work in science and engineering.

*Changes in financial support for graduate students*

The availability of financial support for graduate students in science and engineering has been an important issue since the late 1950s. In contrast to undergraduate education, where support has been principally a vehicle for improving access to a broad cross section of the nation's youth, support for graduate science education has served a variety of other purposes. The most common

20. National Research Council, *Summary Reports, 1970–83*.
21. National Research Council, *Summary Report, 1983*, pp. 5, 38–39.

objective has been "manpower," that is, assuring an adequate supply of highly trained personnel, whether from the university perspective of assisting in teaching and research or from the national perspective of meeting perceived shortages in areas such as health or space.

A second objective has been to promote quality. Graduate education is generally viewed as the end of a long filtering process of the education system. The finest products of the system, or at least a good share of them, will, it is hoped, continue in graduate education to pursue careers in research and teaching. Graduate support is thus typically merit-based and honorific, either explicitly, as in most fellowships, or implicitly, as a reward for succeeding in this highly selective process.

A third objective is to enable individuals to attend graduate school who otherwise might not, either because of an absence of resources or because of the lure of more lucrative careers. Academics in general and doctoral candidates in particular have always operated to some extent in a market-free zone. The relatively lower lifetime earnings of academics (compared with comparably educated people in the private sector) and the nonproprietary nature of basic research have resulted in subsidies for academic research and for graduate education. With a long training pathway to traverse and the prospects of less-than-lucrative careers ahead of them, doctoral students generally require a large measure of subsidy to complete their degrees.

A final objective of graduate student support is to serve vital educational functions. Many forms of support are intimately related to the acquisition of knowledge and skills in the various academic fields. The two major support mechanisms, research assistantships (RAs) and teaching assistantships (TAs), support students and assist faculty while providing apprentice training in research and teaching skills.

Because of these valuable functions, a continuing examination of the availability of financial support for doctoral students is important. How much stipend support is available in the aggregate for various fields? What kinds or types of support are available? What are the sources of the support? Underlying these questions is a more fundamental issue: what is the optimal mix of support that should be available for graduate students? This question will be addressed after recent trends are reviewed. Data examined here are oriented toward doctoral-level education, not simply because this is the primary focus of graduate student support, but also because little data are available on master's-level education.

Historically, support for graduate students followed the same trajectory as the rapidly rising enrollments of the 1960s. While no longitudinal surveys cover that period, in the pre-Sputnik period the majority of graduate science students (58 percent) were primarily self-supported (table 2). By 1969, the number of students primarily self-supported had fallen to 19 percent. During the same period, the portion of students supported by the federal government rose from 10 percent to 37 percent, and those supported by institution or state sources rose from 25 percent to 36 percent. By 1969, for example, the federal government was supporting approximately 54,000 graduate science students—34,000 fellowships and traineeships and 20,000 RAs.[22]

After 1969, however, the climate for support changed radically as economic constraints arose from the Vietnam War, employment shortages turned to surpluses, undergraduate enrollments ceased their rapid ascent, and a change in political leadership brought a less favorable view of government support for higher education. As a result, in the first half of the 1970s the bottom dropped out of federal support for graduate education. Federal fellowships and traineeships declined from 34,000 to 15,000. Precise figures are not available for federal RAs in that era, but they most likely declined as well because of cutbacks in federal research support. As a consequence, the percentage of full-time graduate science students who were primarily supported by the federal government declined from 37 percent in 1969 to 25 percent in 1974, and the share that was self-supported rose by a similar amount, from 19 to 29 percent. Growth in the graduate science education system thus came to an abrupt halt, with enrollments and degree production in the EMP sciences actually declining in this period.

After the mid-1970s, the graduate science education system was more nearly in a condition of steady state. Enrollments and degree production remained relatively constant overall, with notable increases in engineering and computer science. Financial support during this period also remained much less volatile. Federal support, for example, remained virtually level in the 1975–82 period.[23] Beneath the surface, however, significant changes oc-

22. Fellowship data are based on Federal Interagency Committee on Education, *Report on Federal Predoctoral Student Support*, pt. 1: *Fellowships and Traineeships* (Washington, D.C.: GPO, 1970); unpublished FICE data; NIH data for traineeships; and NSF data for RAs. No survey data are available before 1974, when NSF population survey commenced. Excluded are the humanities, professional fields, and, wherever possible, health science fields (such as nursing).

23. National Science Foundation, *Academic Science/Engineering*, pp. 109, 126–38. This source is used for the ensuing discussion, unless otherwise noted.

Table 2. *Percentage Distribution of Sources of Support for Full-Time Graduate Science Students*

| Source | 1954 | 1969 | 1974 | 1980 | 1982 |
|---|---|---|---|---|---|
| All sources | 100.0 | 100.0 | 100.0 | 100.0 | 100.0 |
| Federal | 10.1 | 36.6 | 24.5 | 22.9 | 20.0 |
| Institution and state | 25.3 | 35.7 | 38.5 | 37.6 | 39.3 |
| Other support | 6.6 | 9.1 | 8.4 | 9.2 | 10.0 |
| Self | 58.1 | 18.6 | 28.6 | 30.3 | 30.7 |

Sources: Robert Snyder, "Federal Support of Education in the Natural Sciences: An Inquiry into the Social Impact of Public Policy" (Ph.D. dissertation, Syracuse University, 1981), p. 264; National Science Foundation, *Academic Science/Engineering, Fall 1982* (GPO, 1984), p. 109.

curred. Federal fellowships and traineeships in science and engineering continued to decline, from 15,000 to 9,000, while federal RAs grew from 23,000 to 27,000, thus largely offsetting each other. Enrollment gains that did occur resulted largely from increases in institution- and state-funded TAs and also from self-support. For example, in engineering, whose full-time enrollments rose at an average annual rate of 4.1 percent, the number of students primarily supported on TAs rose at a rate of 7.6 percent per year, with federal support remaining level and self-support increasing at 3.3 percent per year. The large increase in TAs in this field most likely resulted from the large concurrent increases in undergraduate engineering enrollments. Comparable published data are not available for computer science, although similar forces were probably at work.

Such stimuli, however, were not present in other science fields. In the biological sciences, level enrollments obscured two interesting developments. First, the National Research Service Award Act training grants program, the largest ongoing federal graduate training program, experienced continual cutbacks, but these were largely offset by increases in federal RAs. In addition, the number of students primarily self-supported in the biological sciences actually declined in the 1975–82 period by more than 25 percent. This is an interesting development in an era of more limited support; it is perhaps an indication of the importance of support as a training device and not simply as a means of reducing the financial burden.

The fields most adversely affected by the availability of stipend support were the social and psychological sciences. These fields had significant losses in federal support (40 percent) not experienced by other fields in the 1975–82 period. As in other fields, fellowships and traineeships continued to decline. The social and psychological sciences were also affected by cutbacks in federal

RAs. These cutbacks were the result of efforts to curtail social science research. Only 8 percent of the students in the social and psychological sciences were primarily federally supported in 1982, compared with 25 percent of engineering and natural science students. At the same time, 43 percent of social and psychological science students were primarily self-supported, compared with only 25 percent in other fields.

A recently asked question is the extent to which business and industry have taken up the slack in federal support for graduate students, especially in fields like engineering and computer science. Data in this area are far from adequate, but the available data do not indicate a great role at this time at the doctoral level. National Research Council (NRC) data for doctorate recipients in 1983 indicate that 8.4 percent received some (not primary) support from industry. However, data cited earlier indicate substantial support by the private sector for their employees to attend institutions of higher education, in all likelihood part-time at the master's level. Data from the 1978 CPS show possibly 0.9 million such students.

Another recent issue has been the extent to which graduate students have incurred substantial debt as a result of reduced stipend support. Data relevant to this issue are very poor. Even a reliable estimate of the total number of graduate student borrowers is unavailable, let alone the number by field, type of loan, borrowing history, or cumulative indebtedness. A survey of state borrowing agencies by the National Commission on Student Financial Assistance (NCSFA) in 1983 estimated that 410,000 postbaccalaureate (graduate and professional) students borrowed under the guaranteed student loan (GSL) program in fiscal 1982.[24] This was 100,000 fewer students than Department of Education estimates. The distribution of postbaccalaureate borrowers among fields is not known by most state agencies; however, a large portion are students in professional schools, such as law and medicine, and these students are heavy borrowers.

Some information is available about borrowing by doctorate recipients. The percentage of doctoral science and engineering recipients doing *some* borrowing (amount unknown) was 9 percent in 1972; it rose to 25 percent in 1983.[25] The lowest percentage of borrowers was in the EMP sciences (13 percent), and the highest

24. National Commission on Student Financial Assistance, *Signs of Trouble and Erosion: A Report on Graduate Education in America* (New York University Press, 1983), p. 69.

25. National Research Council, *Summary Report, 1972* and *1983*.

was in the social and psychological sciences (42 percent). Data from the same survey in 1981, however, showed that less than 2 percent (less than 0.5 percent in the EMP sciences) used loans as their *primary* source of support. Doctoral students, we may conclude, increasingly use loans as secondary sources of support, especially in the least supported fields (social and psychological sciences), but loans have not become a significant primary source. The growth of loans as secondary sources indicates an erosion in the coverage of stipend sources of support and a growing gap between the cost of attending school and the amount provided by stipend sources.

The apparent erosion in buying power of primary sources of support was possibly the most important development in the steady-state years of 1974–82. Self-support (including work, family support, and loans) as a broad category of support increased somewhat as a primary source, but it apparently increased more as a secondary source. This points to the need for more and better information regarding secondary sources of support than is currently available.

The radical changes in patterns of support over the last quarter century raise the question whether the balance of support among the various mechanisms has changed in ways that have benefited the quality of graduate education. As a general rule, observers have over the years advocated a diversity of mechanisms of financial support as being beneficial to graduate science education. Fellowships and traineeships tend to allow students maximum choice in selecting areas of study, especially in the first years of graduate education course work. TAs provide an opportunity to gain teaching skills as faculty assistants. And RAs provide an opportunity to gain research skills and, frequently, to conduct thesis research under faculty tutelage.

The major change since 1969 has been the declining number of fellowships and traineeships, largely the result of the substantial withdrawal of federal support in this area. Whereas federal fellowships and traineeships exceeded RAs in 1969 (a ratio of 1.5 to 1.0), by 1982 the relationship had more than reversed (with a ratio of 1.0 to 1.9), and fewer than 10,000 students were supported on federal fellowships/traineeships. Only the National Institutes of Health (NIH) training grants and the National Science Foundation fellowships remain significant ongoing programs. The reliance on RAs and TAs, which are most appropriate for students after their first or second year of study, raises the question whether the choices of students may be constrained by premature specialization in a particular area of study. The quality of graduate education could suffer as a result.

The gross fluctuations in federal support have resulted from the fact that personnel needs have been the primary objective of federal fellowship and traineeship support. A perception of major shortages in the 1960s led to massive support; a perception of sufficiency and surplus in the 1970s led to an abrupt curtailment of this support. Since the provision of RAs is largely an unplanned by-product of the research grant process, federal policy in recent years, with the exception of the two programs mentioned, has atrophied into a state of benign neglect. Consideration of the general health of graduate education or the impact of federal policy on the institution of graduate education has thus been too fleeting and too narrowly focused.[26]

*Indicators of quality in doctoral education*

The previous discussion centered on overall trends in enrollments, doctoral degree production, and financial support. Of perhaps greater importance is whether the quality of the graduate education system has improved or declined over the years. Have the best departments maintained or increased their shares of enrollments, degree production, and financial support? Are the nation's best minds entering graduate education?

Information on enrollment, doctorate production, and financial support presented here is based on research that I conducted recently. I used three surveys as the basis for research: the quality ratings of research doctorate departments obtained in a reputational survey conducted by the National Research Council in 1982; the NRC's Survey of Earned Doctorates for the years 1973–83; and the population of doctorate-granting departments from the NSF Survey of Graduate Science and Engineering Students for 1974–82. Matching the program ratings of the first survey with each of the other two surveys shows the distribution of enrollments, doctorate production, and financial support by department and program quality over roughly the last decade.[27]

It is important to note the differences in the overall concentration of resources among the various quality groups. The higher the quality group, the greater the share of enrollments, doctorate

26. One exception is worth noting. For the past nine years, NIH, as part of the National Research Service Award Act (NRSA) program, has supported a continuing study by the National Academy of Sciences to evaluate personnel needs, the training programs under NRSA, and university needs. Seven reports have been issued to date under the title *Personnel Needs and Training for Biomedical and Behavioral Research.*

27. Analysis and findings from this research relating to enrollments and financial support are contained in Snyder, "Graduate Science and Engineering."

output, and financial support. In 1982 the top 25 percent of rated departments had 36 percent of full-time enrollments, the next highest rated group (26–50 percentile) had 22 percent, the lowest-rated group (51–100 percentile) had 26 percent, and a group of nonrated departments (generally with low levels of doctorate activity) had 16 percent. In terms of sources of support, the higher the rated group, the more stipend support is available. This is the result of larger numbers of fellowships-traineeships and RAs and greater use of federal support. Federal fellowships-traineeships and research grants are awarded on a merit basis, so this result should be expected. The concentration with respect to institution and state support is reversed, with departments in lower-rated groups having a higher reliance on this source, primarily because of their greater use of TAs. With regard to doctorate production, the top quartile had more than 40 percent of the doctorates awarded in 1983; lower-rated groups had succeedingly lower shares. These differences are consistent among the various fields, although less markedly so in the social and psychological sciences.

In looking at changes over time, it is worth noting a study done of the years 1968 to 1973 by David Breneman using a similar methodology and similar data sources.[28] Breneman found that in 1968–73, while full-time enrollments declined in science fields (except psychology) and federal support declined sharply overall, the cutbacks were generally absorbed proportionately across various quality groups. Little evidence was found of a "Gresham's Law," whereby mediocre programs absorb greater shares of available resources than the elite ones do.

Research conducted by the author in the steady-state years of 1974–82 indicates that, although the underlying conditions of general stability differed from the conditions of the earlier period of contraction, the results similarly demonstrated little or no change in the distribution of enrollments and support among quality groups. For all fields, in the top 25 percent of the rated departments, full-time enrollments were 37.6 percent in 1974 and 36.3 percent in 1982 (table 3). Interfield changes were also slight, except in mathematics and computer science, where the share of the top 25 percent group declined from 38.6 to 32.3 percent.

With respect to primary sources of support, there were also few overall changes in distribution among quality categories. The share of federal support (both fellowships-traineeships and RAs) going to the top quartile stayed virtually level over the 1974–82

28. David Breneman, *Graduate School Adjustments to the "New Depression" in Higher Education* (Washington, D.C.: National Academy of Sciences, 1975).

Table 3. *Proportion of Full-Time Graduate Enrollments in the Top 25 Percent of Rated Doctorate Departments, by Broad Field, 1974–77, 1979–82*
Percentage enrollment

| Field | 1974 | 1975 | 1976 | 1977 | 1979 | 1980 | 1981 | 1982 |
|---|---|---|---|---|---|---|---|---|
| All | 37.6 | 36.7 | 36.1 | 36.1 | 37.0 | 36.8 | 36.5 | 36.3 |
| Engineering | 43.9 | 43.1 | 44.5 | 44.8 | 45.8 | 44.6 | 44.3 | 42.2 |
| Mathematics and computer science | 38.6 | 37.6 | 36.4 | 36.9 | 37.0 | 34.3 | 33.9 | 32.3 |
| Physical and environmental sciences | 42.6 | 41.8 | 41.7 | 41.9 | 42.3 | 42.2 | 42.4 | 41.9 |
| Biological science | 32.9 | 32.0 | 31.6 | 31.8 | 33.0 | 34.4 | 34.6 | 34.1 |
| Social and psychological sciences | 33.2 | 32.3 | 30.8 | 30.1 | 30.8 | 31.2 | 30.1 | 31.0 |

Source: Robert G. Snyder, "Graduate Science and Engineering Student Enrollment and Support by Department Quality, 1974–1982," paper prepared for the National Science Foundation, Science Indicators Unit, Washington, D.C., 1984.

period at approximately 51 percent, indicating the maintenance of a large share of federal support (table 4). Differences among fields in federal support were also generally small. The largest change for a top quartile group was a 3.6 percent decrease in share in the physical and environmental sciences, although this broad field still had the highest federal share (55.5 percent in 1982) of any broad field. It is also worth noting that there was little change in the distribution of institution and state support among quality groups in this period.

It is important to note that top-quality departments in private institutions not only held their own with public institutions in competition for resources, but actually enhanced their position in the 1974–82 period.[29] Private institutions' share of full-time enrollments rose from 48 percent to 51 percent, while their share of federal support increased from 50 percent to 56 percent, and their share of institution and state support rose from 43 percent to 48 percent.

The distribution of doctorate production appears to have been more volatile from field to field (table 5). For all fields combined, the share of doctorates in the top 25 percent of rated departments remained level from 1973 to 1983 at roughly 40 percent. This figure, however, masks interfield differences. The top quartile engineering group increased its share of doctorates from 45 percent to 53 percent in 1982, then dropped to 51 percent the following year. Similarly, the top quartile in physical and environmental sciences rose in share from 45 percent in 1973 to 50 percent in

29. Snyder, "Graduate Science and Engineering."

Table 4. *Proportion of Full-Time Graduate Enrollments in the Top 25 Percent of Rated Doctorate Departments Whose Primary Source of Support Was the Federal Government, by Broad Field, 1974–77, 1979–82*
Percentage enrollment

| Field | 1974 | 1975 | 1976 | 1977 | 1979 | 1980 | 1981 | 1982 |
|---|---|---|---|---|---|---|---|---|
| All | 50.8 | 50.6 | 49.7 | 49.8 | 51.5 | 50.3 | 49.4 | 51.2 |
| Engineering | 50.0 | 50.1 | 49.5 | 51.6 | 52.7 | 49.5 | 49.0 | 51.4 |
| Mathematics and computer science | 52.5 | 52.7 | 53.4 | 52.8 | 52.9 | 51.6 | 47.7 | 50.5 |
| Physical and environmental sciences | 59.1 | 57.7 | 57.1 | 57.6 | 56.5 | 56.4 | 55.5 | 55.5 |
| Biological science | 48.0 | 47.3 | 47.1 | 47.7 | 48.2 | 49.0 | 48.7 | 49.6 |
| Social and psychological sciences | 45.4 | 47.5 | 44.9 | 40.1 | 44.9 | 41.5 | 39.7 | 43.5 |

Source: Same as table 3.

Table 5. *Proportion of Doctoral Degree Recipients in the Top 25 Percent of Rated Doctorate Departments, by Broad Field, 1973–83*
Percentage recipients

| Field | 1973 | 1974 | 1975 | 1976 | 1977 | 1978 | 1979 | 1980 | 1981 | 1982 | 1983 |
|---|---|---|---|---|---|---|---|---|---|---|---|
| All | 41.3 | 41.4 | 41.4 | 41.6 | 40.9 | 40.9 | 41.6 | 40.1 | 40.6 | 40.6 | 40.2 |
| Engineering | 44.6 | 45.7 | 46.1 | 49.6 | 47.0 | 52.4 | 50.2 | 51.4 | 52.5 | 52.6 | 50.8 |
| Mathematics and computer science | 46.5 | 45.0 | 45.9 | 47.6 | 46.2 | 47.1 | 48.8 | 48.3 | 49.7 | 48.8 | 48.0 |
| Physical and environmental sciences | 44.8 | 45.0 | 45.5 | 46.0 | 45.8 | 48.5 | 50.7 | 49.0 | 50.3 | 50.4 | 49.8 |
| Biological science | 32.3 | 33.4 | 34.8 | 36.2 | 36.8 | 34.5 | 35.6 | 34.5 | 36.3 | 34.8 | 35.4 |
| Social and psychological sciences | 39.9 | 39.9 | 39.1 | 37.9 | 37.2 | 35.6 | 35.4 | 33.5 | 32.7 | 32.5 | 32.3 |

Source: Author's tabulations prepared for the National Science Foundation and based on data from the National Research Council's Survey of Earned Doctorates.

1983. On the other hand, the social and psychological sciences' top quartile experienced a sharp drop in their share over the decade, from 40 percent to 32 percent.

In the period 1968–73, Breneman noted a decline in the shares of doctorates produced in the top-rated groups of departments across all fields.[30] Pointing out the lag time between first enrollment and receipt of degree, he argued that the decline in share by the elite departments was actually attributable to changes occurring in the growth period of the 1960s rather than to changes in the contractive period of the 1970s.

A similar assumption of lag time can be applied to the contractional period 1969–74, which would presumably affect doctorate production in the period roughly around 1974–79. In engineering and in the natural sciences, a greater concentration

30. Breneman, *Graduate School Adjustments*, pp. 40–45.

occurred in 1974–79 (table 5). This concentration implies that the more elite departments were better able to maintain their doctorate output in the face of cutbacks and a declining job market than were the lower rated departments. In the social and psychological sciences, the decline in share by the elite departments is more difficult to explain, but it does follow the atypical pattern of this field in general. That is, in the face of cutbacks in support in the 1970s, enrollments and doctorate output continued to rise through 1977. Growth in the social and psychological sciences was unaffected by cutbacks and continued to take place in lower-rated departments that had little federal support. Hence, the declining share of doctorates in the top-rated departments continued through the late 1970s. The social and psychological science fields appear to have less inherent reliance on research training support; they therefore have less sensitivity to shifts in federal support.

Another potential effect of the reduction in stipend support and the depressed job market is the length of time needed to complete the doctoral degree. As one would expect, the median registered time to complete the degree increased in most science and engineering fields in the 1973–83 period, although generally by very small amounts (table 6). For all fields, the median time increased from 5.7 to 6.2 years; however, most of this increase results from the social and psychological sciences, where the time needed increased from 5.7 years to 6.9 years.

Increases of roughly one-half year occurred in mathematics and computer science and the biological sciences, with little or no change occurring in engineering and the physical and environmental sciences (table 6).

There was considerable variation among fields when one compares the time to degree among different quality levels of departments. In 1983 large differences occurred between the highest- and lowest-rated quality groups in mathematics and computer science (5.6 versus 6.6 years) and in the physical and environmental sciences (5.4 versus 6.6 years). But little or no differences in these groups were evident in engineering, in the biological sciences, or in the social and psychological sciences (table 6).

The top-quality research departments in science and engineering (with the exception of the social and psychological sciences) appear to be maintaining their shares of enrollments, support, and doctorate production. Fundamental questions, however, remain about whether the quality of students undertaking graduate education is high enough and whether there are enough bright

Table 6. *Median Registered Time to Doctoral Degree, by Field and Program Quality Group, 1973–83*
Years

| Field and program quality group[a] | 1973 | 1974 | 1975 | 1976 | 1977 | 1978 | 1979 | 1980 | 1981 | 1982 | 1983 |
|---|---|---|---|---|---|---|---|---|---|---|---|
| All fields | 5.7 | 5.6 | 5.6 | 5.7 | 5.8 | 5.8 | 5.9 | 6.0 | 6.0 | 6.1 | 6.2 |
| Highest | 5.4 | 5.3 | 5.3 | 5.5 | 5.4 | 5.5 | 5.5 | 5.6 | 5.7 | 5.7 | 6.0 |
| Lowest | 5.8 | 5.8 | 5.8 | 5.9 | 6.0 | 6.0 | 6.1 | 6.2 | 6.3 | 6.4 | 6.5 |
| Engineering | 5.6 | 5.6 | 5.5 | 5.7 | 5.5 | 5.5 | 5.5 | 5.5 | 5.5 | 5.7 | 5.6 |
| Highest | 5.3 | 5.3 | 5.2 | 5.3 | 5.3 | 5.3 | 5.2 | 5.3 | 5.4 | 5.4 | 5.5 |
| Lowest | 5.7 | 5.9 | 5.7 | 5.9 | 5.7 | 5.9 | 5.8 | 5.8 | 6.0 | 6.0 | 5.8 |
| Mathematics and computer science | 5.6 | 5.5 | 5.5 | 5.6 | 5.7 | 5.7 | 5.9 | 5.9 | 6.0 | 6.0 | 6.2 |
| Highest | 4.9 | 4.8 | 5.1 | 5.2 | 5.2 | 5.1 | 5.4 | 5.6 | 5.6 | 5.5 | 5.6 |
| Lowest | 6.0 | 6.1 | 5.9 | 6.2 | 6.0 | 6.1 | 6.0 | 6.5 | 6.2 | 6.6 | 6.6 |
| Physical and environmental sciences | 5.7 | 5.6 | 5.5 | 5.6 | 5.7 | 5.7 | 5.5 | 5.6 | 5.6 | 5.7 | 5.8 |
| Highest | 5.3 | 5.2 | 5.2 | 5.2 | 5.2 | 5.3 | 5.2 | 5.2 | 5.2 | 5.2 | 5.4 |
| Lowest | 6.1 | 6.1 | 6.0 | 6.0 | 6.2 | 6.0 | 5.9 | 6.0 | 6.2 | 6.0 | 6.2 |
| Biological science | 5.6 | 5.5 | 5.6 | 5.6 | 5.7 | 5.7 | 5.8 | 5.8 | 5.9 | 6.0 | 6.1 |
| Highest | 5.5 | 5.5 | 5.5 | 5.6 | 5.6 | 5.7 | 5.9 | 5.8 | 5.9 | 6.1 | 6.0 |
| Lowest | 5.6 | 5.5 | 5.6 | 5.7 | 5.8 | 5.7 | 5.7 | 5.7 | 5.8 | 5.9 | 6.2 |
| Social and psychological sciences | 5.7 | 5.6 | 5.7 | 5.8 | 5.9 | 6.0 | 6.3 | 6.4 | 6.5 | 6.7 | 6.9 |
| Highest | 5.6 | 5.6 | 5.6 | 5.9 | 5.8 | 6.1 | 6.3 | 6.4 | 6.4 | 6.6 | 7.0 |
| Lowest | 5.7 | 5.7 | 5.8 | 5.9 | 6.0 | 6.1 | 6.4 | 6.5 | 6.7 | 7.0 | 7.0 |

Source: Same as table 5.

a. The highest group consists of the 10 percent highest rated departments in each field; the lowest group consists of the departments rated in the lowest 51–100 percentile in the field.

young people entering science and engineering fields. How smart is smart enough? How many engineers, chemists, biologists, and sociologists does the nation need? There are no definitive answers to these questions. Furthermore, defining quality and measuring it present virtually insurmountable problems.

The most common measures of quality are admissions test scores—Scholastic Aptitude Tests (SATs) and Graduate Record Examinations (GREs)—because of their availability. While they do provide a common yardstick, certain caveats should be kept in mind, the most important being that the predictive power of these tests is not considered high. Nevertheless, the issue must be addressed because it is the sine qua non of the graduate education system. Using what measures are available, one can at least see whether the trends are up or down. Because GREs are taken by a broad group of people applying for graduate school, they are a good place to start.[31]

31. Without actually matching scores with enrollees or graduates, there is no assurance that the test takers actually attended graduate school. Furthermore, there is no assurance that they are representative of the population of potential or actual graduate students.

A recent study by a researcher from the National Institute of Education examined trends in GRE aptitude and achievement test scores from 1964 to 1982.[32] The study found that in the mid- to late 1960s, when enrollments were rising rapidly, mean GRE scores in engineering and the sciences (except physics) declined substantially. Thus it would appear that the overall level of quality declined in this expansionary period. In the subsequent contractional period of the early 1970s, trends in average GRE scores were mixed. GRE scores in the natural sciences turned upward, while those in engineering remained stable. Psychology scores remained steady and economics scores increased. Scores in political science and sociology, except for a brief climb, continued their downward slide.

The period of the late 1970s and the early 1980s also showed mixed trends in GRE scores.[33] Average GRE scores in this period were stable in engineering and the natural sciences, increased in mathematics, remained stable in psychology and economics, and continued to decline in political science and sociology. It is worth noting, therefore, that in engineering, where enrollments have climbed, average GRE scores have not fallen, while in political science and sociology, GRE scores have continued to fall in the face of level or declining enrollments. One might surmise from these trends that the popularity of engineering has attracted larger numbers of bright students (many of whom are foreign), while some social science fields may be losing a disproportionate share of their brightest potential students to other fields.

Another study using GRE scores was conducted for NSF by the Educational Testing Service to examine trends in GRE scores of applicants for the prestigious NSF fellowship program. These GRE scores were compared with GRE scores of all applicants in their fields and with those of applicants to a selected group of prestigious universities from 1974 to 1980.[34] In general there were significant differences in the mean advanced test scores among the three groups. In biology, for example, in 1980 there were 53 points (617–670) between the mean advanced test scores of all candidates and the scores of those applying to the selected group of elite schools, and an additional 45 points difference (670–715)

---

32. Clifford Adelman, "The Standardized Test Scores of College Graduates, 1964–1982," prepared for National Institute of Education, Study Group on the Conditions of Excellence in American Higher Education, Washington, D.C., December 1984.

33. Ibid.

34. Thomas Hilton, "Trends in the GRE Scores Reported to the NSF and to Selected Graduate Schools: An Update" (Princeton, N.J.: Educational Testing Service, 1983).

between the scores of those applying to the elite schools and those of NSF applicants, a total spread of 98 points. The largest spread was in mathematics (133 points), and the smallest spreads were in geology and psychology (56 and 57 points). The differences generally remained substantial over the six years of the study, thus confirming the selectivity of the prestigious schools and of the NSF fellowship program.

Another piece of recent evidence that is pertinent to the issue of student quality is a survey of opinions of graduate school deans concerning changes in the quality of applicants and doctorate recipients from 1976–77 to 1981–82.[35] While such evidence is soft, these are knowledgeable observers whose opinions are worth noting. With respect to the quality of applicants for science and engineering fields (no differentiation was made among fields), 60 percent indicated that there was no significant change in the last five years, 27 percent indicated significant improvement, and only 14 percent said there was a significant decline in quality. The deans of the top fifty doctorate-granting institutions expressed similar views. Discussing changes in the quality of doctorate recipients, 72 percent of the top fifty deans indicated no change in the last five years, 23 percent indicated a significant improvement, and 5 percent said the earlier group was better qualified. It is clear, then, that graduate school deans have not observed a decline in graduate student quality in the last five years and are in general agreement with the GRE data for this period.

One contention frequently heard is that the nation's brightest arts and science bachelor's-degree recipients are no longer pursuing advanced degrees in these fields, and that there is a kind of brain drain from these fields into professional school fields, such as medicine, law, and business.[36] Rodney Hartnett has attempted to address this issue by identifying two separate groups of graduates (arts and science doctorate recipients and professional degree holders), obtaining their college entrance exam scores (primarily SATs), and then examining the differences in scores between the two groups for four cohorts over the years 1966, 1971, 1976, and 1981.[37]

35. Frank Atelsek, *Student Quality in the Sciences and Engineering: Opinions of Senior Academic Officials*, HEP Report 58 (Washington, D.C.: American Council on Education, 1984).

36. For example, see William G. Bowen, *Report of the President, Princeton University, 1981*. Bowen's concern is with the humanities and the social sciences. A different kind of brain drain has occurred with respect to engineering and computer science—not out of the field, but into business and industry rather than into graduate school.

37. Rodney Hartnett, *Trends in Student Quality in Doctoral and Professional Education* (New Brunswick, N.J.: Rutgers University, 1985).

Hartnett's data reveal similar overall trends in doctorate, professional, and national norm groups over the fifteen-year period of study. Scores of degree recipients gradually increased from 1966 to 1976, then declined slightly to 1981. Throughout this period the mean SAT Math scores of doctorate recipients were consistently higher than those of professional degree recipients by twenty or more points. Trends were also similar in EMP and social science fields, with EMP sciences having higher SAT Math scores. Hartnett also found that the rising and falling trends in these scores of arts and science doctorate recipients were the same in prestigious departments as in less selective departments, with prestigious departments having consistently higher scores. In the most recent period of general decline, the percentage of science doctorate recipients in all fields who scored above 750 on the SAT Math test increased substantially, while the percentage scoring below 600 also increased. The implication here is that the quality of the top doctorate recipients has increased and that the overall decline results from the greater number of lower scores by other doctorate recipients.

The data available on the quality of graduate students entering science and engineering are clearly too sketchy to arrive at either comprehensive or definitive conclusions. Nonetheless, some hypotheses may be posited based on the limited evidence. In the expansionary period of the 1960s, the base of graduate education was broadened through the establishment of new doctoral departments and institutions, the improvement and expansion of existing institutions, and the provision of considerable new amounts of financial assistance. As a result a larger number of excellent students were attracted to graduate study. At the same time the expanding base may have led to some lowering of overall student quality as enrollments and support were distributed to newer and less selective programs.

In the early 1970s, sharp contractions in support and a downturn in the labor market led to declining enrollments in most natural science and engineering fields. Losses in enrollments and support were generally distributed evenly across different quality departments. At the same time, average GRE scores increased, indicating a heightened selectivity. After the mid-1970s, the natural sciences and engineering remained in an overall condition of steady state (although some engineering fields and computer science grew rapidly during the early 1980s). This condition was reflected in the generally unchanged distribution of enrollments and support among departments of different quality levels and in the steady levels of average GRE scores of applicants.

A caveat needs to be made regarding the apparently positive condition reflected in the stable distribution of resources among the quality levels of departments in the natural sciences and engineering. The process of merit and peer review systems in the awarding of fellowships, training grants, and research grants suggests that there should be a greater concentration of financial support among elite research departments as resources contract, rather than the stable distribution that occurred. While the best institutions shared proportionately in the declining pool of financial resources, the essential fact is that their resources did decline in absolute terms. Apparently the increased breadth of the graduate education system has permanently altered the distribution of resources, either because excellence is now more widely distributed or because practical political considerations dictate such a distribution.

For most social and behavioral sciences, in contrast to the natural sciences and engineering, quality indicators have turned consistently downward since the mid-1960s. Top-quality social science departments have had declining shares of enrollments, doctorates, and sources of stipend support. In addition, GRE scores of applicants in these fields (with the exception of economics) have declined consistently since the mid-1960s. While the natural sciences and engineering appear to be maintaining a stable level of attractiveness for bright students, the social and behavioral sciences appear to be experiencing a continuing loss of talent to other fields.

*Research agenda*

The quality of data used in this paper has been uneven, the result largely of inadequate attention to graduate education and the consequent inadequate funding of research necessary to address the pertinent issues. Although research will not answer all questions, especially those requiring normative decisions, policy decisions can and must be based on a better knowledge than currently exists.

The federal policy choices relevant to this paper revolve around the provision of student financial support—how much, to whom, in what areas, and by what means. Such decisions will affect, though they will not wholly determine, levels of enrollment and degree production and the quality of graduate students and graduate education. The underlying questions have not changed over the years. Should the "free market" be allowed to determine student choice, or is subsidy needed to assist free choice? How much subsidy do graduate students in science and engineering merit? Should such subsidies be directed to national manpower needs or should they simply allow free rein to the best minds? Should the individual student or the institution or department be the locus of support? To help address these questions, an improved data base needs to be established, and additional research needs to be conducted.

The major improvement that needs to be made is in the data base for graduate student support not covered in the NSF student support survey. As noted in the above discussion, major changes appear to be occurring. The amount of support devoted to a primary source may have changed over the years; some of the primary sources under the inclusive self-support heading, especially loans, work, and family support, are becoming more important; secondary sources, especially loans, seem to be increasing; and more information is needed about the support of part-time students, both matriculated and nonmatriculated, especially that provided by employers.

Several steps should be taken to meet these needs. Information from the NSF survey about the primary source of support should be augmented to provide information on industry, loan, work, and family support. A periodic sample survey of graduate students is needed to obtain more exact information about the magnitude of various sources, especially secondary sources, and about the costs of graduate education. Such a survey would cover a representative sample of fields, types of institutions, and students' year of study. It would collect detailed information on types of loans and amounts borrowed annually and cumulatively. The Department of Education and state guaranty agencies should routinely collect and report information on types and amounts of Education Department loans to graduate students by field, by year of study, and by amount of annual and cumulative borrowing. Considerably more attention needs to be given to collecting information about the numbers and financing of part-time, master's-degree, and employer-paid graduate students. These groups overlap, but they are also distinct. A more precise definition of these populations is necessary.

Considerable research and analysis need to be performed. The relationship between sources of support and doctorate degree production needs exploration. Are certain types of support more effective than others? How are time to degree and attrition affected?

An additional area for exploration concerns the mechanics of growth and of decline in graduate programs. Why did the system continue to grow in the 1970s? In what kinds of institutions and departments? How were their students supported? What are the characteristics of those departments showing substantial improvement or loss in quality?

Another area needing research is one in which costs are outpacing resources for graduate education. How are loans being used—as a minor supplement or as a major source? Who is borrowing, and in what fields? Does borrowing create incentives to enter certain fields or specialties and disincentives to enter others?

Finally, the nontraditional population of graduate students needs to be defined. Is cyclical retraining a reality in high-technology fields? Are employers financing such training—in what fields, on a full-time or part-time basis, in matriculated or nonmatriculated programs? What employers have these programs, and how much financial support is available? Exploration of this area is increasingly important because of the quickening pace of technological change and the growing awareness of the need for periodic retraining of employees.

The data on student quality presented in this paper show some current trends, but they are too partial, too episodic, and, to some extent, too out of date to command much confidence. We need ways to obtain more up-to-date information on the attraction of highly talented students to graduate study, especially on the pathways of the most talented college students into or out of graduate fields.[38]

A related but largely unexplored area is the relationship between sources of support and the quality of graduate education. How many highly talented students are lost to graduate study because of a lack of adequate financing or career opportunities? High-quality students, however, are only one aspect of high-quality graduate education. I have discussed the importance of mechanisms of support to the education and training process and the notion of a balance in types of support—fellowships, RAs, TAs—as beneficial to the quality of graduate education. Further investigation is needed into what balance is desirable in various fields and whether the cutbacks in federal fellowships and traineeships have had an adverse impact on the quality of graduate education. Has too much reliance been placed on RAs and TAs? Related to

---

38. One study by the Consortium on Financing Higher Education (COFHE), will examine changes in the proportions of talented college seniors who select arts and science graduate education as opposed to professional school study. Frank Goldberg and Ray Koenigsknect, *Highest Achievers*, forthcoming.

this is the issue of stability, which most observers have argued is an important factor in maintaining a quality training environment. Did the roller coaster of support in the 1960s and 1970s adversely affect training quality? If the findings reveal negative effects, how should support be structured to prevent or mitigate such occurrences? Should the manpower rationale be modified to provide more stability? Should longer-term institution-based support, such as training grants, be more frequently used?

Addressing these questions and providing the necessary background data will yield valuable insights into the function and the structure of graduate education and will assist policymakers who wish to evaluate the health of graduate education.

# The State of Academic Labor Markets

MICHAEL S. MCPHERSON

THE STATE of graduate education is closely linked to developments in academic labor markets. Even though more and more Ph.D.'s find themselves seeking employment in nonacademic settings (whether by necessity or by choice), universities and colleges remain the most important employers of doctorate recipients in most disciplines. Graduate institutions, the educators of these Ph.D.'s, must concern themselves with their students' employment destinations. Moreover, graduate institutions are themselves major employers of Ph.D.'s. From that perspective they must take account of developments that may affect their ability to hire qualified personnel. This paper surveys what is happening to the academic employment patterns of Ph.D.'s and tries to detect signs of what may lie ahead. The emphasis is on description and diagnosis rather than on recommended cures.

The paper begins with an overview of recent developments affecting faculty labor markets as a whole and then focuses on two areas where change has been most rapid: the humanities and the technical fields of engineering and computer science. The third section takes up recent attempts to project the longer-run future of academic labor markets and attempts to see how those projections are faring in light of recent experience. The following section attempts to identify some of the principal policy concerns implied by these actual and potential developments and indicates the range of proposals that have been advanced to respond to those concerns. A brief note on data needs precedes the conclusion.

The reference in the title of this paper to academic labor markets in the plural is no accident. Ph.D.'s are highly specialized personnel (as anyone who has listened to professors pronounce on affairs outside their specialty can attest). Employment conditions differ very widely among disciplines and even among subdisciplines, with the result that few generalizations about the market for faculty as a whole are worth much. Unfortunately, thorough discussions of disaggregated data are demanding of space, of the

57

reader's patience, and sometimes of the author's knowledge. The strategy in this paper has been to present data in as disaggregated a form as feasible, to highlight in the text the areas where developments are most striking, and to encourage readers to examine for themselves the data for fields that are not extensively discussed in the text.

*Recent changes in demand for faculty*

Four important trends characterize recent developments in academic labor markets. (1) The demand for new faculty has shifted noticeably among academic disciplines, with rapid growth in computer science and in some fields of engineering accompanied by a marked weakening of the market in the humanities and in some physical and social sciences. (2) The proportion of recent Ph.D.'s obtaining academic appointments has gradually declined across a wide range of disciplines. The decline has occurred slowly in some fields and much more rapidly in others. (3) Salary differentials among academic disciplines have widened. Technical fields, including engineering, computer science, and economics, have maintained or improved real salaries as other academic salaries have dropped. (4) The overall rate of growth of academic employment has gradually slowed; the slowdown has been more apparent in the past few years.

All four trends are closely related to changes in the level and composition of undergraduate enrollments and in student preferences among courses and majors. This close linkage should be expected, since the demand for teaching services is the most important single determinant of faculty employment levels.[1]

The most dramatic development in the enrollment market has been the large and sustained shift among undergraduate course selections and majors away from traditional arts and sciences subjects and toward such technical subjects as computer science and engineering, as well as business and economics (see table 1). This shift in choice of majors has been the main factor explaining the much discussed academic hiring shortages in engineering and computer science. It also is a factor in the noticeable worsening of the already weak academic market for humanists. The number of students majoring in traditional science fields like mathematics and physics has dropped, too, but the effects of this drop on

1. Research support is another determinant of academic employment and is especially important in the major universities. In recent years, however, overall funding levels have changed slowly and probably have not had much effect on aggregate academic employment trends. Shifts in the patterns of research funding—toward applied science and away from social science and humanities—have, if anything, reinforced the effects of enrollment shifts.

Table 1. *Percentage Change in Bachelors' Degrees Conferred by Institutions of Higher Education, by Field of Study, 1976–77 to 1981–82*

| Field of study | Change |
| --- | --- |
| All | 3.64 |
| Agriculture and natural resources | −2.04 |
| Architecture and environmental design | 5.49 |
| Area studies | −15.04 |
| Biological sciences | −22.32 |
| Business and management | 41.90 |
| Communications | 47.42 |
| Computer and informational sciences | 216.33 |
| Education | −29.65 |
| Engineering | 62.34 |
|   Civil, construction, transportation | 27.90 |
|   Electrical, electronics, communication | 65.61 |
|   Mechanical | 80.73 |
| Fine and applied arts | −3.28 |
| Foreign languages | −29.42 |
| Health professions | 11.03 |
| Letters | −13.55 |
|   English, general and English literature | −18.89 |
|   Philosophy | −23.64 |
| Mathematics | −18.29 |
| Physical sciences | 6.91 |
|   General; physics: general, molecular, nuclear | −12.53 |
|   Chemistry: general, inorganic, organic, physical, analytical, pharmaceutical | −1.36 |
|   Astronomy and astrophysics | −25.66 |
|   Geology | 42.70 |
| Psychology | −13.39 |
| Public affairs and services | −5.26 |
| Social sciences | −14.89 |
|   Anthropology | −36.50 |
|   Economics | 29.94 |
|   History | −32.58 |
|   Geography | −4.15 |
|   Political science and government | −2.85 |
|   Sociology | −35.01 |
| Theology | −1.82 |
| Interdisciplinary studies | 5.55 |

Source: U.S. Department of Education, National Center for Education Statistics, *Earned Degrees Conferred* (Government Printing Office, 1979 and 1984).

faculty demand have apparently been partly offset by increased enrollments in mathematics and science courses by engineering and computer science majors.

The shifts among disciplines in demand for and employment of faculty are shown in tables 2 and 3 (fully comparable data are not available for science and engineering Ph.D.'s and for human-

Table 2. *Number of Ph.D. Scientists and Engineers, by Occupation and Type of Employer, 1979, 1981, 1983*

| Occupation | Total employment | | | Educational institutions | | | Four-year colleges, universities, medical schools | | |
|---|---|---|---|---|---|---|---|---|---|
| | 1979 | 1981 | 1983 | 1979 | 1981 | 1983 | 1979 | 1981 | 1983 |
| Physical scientists | 64,318 | 63,198 | 63,986 | 27,248 | 28,333 | 27,931 | 25,928 | 26,897 | 26,453 |
| Mathematical scientists | 16,060 | 15,594 | 16,379 | 12,606 | 12,739 | 13,244 | 12,113 | 12,294 | 12,770 |
| Computer specialists | 6,758 | 9,048 | 12,164 | 2,457 | 3,010 | 4,031 | 2,443 | 2,954 | 3,905 |
| Environmental scientists and economists[a] | 27,590 | 29,455 | 33,425 | 13,861 | 15,789 | 18,044 | 13,589 | 15,425 | 17,783 |
| Engineers | 51,532 | 56,953 | 61,545 | 17,048 | 18,083 | 20,320 | 16,929 | 18,018 | 20,249 |
| Life scientists | 86,322 | 86,715 | 92,802 | 52,207 | 56,787 | 58,906 | 50,938 | 55,528 | 57,315 |
| Psychologists | 40,262 | 43,064 | 46,645 | 19,949 | 21,833 | 22,182 | 17,670 | 19,195 | 19,377 |
| Social scientists less economists[a] | 39,438 | 39,520 | 42,374 | 28,550 | 30,235 | 31,392 | 27,371 | 28,699 | 29,702 |
| Total | 332,280 | 343,538 | 369,320 | 173,966 | 186,809 | 196,050 | 166,985 | 179,010 | 187,554 |
| | *Annual percent change[b]* | | | | | | | | |
| Physical scientists | ... | −0.9 | 0.6 | ... | 2.0 | −0.7 | ... | 1.8 | −0.8 |
| Mathematical scientists | ... | −1.5 | 2.5 | ... | 0.5 | 2.0 | ... | 0.7 | 1.9 |
| Computer specialists | ... | 16.9 | 17.2 | ... | 11.3 | 17.0 | ... | 10.5 | 16.1 |
| Environmental scientists and economists[a] | ... | 3.4 | 6.7 | ... | 7.0 | 7.4 | ... | 6.8 | 7.6 |
| Engineers | ... | 5.3 | 4.0 | ... | 3.0 | 6.2 | ... | 4.5 | 1.6 |
| Life scientists | ... | 0.2 | 3.5 | ... | 4.4 | 1.9 | ... | 4.3 | 0.5 |
| Psychologists | ... | 3.5 | 4.2 | ... | 4.7 | 0.8 | ... | 3.7 | 4.6 |
| Social scientists less economists[a] | ... | 0.1 | 3.6 | ... | 3.0 | 1.9 | ... | 2.4 | 1.7 |
| Total | ... | 1.7 | 3.8 | ... | 3.7 | 2.5 | ... | 3.6 | 2.4 |

Sources: National Science Foundation, *Characteristics of Doctoral Scientists and Engineers in the United States, 1979, 1981* (GPO, 1982 and 1984); unpublished NSF data from the Survey of Doctorate Recipients.

a. In 1979 and 1981 "agricultural economics" was included in "environmental sciences," but in 1983 it was moved to "economics" (there were estimated to be 2,333 such persons in 1983; their distribution among types of employers is not known). The "environmental science" and "economics" categories have been combined here to avoid allowing this definitional change to influence apparent trends.

b. Two-year percentage change divided by two.

ities Ph.D.'s).[2] During the period 1979–83 combined computer specialty and engineering employment in four-year colleges and universities increased annually by 25 percent. In the same period, total employment in seven humanities fields at the same group of institutions grew by only 11 percent a year, the same growth as was experienced in all science and engineering fields together, exclusive of computer science and engineering. The growth rate in computer science and engineering academic employment rose substantially after 1981 while falling sharply in other fields. These data provide clear evidence that colleges and universities are

2. The science and engineering data in table 2 count Ph.D.'s by field of employment, while the humanities data count people by the field in which they earned their Ph.D. Since people tend to switch out of declining fields and into expanding fields, the statistics on science and engineering "field of employment" will tend to show larger swings than the humanities data based on "field of doctorate."

Table 3. *Number of Ph.D. Humanists, by Field of Doctorate and Type of Employer,*
*1979, 1981, 1983*

| Field[a] | Total employment | | | Educational institutions | | | Four-year colleges, universities, medical schools | | |
|---|---|---|---|---|---|---|---|---|---|
| | 1979 | 1981 | 1983 | 1979 | 1981 | 1983 | 1979 | 1981 | 1983 |
| History | 16,300 | 18,400 | 18,516 | 13,268 | 14,959 | 14,736 | 11,883 | 13,266 | 13,010 |
| Art history | 1,500 | 1,700 | 2,110 | 1,254 | 1,391 | 1,619 | 1,244 | 1,358 | 1,600 |
| Music | 4,000 | 4,700 | 5,378 | 3,460 | 3,966 | 4,467 | 3,176 | 3,652 | 4,018 |
| Philosophy | 5,200 | 5,600 | 6,059 | 4,446 | 4,872 | 4,996 | 4,129 | 4,625 | 4,600 |
| English and American language and literature | 17,700 | 19,000 | 20,286 | 15,753 | 16,682 | 17,258 | 14,656 | 15,162 | 15,462 |
| Classical language and literature | 1,500 | 1,600 | 1,662 | 1,266 | 1,357 | 1,365 | 1,143 | 1,234 | 1,279 |
| Modern language and literature | 11,000 | 12,400 | 13,339 | 9,944 | 10,949 | 11,488 | 9,218 | 9,994 | 10,530 |
| Total | 57,200 | 63,400 | 67,350 | 49,391 | 54,176 | 55,929 | 45,449 | 49,291 | 50,499 |
| | | | | *Annual percent change*[b] | | | | | |
| History | . . . | 6.4 | 3.2 | . . . | 6.4 | −0.7 | . . . | 5.8 | −1.0 |
| Art history | . . . | 6.7 | 12.1 | . . . | 5.5 | 8.2 | . . . | 4.6 | 8.9 |
| Music | . . . | 8.8 | 7.2 | . . . | 7.3 | 6.3 | . . . | 7.5 | 5.0 |
| Philosophy | . . . | 3.8 | 4.1 | . . . | 4.8 | 1.3 | . . . | 6.0 | −0.3 |
| English and American language and literature | . . . | 3.7 | 3.4 | . . . | 3.0 | 1.7 | . . . | 1.7 | 1.0 |
| Classical language and literature | . . . | 3.3 | 1.9 | . . . | 3.6 | 0.3 | . . . | 4.0 | 1.8 |
| Modern language and literature | . . . | 6.4 | 3.8 | . . . | 5.1 | 2.5 | . . . | 4.2 | 2.7 |
| Total | . . . | 5.4 | 3.1 | . . . | 4.9 | 1.6 | . . . | 4.2 | 1.2 |

Sources: National Research Council, *Science, Engineering, and Humanities Doctorates in the United States, 1979, 1981* (National Academy of Sciences, 1980; National Academy Press, 1982); unpublished data from NRC.
a. The categories "speech and theater" and "other humanities" are excluded because of definitional changes over time.
b. Two-year percentage change divided by two.

adjusting their staffing patterns to accommodate strong student interest in technical fields.

Reduced growth in academic employment in the humanities as well as in some social science and natural science fields has constricted academic job openings in those areas and has encouraged Ph.D.'s in those areas to seek nonacademic employment. The shift in the humanities has been rapid indeed. From 1979 to 1983, the percentage of Ph.D.'s in seven major humanities fields employed in educational institutions fell from 86 percent to 75 percent. To make the same point another way, fully half the growth in employment in those humanities fields has been in nonacademic jobs since 1979—and this in fields where traditionally more than four out of five Ph.D.'s entered the academic profession.

Perhaps more surprising, even in technical fields, where the academic demand for Ph.D.'s has strengthened, the percentage of

Ph.D.'s employed in educational institutions has gradually declined. Among computer science Ph.D.'s specifically, the share of educational employment has fallen substantially since the early 1970s, while in engineering it has been roughly constant.[3] If new Ph.D.'s in the humanities and other nontechnical fields are being "pushed" out of academe by the lack of good jobs, engineering and computer science Ph.D.'s are being "pulled" away by the same booming market for technical people that has been driving the shift in undergraduate majors.

A further consequence of the shifting course and major preferences of undergraduates has been pressure on university and college salary scales. Partly because competition to enroll the best students is intense, universities and colleges are eager to expand faculty in areas where student demand is rising. Stiff competition from nonacademic employers is forcing the universities to offer premium starting salaries to do so. At the same time inflation and budgetary pressures have encouraged universities and colleges to permit salaries in low-demand fields to drop in real terms. The result has been a noticeable widening of salary differentials for faculty in different fields, especially at the assistant professor level. Data for the land grant schools show that assistant professor salaries in many fields, including biology, social science, and foreign languages, fell by over 15 percent in real terms from 1976 to 1981; real salaries in engineering and computer science stayed roughly constant.[4]

The rate of growth in faculty employment as a whole has gradually slowed, though the slowdown has been less obvious than the shifting fortunes of employment in different academic disciplines. Good recent data on total faculty size are hard to find; however, data from the National Center for Education Statistics (NCES) suggest that total numbers of full-time-equivalent faculty grew by 31 percent from 1972 to 1977, but by only 10 percent from 1977 to 1982.[5] This finding is bolstered by more precise data on science and engineering Ph.D.'s. A long-term slowdown in growth of employment for Ph.D. scientists and engineers in educational institutions is evident in data from the National Research Council's (NRC) Survey of Doctorate Recipients. Such

3. National Science Foundation, *Characteristics of Doctoral Scientists and Engineers in the United States, 1981* (Government Printing Office, 1982); unpublished data from NSF.

4. Reported in *Academe*, July–August 1982, p. 9.

5. Unfortunately, in recent years, NCES has resorted to estimating faculty size on the basis of enrollments instead of on the basis of direct counts. See National Center for Education Statistics, *Condition of Education, 1984* (GPO, 1984), p. 78.

employment grew by more than 15 percent between 1973 and 1975 and by only 5 percent between 1981 and 1983. Unfortunately, comparable long-term data are not available for humanities Ph.D.'s, but they would most likely show a more severe drop in faculty growth.

Even a gradual slowing in employment growth has a magnified effect on hiring, since the amount of new hiring depends on the increment in faculty size. Suppose, for example, replacement demand for faculty—the amount of hiring needed to compensate for deaths, retirements, resignations, and dismissals—amounts to 4 percent of total faculty (a reasonable estimate based on past experience). Then a decline in the annual growth rate of faculty from 7 percent to 4 percent would reduce the number of new hires from 11 percent of the faculty to 8 percent, a decline of more than 25 percent. Although accurate data on hiring rates are not available, this is probably a fair estimate of the contraction in academic hiring that occurred between the early 1970s and the early 1980s.

This slowdown in faculty hiring naturally correlates with the comparable slowdown in enrollment growth over the same period. Thus from 1970 to 1976 full-time-equivalent enrollments grew by 24 percent, while from 1976 to 1982 (the most recent year for which data are available) those enrollments grew by just 11 percent. Shifts in the composition of enrollment among types of institutions and students have also contributed to the slowdown in faculty demand, especially for Ph.D. faculty. Part-time enrollments and enrollments at two-year colleges have been growing more rapidly than other enrollments, in part because of the increasing enrollment of older students, who are more likely to be in these categories. Because such enrollments tend to be associated with higher student-faculty ratios and with institutions where Ph.D.'s are a smaller fraction of the faculty, they generate less demand for faculty and for Ph.D. faculty than do equivalent full-time enrollments or enrollments at four-year institutions.

The enrollment trends described here, both in total and in composition, can probably be linked to underlying demographic movements—the slowed growth and now shrinkage in the college-age population. Continuation of these trends could easily lead to shrinkage in total Ph.D. faculty in American higher education within the next few years.

The shift in enrollment and faculty demand among disciplines described earlier has been taking place against this background of sluggish growth in overall faculty demand. A comparable shift in student interests during an enrollment boom like that of the 1960s would have served only to influence relative rates of employment growth. Managing such shifts is much more difficult in the face of overall enrollments and the total number of faculty, which are growing slowly and which may soon decline.

*Engineering and humanities: two kinds of distress*

The impact of shifts in undergraduate major preferences can be understood more clearly by examining two areas where change has been most rapid: the humanities on the one hand and computer science and engineering on the other.[6] The reader should keep in mind that these are extremes on a continuum: business and economics have shared in the gains experienced in technical fields, while some arts and sciences fields, among them sociology, mathematics, and physics, have suffered declines paralleling those in the humanities. Thus much of the following discussion would apply, with appropriate adjustments, to these other areas as well.

Paradoxically, the boom in engineering and computer science enrollments and the depression in humanities enrollments give rise to sometimes parallel worries about the faculty hiring situation in those fields. Both surplus and shortage areas cause worry about the capacity of academic institutions to attract enough high-quality personnel to those fields—in the case of engineering because nonacademic job prospects are so strong, in the case of the humanities because academic job prospects look so weak. Ultimately the problems facing the two areas must be considered jointly, since the enrollment upturn in technical disciplines and the downturn in humanistic disciplines are two sides of the same coin. After examining issues for the two sectors separately, the discussion considers their combined effect on universities and graduate schools.

### Humanities

The extent of distress in the academic job market for humanists is clearly shown in a recent survey of colleges and universities conducted by the American Council on Education (ACE). These results corroborate the NRC survey's indication that total academic employment has actually fallen in recent years in some humanities fields. Table 4 indicates that between 1979 and 1982 the number of full-time faculty in history and philosophy decreased by several

6. This paper adopts the classification scheme of the NRC surveys, which group history with the humanities; NCES groups history with the social sciences.

Table 4. *Comparison of Full-Time Humanities Faculty, by Discipline and Type of Institution, Fall 1979 and Fall 1982*

| Discipline and institution | Fall 1979 | | Fall 1982 | | Percent change |
|---|---|---|---|---|---|
| | Number | Percent | Number | Percent | |
| English, total | 28,076 | 100.0 | 28,267 | 100.0 | 0.7 |
| Universities | 6,801 | 24.2 | 6,912 | 24.5 | 1.6 |
| Four-year colleges | 12,254 | 43.6 | 12,532 | 44.3 | 2.3 |
| Two-year colleges | 9,022 | 32.1 | 8,823 | 31.2 | −2.2 |
| History, total | 13,613 | 100.0 | 13,159 | 100.0 | −3.3 |
| Universities | 3,824 | 28.1 | 4,019 | 30.5 | 5.1 |
| Four-year colleges | 6,933 | 50.9 | 6,446 | 49.0 | −7.0 |
| Two-year colleges | 2,856 | 21.0 | 2,695 | 20.5 | −5.7 |
| Modern languages, total | 11,009 | 100.0 | 11,552 | 100.0 | 4.9 |
| Universities | 4,167 | 37.9 | 4,598 | 39.8 | 10.3 |
| Four-year colleges | 5,470 | 49.7 | 5,464 | 47.3 | −0.1 |
| Two-year colleges | 1,372 | 12.5 | 1,489 | 12.9 | 8.6 |
| Philosophy, total | 5,889 | 100.0 | 5,704 | 100.0 | −3.1 |
| Universities | 1,813 | 30.8 | 1,986 | 34.8 | 9.6 |
| Four-year colleges | 3,261 | 55.4 | 3,092 | 54.2 | −5.2 |
| Two-year colleges | 815 | 13.8 | 625 | 11.0 | −23.3 |

Source: I. Gomberg and F. Alelsek, *Full-Time Humanities Faculty, Fall 1982* (American Council on Education, 1984). Figures are rounded.

percent,[7] while faculty growth in the field of English literature, a very large field for humanists, was extremely low.

Although a decline of a couple of percent may not seem dramatic, it is important to stress that even small declines in total faculty size imply rather severe restrictions on new hiring. If, for example, 2 percent of the faculty retire or die in a given year, and another 2 percent leave academic employment for other reasons, a 1 percent annual drop in total faculty will cut new hiring by a quarter, compared with a situation in which total faculty demand is constant. In history these percentages would imply that about 500 new positions for Ph.D.'s open up each year because of retirements and other departures, but, if the ACE data are correct, about 125 of those positions are disappearing because of shrinkage in faculty size.

The slowing demand for faculty has also caused a change in the kinds of appointments colleges and universities offer to young humanists. The ACE survey data indicate that approximately 57 percent of the new appointments in humanities fields in recent

7. The NRC data indicate somewhat smaller declines in academic employment of Ph.D.'s in history and philosophy than the ACE's counts of full-time faculty suggest. The differences may simply result from sampling error, or they may follow from changes in the role of part-time or non-Ph.D. faculty. It is important to stress that the trends suggested by these alternative data sources are similar.

Table 5. *Comparison of Full-Time Humanities Faculty Appointments, by Discipline, Academic Years 1979–80 and 1982–83*

| Faculty appointments | English | History | Modern languages | Philosophy |
|---|---|---|---|---|
| *Total* | | | | |
| 1979–80 | 2,055 | 453 | 694 | 456 |
| 1982–83 | 1,697 | 505 | 845 | 358 |
| Percent change | − 17.4 | 11.4 | 21.7 | − 21.5 |
| *Tenured or in tenure track* | | | | |
| 1979–80 | 862 | 213 | 377 | 228 |
| 1982–83 | 664 | 258 | 331 | 132 |
| Percent change | − 23.0 | 21.1 | − 12.2 | − 42.1 |
| *Not in tenure track* | | | | |
| 1979–80 | 1,193 | 240 | 317 | 228 |
| 1982–83 | 1,032 | 247 | 514 | 225 |
| Percent change | − 13.5 | 2.8 | 62.2 | − 1.2 |

Source: Same as table 4.

years have been to nontenure-track positions. These positions are typically temporary. The number of such positions is high, and it is apparently increasing. As table 5 shows, the ratio of nontenured to tenured or tenure-track appointments rose in every humanities discipline except history between 1979 and 1982. In fact, by 1982, 47 percent of full-time nontenured humanities faculty were in nontenure-track positions.

Even with these substantial declines in humanities hiring, it appears that colleges and universities may not have adjusted fully to recent enrollment shifts. According to NCES data cited earlier, history majors have dropped by 33 percent since the mid-1970s, while total numbers of history faculty have stayed roughly constant. If these low history enrollments continue, there will most likely be a further downward adjustment in the number of persons teaching history. Drops in numbers of philosophy, English, and foreign-language faculty are probable too.[8]

As one would expect, the substantial decline in actual and prospective academic employment prospects in the humanities has had a considerable impact both on the numbers of persons seeking humanities Ph.D.'s and on employment patterns for young humanists. In the fields that have been hardest hit, including history, English, and philosophy, Ph.D. production has been declining steadily since the early 1970s, and it is now down to 50 percent or 60 percent of its 1974 level (see table 6). Substantial

8. Faculty demands tend to be more stable than numbers of majors, because of enrollments in survey courses and other courses taken by students not majoring in the field.

Table 6. *Number of Doctorate Recipients, by Field and Year, Selected Years, 1974–83*

| Field | 1974 | 1977 | 1980 | 1983 |
|---|---|---|---|---|
| Physical sciences | 4,976 | 4,379 | 4,111 | 4,424 |
| Mathematical sciences | 1,211 | 933 | 744 | 701 |
| Computer sciences | . . . | 31 | 218 | 285 |
| Physics and astronomy | 1,339 | 1,150 | 983 | 1,042 |
| Chemistry | 1,797 | 1,571 | 1,538 | 1,759 |
| Earth, atmosphere, and marine | 629 | 694 | 628 | 637 |
| Engineering | 3,147 | 2,643 | 2,479 | 2,780 |
| Life sciences | 4,962 | 4,920 | 5,460 | 5,540 |
| Social sciences | 5,884 | 6,073 | 5,855 | 6,055 |
| Anthropology | 379 | 385 | 370 | 373 |
| Economics | 834 | 811 | 744 | 792 |
| Political science | 776 | 614 | 505 | 397 |
| Sociology | 645 | 725 | 601 | 525 |
| Psychology | 2,598 | 2,990 | 3,098 | 3,307 |
| Humanities | 5,170 | 4,562 | 3,868 | 3,494 |
| History | 1,186 | 961 | 745 | 616 |
| Classics | 88 | 60 | 54 | 44 |
| Philosophy | 417 | 331 | 255 | 242 |
| American and English language and literature | 1,369 | 1,076 | 952 | 714 |
| Modern language and literature | 770 | 628 | 448 | 446 |

Source: National Research Council, *Summary Report, 1983: Doctorate Recipients from United States Universities* (National Academy Press, 1984).

reductions in rates of Ph.D. production are evident in some scientific fields as well.

Even at these sharply reduced rates of production, the market in these fields remains in considerable difficulty. Table 7 summarizes data on employment plans of new Ph.D.'s from the NRC's Survey of Earned Doctorates. The number of humanities Ph.D.'s still seeking employment at the time of the survey remained at the 30 percent level reached in the mid-1970s, about double the rate in 1971. This suggests that the decline in Ph.D. production since the mid-1970s did not succeed in tightening the market for new Ph.D.'s in humanities. Moreover, even though the rate of Ph.D. production in the humanities dropped by 30 percent since the mid-1970s, the portion of new Ph.D. humanists who had secured academic employment by the time of the survey stayed below 50 percent, much lower than the 70 percent rate of academic employment at the beginning of the 1970s. As noted, much of the recent employment has been in temporary positions.

Thus the academic market for humanists has stayed soft even as Ph.D. production has declined, and it may well soften further if recent trends in enrollment patterns continue. In history, for

Table 7. *Postgraduation Plans of Doctorate Recipients Entering the U.S. Labor Force, by Field of Doctorate, Selected Years, 1971–83*
Percent

| Field[a] | 1971 | 1975 | 1979 | 1983 |
|---|---|---|---|---|
| *Total doctorates*[b] | | | | |
| Seeking appointment | 20.4 | 25.6 | 26.1 | 27.1 |
| Definite academic plans | 56.7 | 49.5 | 46.6 | 45.7 |
| *Physics and astronomy* | | | | |
| Seeking appointment | 25.8 | 29.3 | 21.7 | 29.0 |
| Definite academic plans | 44.4 | 42.1 | 45.2 | 43.5 |
| *Chemistry* | | | | |
| Seeking appointment | 19.4 | 20.8 | 17.7 | 22.5 |
| Definite academic plans | 47.0 | 43.5 | 41.7 | 36.9 |
| *Mathematics* | | | | |
| Seeking appointment | 22.9 | 28.6 | 26.0 | 22.3 |
| Definite academic plans | 61.0 | 48.7 | 48.8 | 56.5 |
| *Engineering* | | | | |
| Seeking appointment | 27.1 | 27.3 | 22.6 | 27.6 |
| Definite academic plans | 24.6 | 21.7 | 24.8 | 26.7 |
| *Biological and health sciences* | | | | |
| Seeking appointment | 20.2 | 21.9 | 20.6 | 23.4 |
| Definite academic plans | 61.5 | 59.3 | 62.3 | 60.4 |
| *Agricultural sciences* | | | | |
| Seeking appointment | 26.1 | 26.6 | 30.8 | 33.9 |
| Definite academic plans | 45.5 | 41.3 | 40.5 | 34.8 |
| *Social sciences* | | | | |
| Seeking appointment | 16.0 | 24.0 | 27.3 | 30.4 |
| Definite academic plans | 61.4 | 49.1 | 40.7 | 36.9 |
| *Humanities* | | | | |
| Seeking appointment | 17.8 | 34.5 | 36.9 | 34.4 |
| Definite academic plans | 70.5 | 50.5 | 44.8 | 48.0 |

Source: National Research Council, *Summary Report, 1983*.
a. "Definite academic plans" comprise those reporting definite plans for either postdoctoral and doctoral study or academic appointment.
b. Includes doctorates in professional fields and education, not shown separately.

example, Ph.D. production is around 600 per year, and it is unlikely that more than 200 tenure-track positions in history are being created each year.[9]

Given the inability of the academic market to absorb the bulk of these new doctorates, the quality of nonacademic job opportunities for humanists (as well as for Ph.D.'s in some social science fields) is central to an evaluation of their job prospects. The picture here remains unclear, but the experience of the last decade, during which substantial numbers of Ph.D. humanists have sought

9. This estimate is based on the assumption that attrition of 4 percent a year creates a replacement demand for history faculty of about 500 a year, but a third of that is disappearing through shrinkage in total faculty. Even if as many as three-fifths of new positions are tenure track—a generous estimate—this would imply 200 new tenure-track openings a year.

nonacademic employment, provides some information. Actual unemployment of these highly educated personnel does not seem to be a serious problem: an NRC study of recent Ph.D.'s shows that only about 2.2 percent of humanities Ph.D.'s were unemployed and seeking employment five to eight years after receiving the doctorate.[10] The quality of the employment they obtain is much harder to assess. It remains true that most Ph.D. humanists initially aspire to academic careers and that many of those who obtain nonacademic jobs regard them as a second-best alternative.[11] The flood of applications a good academic job opening can attract is evidence of the eagerness with which fresh Ph.D.'s seek such positions. No clear evidence exists, however, to show that those who are employed outside academe report lower salaries or lower levels of job satisfaction than those with academic employment. Few say that they regret their graduate training.[12] The overall result is a little like discovering that, although the bus people boarded for a trip to Chicago actually deposited them in Detroit, interviews with the passengers indicate that, on balance, they like Detroit well enough.

The large numbers of humanists entering nonacademic jobs and nontenure-track jobs within academe make the present and the near future times of unusual uncertainty for both humanities graduate students and graduate departments. The scarcity of traditional academic jobs may adversely affect the quality of students seeking advanced training in the humanities, perhaps enough to reduce the quality of applicants for the limited number of good academic jobs available. Depending on how promising nonacademic alternatives appear, pressure may well emerge to reduce Ph.D. production further in some humanities fields and in other arts and sciences fields, even beyond the large reductions that have already occurred.

### Engineering and Computer Science

Engineering baccalaureates were at a cyclical low in the mid-1970s, but their growth since then has far surpassed any previous level, while the number of computer science majors has simply

10. National Research Council, *Departing the Ivy Halls: Changing Employment Situations for Recent Ph.D.'s* (Washington, D.C.: National Academy Press, 1983), p. 54.

11. One way of substantiating this point from available data is to note that humanities Ph.D.'s employed outside academe are much less likely to be employed in their Ph.D. field than are those in academe. A lack of job opportunities within the field is the reason people cite most frequently for being employed outside their Ph.D. field.

12. For supporting evidence, see Lewis C. Solmon and others, *Underemployed Ph.D.'s* (Lexington, Mass.: Lexington Books, 1981); Ernest May and Dorothy Blaney, *Careers for Humanists* (Academic Press, 1981); National Research Council, *Humanists on the Move: Employment Patterns for Humanities Ph.D.'s* (National Academy Press, 1985).

mushroomed since such degrees began to be counted in the early 1970s. As noted earlier, colleges and universities have responded by expanding engineering and computer science faculties much more quickly than other faculties. Despite these increases, there is considerable evidence that staffing adjustments are not complete. While the number of engineering B.A.'s increased by more than half and the number of computer science graduates more than tripled from the mid-1970s to the early 1980s, numbers of Ph.D. faculty in these areas increased by rather smaller proportions over a comparable period—about 92 percent in computer science and 41 percent in engineering from 1977 to 1983. Surveys conducted by the Engineering Manpower Commission for the Engineering College Faculty Shortage Project document the resulting gap between student loads and faculty availability. The 1982 survey of engineering deans indicated that 7.9 percent of all engineering faculty positions went unfilled in 1982 (more then 20 percent of vacancies at the level of assistant professor were unfilled).[13]

The majority of schools in the survey reported that faculty shortages had resulted in higher teaching loads and in some curtailment of course offerings. Schools also reported heavier reliance on part-time faculty and on foreign nationals in staffing positions. Engineering deans regard some of the faculty they are hiring as not fully qualified to teach (partly because of language problems). That and the increase in course loads have led to widespread worry in engineering schools about the quality of undergraduate engineering education.

Is the supply of new Ph.D.'s adequate to meet this demand? Ph.D. production has been growing rapidly in computer science (from a very low base) and, after a dip in the late 1970s, it is rising in engineering as well, a trend that is expected to continue (see table 6). As noted earlier, however, the share of these Ph.D.'s seeking academic employment is low compared with other Ph.D. fields and has not risen in response to the academic hiring shortages. Even though starting salaries for faculty in engineering and computer science have increased substantially faster than other academic salaries, the nonacademic market for technical people with advanced training has apparently stayed strong enough to compete effectively with academe for new Ph.D.'s. Although good data on comparative academic and nonacademic compensation are difficult to obtain, the attraction of nonacademic jobs appears to lie less in high starting salaries than in better long-run

13. A report on the survey appears in *Engineering Education*, vol. 73 (October 1983), pp. 47–53.

salary and career prospects and working conditions. The latter include, in many cases, better facilities and support for advanced research in industry than in academe.[14]

Still, enough Ph.D.'s are entering academic engineering and computer science to permit faculty in those areas to grow, despite the inevitable flow of resignations and retirements. If the number of majors in these fields stays constant or grows more slowly than the number of faculty, the shortages will eventually abate. The growth rate of engineering Ph.D. faculty is not high, however; only recently has it averaged more than 3 percent per year. If present trends continue, the shortages will not disappear quickly.[15] The outlook and appropriate responses to the shortages depend heavily on whether undergraduate interest in technical fields continues at present levels, grows, or declines.

### Managing Swings in Faculty Demand

If one looks at developments in the humanities and in technical fields simultaneously, it seems clear that universities and colleges have been reluctant so far to respond fully to recent swings in undergraduate course and major preferences. In shortage areas such as engineering and computer science, schools have responded in part through increased recruiting and improved salary offers, but they have also responded in important ways by allowing class sizes to rise, by enlisting faculty to teach outside their specialties, and (to some degree) by rationing enrollments into high-demand fields. In surplus areas, they have not allowed faculty levels or rates of hiring to drop as rapidly as movements in course preferences alone would call for. The desire to maintain staffing levels while preserving flexibility for further adjustments is reflected in the increasing reliance on nontenure-track appointments in humanities fields. This trend, in turn, probably reflects strain on university budgets, especially in the humanities.

The universities seem, in effect, to be playing for time, reluctant to curtail humanities programs they consider important and uncertain of how long the enrollment boom in engineering and computer science will last. They surely remember that past booms

14. See the discussion in National Research Council, *Labor Market Conditions for Engineers: Is There a Shortage?* (National Academy Press, 1984), and in Eugene Chesson, "The Future Shortage of Faculty: A Crisis in Engineering," *Engineering Education*, vol. 70 (April 1980), pp. 731–38.

15. Percentage growth rates in computer science faculties are much higher, but the base remains quite small, so the absolute growth is not great.

in engineering enrollments have been followed by sharp declines in which engineering staff have been temporarily redundant.

The current patterns of university adjustment are probably reasonable ones if the shift in undergraduate preferences is essentially transitory. But if the present trends prove lasting, more fundamental adjustments will probably occur. One would expect, in that event, firmer efforts to improve salaries and working conditions in technical fields and more rigorous curtailment of hiring in traditional arts and sciences fields. Other developments might include attempts by universities to systematize arrangements for employing leading engineers from industry and government as part-time faculty and a sharper differentiation between technical faculty and arts and sciences faculty in the governance of universities (following the model of law, medical, and business schools).

Are the recent trends away from arts and sciences and in favor of computer science and engineering likely to continue, or will they reverse themselves? One route by which a reversal could take place would be the imposition of more stringent liberal arts requirements for technical students, as proposed, for example, in the recent report by the National Institute of Education (NIE) panel on excellence in undergraduate education. Such requirements, even if they did not affect undergraduates' choice of majors, would lead to larger enrollments in humanities and related courses, and would thus reduce the trend away from those disciplines. There is, however, room for doubt that universities and colleges will move voluntarily to impose such requirements at a time of intense competition for students.

What is the likelihood that students themselves will migrate back toward arts and sciences majors and away from technical fields in the near future? Predicting undergraduate behavior (of any kind) is a notoriously hazardous business, but we can identify two principal sources of the trend toward engineering and computer science enrollments. One is the strong demand for technical people that has been associated with economic recovery, the rapid spread of computer technology, and the defense buildup. The other is the weak job market for liberal arts B.A.'s, the product, apparently, of rapid growth in the supply of such personnel in the 1960s and early 1970s and of relatively weak growth in employment demand in these areas in recent years.

Predictions of future demand for engineers and computer scientists vary widely, but a recent symposium sponsored by the National Research Council generated some consensus that the supply and demand for engineers as a whole are likely to be in rough balance for the rest of the decade.[16] This conclusion was predicated on the assumption that engineering enrollments would stay roughly at the high level reached in the most recent years. This analysis, then, does not suggest that the proportion of baccalaureates in technical fields will continue to increase, but neither does it point toward a sharp downturn in those labor markets that would result in a rapid drop in undergraduate enrollments.

The labor market for liberal arts B.A.'s will more likely show some improvement in the rest of the decade if economic growth continues and as growth in supply of personnel to that market diminishes. Such a development, if it occurs, might encourage a return to undergraduate major preferences more like those of the past. The result would be some easing in the academic hiring situation in both engineering and humanities, with more hiring opportunities in the humanities and a reduction in engineering faculty shortages. Any strong move in this direction, however, might well be blocked by reemergence of shortages in the market for B.S. engineers.

A reasonable guess is that undergraduate major preferences are likely to stabilize at something like their present levels for the next five to eight years. Such a future would most likely imply continuing low levels of academic hiring in the humanities and in some other arts and sciences fields and continuing shortages of highly qualified engineering and computer science faculty for some time to come.

Recent pressures on universities created by this large shift in student preferences seem likely to continue. Budgetary stringency is likely to produce downward pressure on academic salaries in arts and sciences, while competition with nonacademic alternatives will encourage continued increases in faculty salaries for engineers and computer scientists. Universities and colleges have a strong traditional resistance to responding to market pressures in this way, a tradition based partly on concerns about equity in institutions where faculty carry significant responsibility for governance. Salary differentials will continue to be a difficult problem for universities and colleges. Pressures to adjust staffing arrangements to enrollment patterns may present colleges and universities with other difficult choices about maintaining adequate programs in some traditional liberal arts areas and about making commit-

16. Shortages were thought to be likely in narrower subfields, including electrical engineering and computer-assisted design and manufacture. See National Research Council, *Labor Market Conditions.*

ments to technical education that may prove difficult to reverse. The poor academic market in some traditional liberal arts areas and the strong nonacademic market in some other areas raise doubts about the capacity of academe to attract enough of the very best people to sustain the vitality of scholarship and research. This concern is present in both technical and liberal arts fields, even though the forces at work are different.

*Future demands for faculty*

Difficulties created by interfield shifts in demand for faculty could be either eased or exacerbated depending on what happens to the overall demand for faculty. Several influential studies, which appeared between 1978 and 1981, argued that demographic trends portended serious future declines in faculty hiring. Perhaps the most careful and influential of these studies were the ones by Roy Radner and Charlotte Kuh for the Carnegie Council on Policy Studies in Higher Education and by William G. Bowen for the 1981 *Report of the President* at Princeton University.[17] The bleak picture presented by these studies was based in part on low faculty retirement rates in the 1980s owing to the skewed age distribution of the faculty. The studies relied even more heavily on projections of declining enrollment resulting from a declining college-age population. Many observers have come to question the relevance of these studies, since the anticipated decline in college enrollments has yet to occur, even though a decline in the college-age population has begun. Yet it is also true, as noted earlier, that recent declines in the faculty growth rate can be plausibly linked to a demographics-related slowdown in enrollment growth. It is therefore worth looking more carefully at recent developments to see how well these demographically driven projections are holding up so far.

It has also been widely noted that the demographic decline is only temporary, so that even if it does reduce enrollments, recovery can be anticipated in the 1990s, a time when retirements are also expected to rise. It therefore makes sense to take a brief look at the "further future," to see how strong a recovery it might be reasonable to expect.

Bowen projected a decline in full-time-equivalent faculty of about 15 percent from a peak in 1982 to a low point in 1996.

17. Roy Radner and Charlotte Kuh, *Preserving a Lost Generation: Policies to Assure a Steady Flow of Young Scholars Until the Year 2000*, Report to the Carnegie Council on Policy Studies in Higher Education (New York: The Council, October 1978); William G. Bowen, *Report of the President, Princeton University, 1981*.

Radner and Kuh, using a basically similar model, projected a slightly smaller decline of about 10 percent in total faculty, with the low point occurring a couple of years earlier. Behind these numbers lie projected declines in enrollment: Radner and Kuh projected a 12 percent fall in full-time-equivalent enrollments from a 1982 peak to a 1995 trough, while Bowen projected a 15 percent decline to a 1996 trough.[18] A steady and gradual drop of this sort in total faculty numbers, should it materialize, would have quite a serious effect on new academic hiring. With total faculty falling steadily, new hiring would be pushed below the number of openings created by replacement demand (and replacement would itself be somewhat depressed by below-normal retirement rates).

Is it safe, however, to dismiss these projections because enrollments have not yet fallen? Several considerations suggest that such a reaction is premature. First, neither study projects really noticeable enrollment declines until 1983, and the most recent firm data on enrollment only go through 1982. A comparison of the Radner-Kuh enrollment projection through 1982 with actual experience indicates that so far the projection is tracking well. The authors projected a 9.8 percent enrollment increase between 1976 and 1982; the actual increase was 10.8 percent. Substantial drops in the population of 18- to 24-year-olds are expected in 1985 and 1986; not until data are available for those years will a clear picture of the effectiveness of demography-driven enrollment projections emerge.

Second, the shift toward two-year colleges and the increased number of older students imply that each increment of enrollment is generating a smaller added demand for faculty than in the past. Many of those who expect enrollment declines to be avoided base their hopes on an anticipation of rapid growth in numbers of such nontraditional students; to the degree that it occurs, the result may not be as favorable for faculty demand (and especially demand for Ph.D. faculty) as aggregate enrollment numbers might suggest.

Finally, a closer look at the most recent available enrollment data from NCES provides hints that the effects of demographic decline are indeed already being felt. Even though total enrollment increased modestly from 1981 to 1982, first-time freshman en-

18. There are a number of differences in detail between these analyses. The timing difference in the low point of total faculty apparently results from Radner and Kuh's use of an 18- to 21-year-old population in projecting enrollment demand. Bowen used an approach that weighted enrollments of different age groups according to their representation in the population.

rollment actually fell sharply during that time. Only proprietary institutions showed growth in freshman enrollment. Moreover, enrollments of 18- to 19-year-olds—the group that should reveal demographic effects first—also fell between 1980 and 1982, by 6 percent.[19]

It is certainly too soon to say whether projections of enrollment and faculty decline will be realized. All such projections contain important uncertainties. But there is little evidence in developments so far that tends to discredit the projections, whose implications must therefore be taken seriously.

Should enrollment declines take hold, they could affect the trends discussed earlier. A shrinkage in total enrollments would tend to reduce the excess demands for engineering and computer science faculty if the enrollment declines are shared evenly among disciplines. On the same assumption, such declines would lead to further erosion in the demand for arts and sciences faculty. If a strong market for bachelor's-level personnel in technical fields keeps those enrollments up, faculty shortages in those areas will continue to be felt. The downward effects on demand for arts and sciences faculty could be even more severe. Those disciplines would then bear the full brunt of overall enrollment declines, and they might well experience large declines in their capacity to hire new faculty.

Retirement rates for faculty are expected to be higher in the late 1980s and the 1990s as faculty hired during the 1960s boom approach retirement age. The decline in the college-age population will reverse itself in the 1990s as well. Since the pipeline for production of faculty is long, it is useful to look ahead to get some sense of the extent of expansion we might anticipate.

Prediction of student preferences, or even the nature of higher education, a decade and more away is difficult. Data based on student and faculty demographics, however, suggest that recovery will come quite late in this century and will not be strong. The growth in replacement demand from rising retirement rates will be, as William Bowen put it, "steady and modest," a source of some relief but not of rapid recovery.[20] Death and retirement rates are expected to rise fairly steadily, from about 1 to 1.5 percent of the faculty a year now to 2.5 or 3 percent of the faculty a year by the end of the century. Changes of this magnitude can, however, easily be swamped by relatively small fluctuations in the size of the total faculty, or by changes in the rate at which faculty quit or are dismissed from academic jobs.

19. National Center for Education Statistics, *Condition of Education, 1984.*
20. Bowen, *Report of the President, Princeton University, 1981,* p. 16.

Changes in size of total faculty will be shaped largely by enrollment movements, which are in turn influenced by the size of the college-age population. Census projections indicate that the number of persons aged 18 to 24 will not start growing until 1997 and that then the growth will be quite modest.[21] During the early recovery years growth of that population group will average well under 2 percent per year. The census projects that by the year 2010, the size of that age group will still be nearly 10 percent below its peak of the early 1980s. Thus, if demography rules, faculty expansion will be late in coming and will be gradual.

These paragraphs fall far short of a careful projection of long-term conditions in academic labor markets. They do, however, suggest that the recovery to be expected from demographic forces alone—both faculty and student—is only modest and will not occur until quite close to the year 2000. Some observers have suggested that there is need to worry about a rather sudden emergence of faculty shortages in the early 1990s as a result of reversals in downward demographic trends. This worry may well prove exaggerated.

*Policy issues*   Graduate institutions must be concerned about trends in academic labor markets from two perspectives. First, as producers of Ph.D.'s, graduate institutions have a responsibility to supply the highly skilled personnel colleges and universities require and to try to ensure that their graduates have reasonable employment prospects. Second, as employers of Ph.D. faculty, graduate institutions must be alert to trends in academic labor markets that may affect their capacity to accomplish their research and educational tasks effectively.

Perhaps the main message to be drawn from this survey of trends in academic labor markets is that the policy issues identified in the late 1970s and early 1980s remain central and largely unresolved today. Five or so years ago several reports warned of an impending weakening in academic employment prospects in many arts and sciences disciplines, with attendant concerns about surplus Ph.D.'s, potential declines in quality of graduate students, and difficulties for academic departments in maintaining adequate flows of new faculty. At about the same time, warnings emerged of shortages of Ph.D.'s available for academic employment in certain critical technical fields, especially computer science and electrical engineering, with adverse effects foreseen on the capacity

21. U.S. Bureau of the Census, *Current Population Reports,* series P-25, no. 952, "Projections of the Population of the United States, by Age, Sex, and Race, 1983 to 2080" (GPO, 1984), table 6.

of universities to train needed technical personnel and to perform effective research.

In fact, both sets of concerns appear to be real, with excess demand for and excess supply of Ph.D.'s existing in different academic disciplines simultaneously. There is no contradiction in this—in fact, as academic labor markets reflect swings in undergraduate course preferences, we should expect such a result—but it does seem difficult for the policy process to take hold of both sets of problems at once. Concern about shortages of Ph.D.'s drives out concern about inadequate demand, and conversely. Perhaps the greatest need for intelligent policy is to recognize the differing circumstances and prospects facing highly educated personnel in different fields and to avoid simplified or generalized prescriptions.

Policy issues and alternatives regarding both high-demand and low-demand areas have been extensively and carefully discussed elsewhere.[22] All that can be done here is to highlight the principal areas of concern and to mention the kinds of remedies that have been discussed.

### Balance of Supply of and Demand for Ph.D.'s

In shortage areas, well-qualified people to staff teaching positions are difficult to find. Beyond temporary solutions, like hiring less qualified people or increasing course loads, two more basic kinds of alternatives have been entertained: increasing the total supply of new Ph.D.'s in such fields more rapidly or encouraging a larger fraction of Ph.D.'s to seek academic employment. The obvious route to the first strategy would be to increase graduate stipends offered to students who are strong in such fields as computer science and electrical engineering to offset the high earnings such students can receive with bachelors' degrees. But as a method of increasing academic employment of Ph.D.'s, this strategy has the important defect that only a minority of Ph.D.'s in these fields enter academic jobs. Presumably such stipend

---

22. For discussions of implications of declining demand, see National Research Council, Committee on Continuity of Academic Research Performance, *Research Excellence through the Year 2000* (National Academy of Sciences, 1979); Bowen, *Report of the President, Princeton University, 1981* and *1984*; and Carnegie Council on Policy Studies in Higher Education, *Three Thousand Futures*, Attachment K, "Smoothing the Flow of New Faculty" (San Francisco: Jossey-Bass, 1980). On Ph.D. shortages, see National Science Foundation and Department of Education, *Science and Engineering Education for the 1980s and Beyond* (Government Printing Office, 1980), and reports on the Engineering College Faculty Shortage Project reported in various issues of *Engineering Education*. Both sets of issues are discussed in Solmon and others, *Underemployed Ph.D.'s.*

support would help to subsidize the training of Ph.D.'s destined for industry. But the case needs to be made to justify a public subsidy for such advanced training of industrial workers when the employers involved do not find it worthwhile to pay large enough salaries to encourage more young people to seek such training.

Attracting more Ph.D.'s to academe, presumably by improving salaries and working conditions, would avoid the problem of subsidizing students who are headed for industry, but it is not unproblematic either. Government subsidies for salary support would be outside the usual line of government funding of higher education, and the method for selecting appropriate institutions and faculty to receive such subsidies is not clear. Such subsidies would tend to widen salary differentials within universities, raising issues about morale and the effectiveness of faculty governance.

In fields where academic demand is declining or may decline, the principal concerns regarding overall supply-demand balance are the possible personal and social costs of directing people into unproductive career paths; the possible adverse effects of a poor job market on the quality of graduate students in such disciplines; and the serious adverse effects on the prospects for increasing the representation of women and minorities in academe. Any large reduction in rates of academic hiring will reduce the rate at which the racial and sexual composition of faculties can change. Poor academic job markets have been particularly discouraging to minority candidates, who face strong opportunities elsewhere in the economy.

One response to declining academic demand is to encourage more rapid entry of Ph.D.'s into good nonacademic jobs. Potential employers need to learn more about the versatility and skill (and winning personalities?) of humanities and social science Ph.D.'s, just as the doctorate holders need to stop viewing all nonacademic jobs as unworthy. Beyond such counseling and brokering, there is also support for modifying the training of Ph.D.'s to increase their capacity to perform in a wider range of employment settings.

A second, complementary approach to potential oversupply is to increase academic demand in surplus fields, presumably through government funding of some form of academic positions. If, in fact, serious declines in hiring emerge in a wide range of fields, generating enough academic positions to make a dent in the overall labor market would be no small order. (Note that this proposition is different from that of providing enough support to create a limited number of positions at research-oriented institutions to ensure a flow of new faculty to those places.) Such a policy would also move outside traditional channels of government support for higher education, raising difficult issues of program design.

Graduate enrollments in some fields may need to decline further to avoid serious disruptions in the market for new Ph.D.'s. There have already been dramatic declines in Ph.D. production in some disciplines, and it is important to understand how these have been accomplished and with what consequences. Has there been a shrinkage mainly in number or in size of programs? If the latter, are many programs reaching some critical minimum size? Although further cuts in Ph.D. production are unpleasant to contemplate, the possibility of their occurring cannot be ruled out. It is therefore wise to try to think in advance how they might best be accomplished, if necessary, and to get a sense of what would most likely be the costs and how they might influence the effectiveness of remaining programs.

A final issue about overall supply-demand balance is that of preparing for an upturn in academic demand for Ph.D.'s later in the century. Overreaction to a temporary decline could lead to a shortage of Ph.D.'s later. The discussion has indicated that, at least as far as demographics are concerned, this does not appear to be a problem for the immediate future. Still, the timing and magnitude of potential recovery are important subjects for study. Any contractions that occur in the near future should not be so severe as to prevent the possibility of modest expansion in graduate enrollments by the early 1990s.

### Attracting Exceptional Performers

The academic community, concerned about the overall quality of graduate students, is especially concerned about the role of exceptional students. This concern is based on the premise that major advances in research and scholarship are uniquely dependent on a relatively small number of outstanding performers. In shortage fields like engineering, in which top students may be attracted to industrial opportunities, and in potential surplus fields like history, in which top students may be discouraged by poor overall job prospects, academe may fail to get the few exceptional students that it needs. Creation of a limited number of prestigious, attractive, and competitive fellowships in all fields to help ensure an enticing path into academe for some able young people might be a way to combat this potential problem. Such a program might be complemented, especially in low-demand fields, by the creation of a comparable number of awards to support attractive entry-level positions in academe for outstanding young scholars. NSF's recently initiated Presidential Young Investigator program has this aim. The scope of such a program, aimed at a limited group of exceptionally promising people, could be much less than is needed to influence the overall supply-demand balance for Ph.D.'s.

### Sustaining Research Vitality

The effectiveness of research-performing academic departments may, in the view of some, suffer from a reduced flow of new faculty for reasons apart from a failure to attract enough of the best minds to academic research. The inflow of new faculty provides fresh insights on research problems, allows departments to adjust their staffing to shifting research interests, and maintains healthy communications across generations of researchers.

The ability of research-performing colleges and universities to hire new faculty is, of course, linked not to overall enrollment movements but to movements in enrollments at that more limited set of institutions, and also to movements in research funding levels. Thus the extent of hiring constrictions is difficult to predict. The shift in course preferences away from many arts and sciences disciplines is already clearly constricting the creation of regular faculty positions in those areas, even at some leading universities. If these developments are accompanied by significant overall enrollment declines, such constrictions may well become both more severe and more widespread among research institutions.

Two broad and complementary approaches to combatting the effects of such a restriction in the flow of new faculty have been discussed. One approach is to add to the capacity of affected departments and disciplines to hire new personnel. Suggestions have included financing of larger numbers of postdoctoral awards, perhaps with longer than usual terms; providing resources to departments to create new faculty positions; or simply ensuring adequate research support to allow for the creation of research positions with reasonable levels of job security. Another suggestion has been to create openings for new faculty by encouraging the retirement or relocation of older faculty. The second approach is to compensate for the loss of new blood by investing more heavily and more thoughtfully in maintaining the vitality of older faculty. The idea of such proposals is to encourage faculty development through increased support for investments in training in new techniques and research areas, sabbaticals, and other areas.

**A note on data**

It is easy to produce wish lists of data that one would very much like to have. But the gap that seems most severe as one tries to understand developments in faculty labor markets is the absence of good data on staffing patterns developed from the institutions' point of view. The two surveys conducted by the Office of Scientific and Engineering Personnel of the National Research Council provide useful information on the Ph.D. population, from the doctorate holders' point of view. But no one currently assembles counts of faculty and of new appointments to faculty by discipline, by type of institution, and by faculty rank. The picture of what employment patterns are like, and of how they are changing, is therefore incomplete. If, as seems likely, some of these markets become the focus of close attention in the next five years, detailed and up-to-date information on these developments will be useful. The National Science Foundation develops some information of this kind through its Survey of Scientific and Engineering Personnel Employed at Universities and Colleges. But this source does not provide data on hiring and is limited, of course, to science and engineering personnel. A survey that was comprehensive among disciplines and gathered information on hiring would be of considerably greater use.

## Conclusion

On the surface, recent movements in the overall employment of faculty and in enrollment levels may seem somewhat reassuring, as both faculty and enrollment totals continue to grow. But below the placid surface are signs of considerable turmoil. Most striking is the rapid shift in undergraduate course and major preferences that has produced substantial shortages of technical faculty and a noticeable slowdown in academic demand for teachers in many arts and sciences fields. Academic salary differentials across disciplines are widening even as real salaries in many academic disciplines continue to fall. University staffing has not yet adjusted fully to the shift in undergraduate choice of majors. We can therefore expect further declines in the academic job market for humanists and for some others and continued shortages of technical faculty for some time to come.

Less obvious but potentially just as important are signs of a gradual slowing in enrollment growth that are reflected in a slowing overall pace of faculty expansion. Demographic forces will most likely cause undergraduate enrollments to turn down in the next couple of years, thereby inducing a further slowdown in hiring in many academic disciplines.

Further research is crucial on the issue of disaggregating Ph.D. employment trends according to the quality or type of graduate institution granting the degree and, for academic employment, the quality or type of employing institution. Ph.D.'s from the top handful of departments in any field face career paths that are very different from those faced by other Ph.D.'s. One suspects, though, that the structure of these relationships will change over time. In particular, in declining fields, one can advance the hypothesis that employment markets are becoming more stratified, with most of the academic jobs gobbled up by graduates of top institutions. This and analogous shifts in employment patterns— if they are really happening—may have important implications both for individual institutions and for national policy. The data exist, largely at the National Research Council, to investigate these questions; it is an important task.

# The Status of Engineering Education in the United States

## F. KARL WILLENBROCK

GRADUATE engineering education in the United States is best viewed as part of a continuum that includes undergraduate programs and extends to continuing education programs for practicing engineers.

Undergraduate enrollments in engineering in the United States are at an all-time high. The strong industrial demand for engineers, particularly in rapidly expanding fields such as computers and electronics, has sharply increased enrollment, reversing the decline that occurred in the early 1970s.[1] The increase has strained the capacity in most of the approximately 300 schools in the United States that offer accredited engineering programs. In the major schools admission has become highly competitive. This competition in turn has raised the quality of the students admitted, so that it is probably safe to assert that U.S. engineering schools have never had as many highly qualified undergraduates as they have now.

Undergraduate engineering education, nevertheless, is not in a healthy condition. There are a number of chronic problems that, if uncorrected, could lead to an inability to supply the engineering talent needed to maintain U.S. technological strength. These problems can be categorized as follows: inability to attract and retain top-quality U.S. faculty members; inability to obtain and to maintain the equipment and facilities needed for state-of-the-art engineering instruction; inability to attract top-rank U.S. graduate students into full-time graduate work and teaching assistantships; and inability to adjust to the changing demand among the present engineering disciplines and to respond to newly emerging engineering fields.

The quality of current students has hidden the effect of these weaknesses in engineering undergraduate education from employers of baccalaureate degree recipients. Many engineering

1. Sources of data on engineering student enrollments include the Engineering Manpower Commission and the National Science Foundation.

educators, however, have a deep concern that they are decreasingly able to provide their students with the depth and breadth of educational experience that the talents of the students merit. The accreditation process for undergraduate engineering programs shows clearly that the quality of the undergraduate engineering educational programs has undergone a steady erosion during the past several years. The major causes cited for the deterioration are overloaded faculty, inadequate facilities, and weaknesses in curriculum content.[2]

Lack of state-of-the-art equipment and facilities for research, in addition to inadequate instructional equipment and facilities, also plagues graduate engineering education. The research opportunities available to both faculty and students are therefore severely limited in many fields of technology. Graduate engineering programs also depend on foreign-born students. Full-time students from third world countries predominate in many engineering schools. Many of these students have had little opportunity to work with contemporary laboratory equipment; many have difficulties mastering the English language.

A problem of increasing national importance is how to keep practicing engineers and faculty members professionally up to date during professional careers that may extend to more than forty years. The increasingly rapid rate of technological change and the tendency to raise the retirement age make this a problem of great urgency.

Significant variations among the traditional engineering fields make generalizations about the status of engineering education difficult. Perhaps the most significant variation is the extent to which new engineering knowledge is generated in universities or in industrial, governmental, or other nonacademic laboratories. When the university community is the locale in which seminal research is carried on, the traditional methods govern the transfer of new knowledge in engineering practice. Graduating students, who participate in the generation of new knowledge or have studied under the faculty members who are carrying on such research, transfer this knowledge to their employers. Faculty members, through their consulting, their publications, and their participation in technical meetings, transfer their research results rapidly to industrial or governmental engineers who are concerned with applications.

2. The accreditation of engineering programs is carried on by the Accreditation Board for Engineering and Technology (ABET). The annual ABET reports document a decrease in the percentage of inspected programs that qualify for the maximum (six-year) accreditation.

When nonacademic organizations are the primary locus of new knowledge generation, new knowledge is less effectively transmitted. Industrial engineers are not as committed to rapid publication of research results as are their academic colleagues, and in many cases there are proprietary or classification constraints on publicizing their information. Although some nonacademic engineers teach university courses or write textbooks, their academic contacts are minimal, and the knowledge-transfer process is hindered.

When knowledge transfer is inadequate, a significant gap can develop between current engineering practice and the content of academic programs. If the gap is large, the academic programs are out of date or irrelevant, with deleterious effects on the students and faculty involved and also on the ultimate employers of the students.

Another variation among the engineering fields is the rate at which new technology is introduced into engineering-dependent products and services. In the fields of rapid change, the engineering schools face the difficulty of keeping their faculty, facilities, and curricula up to date. In fields of slower change, engineering practice may not make full use of existing knowledge.

A third variation among the engineering fields is the relative content of theory and practice. Some fields, such as chemical and electronic engineering, have always maintained close ties to the related sciences, while other fields contain a larger component of the art of engineering. In these fields a major part of the engineer's knowledge base comes from experience, and extended graduate study is less needed.

*Engineering faculty capability*

The most crucial problem facing U.S. engineering schools is their decreasing ability to attract and to retain faculty members who are in the top rank of their technical specialties. Immediately after World War II the most academically able undergraduates customarily undertook full-time graduate work, and, upon completion of their Ph.D. programs, the students with the strongest research capabilities sought university appointments. Many university research groups were thus at the forefront of their engineering fields; in some fields they were the dominant source of new ideas.

The present situation is different. Now, many of the most academically capable U.S. engineering undergraduates will, after completion of the baccalaureate, accept industrial positions. Many industrial employers encourage such employees to pursue an M.S. program on either a part-time or full-time basis. Some of the students go on to a Ph.D. degree under company sponsorship.

Relatively few of the most intellectually able U.S. citizens seek an academic career in engineering.

In another popular career pattern, top-ranking engineering baccalaureate recipients do graduate work in business or law schools. Such students use their undergraduate engineering background for a career in technical management or in law.

This general situation has prevailed long enough so that the number of U.S. citizens with credentials for faculty appointments is small compared to the vacancies. The availability of foreign-born candidates for faculty positions has enabled the engineering schools to partially fill the vacancies. The dearth of U.S. citizens among qualified candidates for faculty positions indicates that faculty careers are no longer held in high regard by the most academically able Americans.

The continuation of the present trend away from U.S.-born faculty members can have a number of undesirable results. An engineering faculty that is primarily composed of non-U.S. citizens is not likely to develop a close relationship with the Department of Defense and with defense-related industries. The traditionally close relationship, while not entirely free of problems, has been of great mutual benefit to both the academic and the military communities. Unless academic careers in engineering can be made attractive to exceptionally well-qualified Americans, relations between the engineering schools and the governmental and industrial sectors may undergo significant changes. The linkages, which have produced many past benefits—intellectual stimulation, access to costly experimental facilities, and the interplay of individuals with common interests but different perspectives— may be weakened.

*Instructional and research equipment and facilities*

Successful engineering research and development requires a balanced effort in which both the analytical work and the experimental work are carried on in parallel. In most universities there is much less emphasis on the experimental and far greater emphasis on the analytical.

This imbalance does not stem from an inherent characteristic of academic research; rather, the support structure needed for front-rank experimental work is lacking in most universities. Up-to-date equipment and facilities, paraprofessional support, and powerful computing services are simply not as readily available. As a result, the academic researcher finds theoretical work more productive than experimental work. The imbalance is deleterious to the students' development, because they do not have the opportunity to participate in the crucial interplay of theory and experiment as an integral part of their academic preparation.

Some active fields of engineering research need increasingly expensive and sophisticated instrumentation. The capital investment and support services needed to make such instrumentation available are far beyond the financial resources of the great majority of engineering schools. Most engineering schools do not even attempt to develop the in-house facilities needed to carry on first-rate research in equipment-intensive fields.

Some universities are exploring new mechanisms. The physics and astronomy communities abandoned the practice of seeking to equip each university with its own accelerators and telescopes; they joined together to develop regional facilities. The medical schools have developed the concept of teaching hospitals. Similarly, the academic engineering community should develop cooperative mechanisms for gaining access to state-of-the-art facilities. In some cases regional facilities may be the most appropriate technique. In other cases industry may be able to provide academic research groups with access to company facilities. In still other cases a government agency may provide access to its facilities for academic groups. A proposed national laboratory to house a large-scale shake table for earthquake engineers to study seismic loading of buildings will share access with academics.

Until more progress is made on this problem, the imbalance in academic engineering research and education will continue, and many engineers oriented to experimental research will not be attracted to academic careers.

*Attracting U.S. graduate students*

The typical U.S. recipient of an engineering baccalaureate degree has several career alternatives. The most popular is an industrial career, which has a current starting salary on the order of $25,000 to $30,000 a year, a salary range considerably higher than that available to most other baccalaureate recipients.

Students with strong undergraduate academic records can also become full-time graduate students. The income available from a fellowship or from a teaching assistantship is usually less than $10,000 per year. If this choice is made, however, another career choice must be made upon completion of the graduate program. Again the financial advantages will weigh toward the industrial.

To many students, the opportunity to work in an atmosphere of intellectual excitement and adventure is of greater importance than salary. Some engineering departments and schools maintain such an atmosphere; others do not. Increasingly, industrial laboratories provide very stimulating environments that, together with well-equipped facilities and extensive support services, are very attractive to the research-oriented engineer.

The attractiveness of U.S. graduate engineering education to foreign-born students highlights the unattractiveness of full-time graduate work to U.S. students. Engineering is by far the most popular field of study for foreign graduate students in the United States. Most of the foreign students come from the third world countries of the Middle East and Asia. Relatively few European predoctoral students enroll in U.S. engineering schools.

The lack of U.S. graduate students has had the side effect of degrading the quality of undergraduate engineering programs, since graduate students have traditionally served as teaching and laboratory assistants in undergraduate engineering courses. Many foreign students do not know the language and do not have the experience in experimental techniques needed to serve in these capacities.

The following should be among the measures taken to increase the attractiveness of full-time graduate work to U.S. students: creation in more engineering schools of a community with sufficient intellectual excitement and stimulation; improvement in the equipment and support facilities available for academic instruction and research; and an increase in graduate stipends to about one-half of the prevailing industrial-company salary offer.

*Adjustment to changing or newly emerging fields*

Engineering practice has been strongly affected by the wide availability of programmable computing machines. This change has forced the university community in general and the engineering schools in particular to make a number of adjustments. Universities are beginning to provide computing resources to the faculty and to the graduate students involved in research. Universities have modified curricula to allow for the new capabilities provided by computers. Faculty members who are not computer specialists receive training in the use of computers in their teaching and research. The rapidity with which the various engineering schools have adjusted to these changes has varied widely.

Recent advances in biotechnology also point to a number of changes in future engineering practice. The exploitation of genetic engineering techniques can have a major effect on many industrial chemical processes, on pharmaceutical manufacture, on plant agriculture, and on animal husbandry. Relatively few academic curricula have adjusted to this anticipated development, however. The resources available to most schools of engineering are so limited that it is difficult to prepare for future academic opportunities. New educational materials and curricula are needed to provide the engineering talent for these emerging fields.

*Role of federal government funding*

The engineering and the scientific academic communities have been major beneficiaries of the public support for academic research that was called for in the 1945 Bush report "Science, the Endless Frontier." This federal policy enabled schools of engineering to expand their faculties and to improve their equipment and facilities. It was thus possible to undertake significant curricula modifications and improvement and to handle the bulge in student enrollments that followed World War II. The effect was not uniform over the various engineering fields, however, nor was the effect felt proportionally by all schools of engineering.

The fields of engineering that benefited most from the post–World War II funding were those most directly related to military technology, such as aerospace and electronics. Later, as other mission-oriented federal funding programs for universities were established, support was extended to engineering fields such as nuclear engineering, energy-related engineering, and transportation-related engineering.

The advent of federal funding, however, in addition to strengthening particular fields of engineering research in universities, has had some side effects.[3] Engineering faculty members have developed closer interaction with federal program managers than with industrial program managers. Universities as a result are stressing engineering performance rather than engineering costs. Stretching the limits of technical feasibility is more important than accenting manufacturability and cost containment.

An additional effect of federal funding is a greater concentration of engineering faculty talent in the major research-oriented universities. The number of engineering schools that merit this classification is relatively small. Of the approximately 300 universities that offer accredited undergraduate engineering programs, fewer than 20 had external major research funding in excess of $10 million a year in 1983. Government-funded research has generally strengthened the research-oriented schools and widened the gap between the strong schools and the others.

The growth of the National Science Foundation as a major

---

3. F. K. Willenbrock, *The Impact of Federal Research Funding on Schools of Engineering in the U.S.,* Report on Natural Science and Technology Policy Issues, 1979, House Committee on Science and Technology, 96 Cong. 1 sess. (Government Printing Office, 1979), pp. 84–92.

source of funding for academic research has enabled some non-military fields of engineering, such as civil and chemical, to obtain more access to federal funds. The primary emphasis of the NSF on scientific in contrast to engineering research has resulted in a bias toward the type of engineering research that resembles the scientific. The accent on single principal investigators with yearly grants averaging considerably less than $100,000 a year has not encouraged the development of broadly based engineering research programs involving several different disciplines. Until recently studies of engineering design or of manufacturing processes have been slighted.

The current plans of the NSF to strengthen its engineering programs are desirable. To be successful, however, it should recognize the distinctive characteristics of engineering and design its programs to take these characteristics into account. The newly established Engineering Research Centers program, which requires the engineering schools to include industrial companies as active participants in their research efforts, is an important step in this direction.

*Relation of engineering schools to industry*

Interest on the part of technology-based industrial companies in the status of engineering education in the United States and in other industrialized countries has revived in the past several years.[4] The increase in international competitiveness in a number of engineering-dependent technologies, a shortage of engineering graduates in some rapidly developing fields, and the education of more engineers by leading international military and industrial competitors than by the United States have contributed to the renewed interest.

Increased industrial interest has had positive effects on graduate engineering education. Some specific benefits have been the increased number of equipment gifts to engineering schools as a result of tax credit for industrial research and development (R&D); the initiation by a major electronics industry trade association (the American Electronics Association) of a program of forgivable loans to U.S. students who agree to undertake careers as engineering faculty members; and the funding of university research programs by a group of chemical manufacturers and an association of semiconductor companies. These efforts have had the effect of strengthening ties between schools of engineering and the industrial community.

4. See, for example, "Industry and University, New Forms of Cooperation and Communication," Organization for Economic Cooperation and Development Report, 1984.

Closer industrial interaction has helped to attract U.S. graduate students and to update engineering school equipment and facilities, and it has also influenced the content of engineering curricula. For example, the IBM program in support of graduate programs in manufacturing engineering has resulted in the introduction of a number of graduate programs in manufacturing. Until recently, this aspect of engineering had been largely neglected by the academic engineering community.

Other effects of the increased industrial interest in engineering education can be anticipated. The gap between academic program and the state of the art in some of the rapidly developing technological fields may be closed, more joint research programs by companies and schools may be developed, and the participation of industrially employed engineers as part-time university instructors and members of academic visiting committees may be increased. There are indications, however, that most industrial support will go to the major schools, so that the strong will become stronger and the lower-rank schools may become relatively weaker.[5]

Engineering-dependent industrial companies and their trade associations have considerable legislative influence. While they have applied this influence effectively at the state legislative level in support of engineering school budgets, they have not applied it as effectively at the federal level. Industrial influence on Congress has, for example, assisted engineering schools by supporting a tax credit to companies donating equipment to universities and by opposing a proposal that all foreign-born student graduates be required to return to their native countries for two years before being eligible for employment in the United States. The potential for influencing engineering education through legislation is great. If, for example, the industrial community became a more active participant in the operations of the National Science Foundation, its engineering program might be considerably strengthened.

**Continuing engineering education**

One successful effort to provide educational services to employed engineers has been the use of instructional television channels to make graduate courses in engineering available at locations remote from the originating campus. Some of the engineering schools that have used the television technique are making graduate courses available on videotape through the Association for Media-based Continuing Engineering Education (AMCEE). This association, which was started with NSF and industrial support, is now an

5. J. Truxal and M. Visich, "Engineering Education and National Policy," *Science,* vol. 218 (October 8, 1982), p. 113.

economically successful organization with a current catalog of more than 400 graduate-level courses available on videotape. An offshoot of this program is the National Technological University (NTU), which is offering M.S. degrees based on videotaped courses from a number of different universities.[6]

The more difficult task of modifying the course content and designing curricula appropriate for practicing engineers throughout their careers has not been systematically undertaken. Engineers who are within five to ten years beyond their full-time educational experience find graduate courses as they are offered to full-time graduate students on campus valuable educational experiences. Such courses may not, however, satisfy the needs of midcareer engineers.

According to recent studies,[7] only 5 percent of practicing engineers are currently involved in continuing education programs. The problem of providing appropriate educational services to the employed engineers throughout their entire professional careers thus remains largely unsolved.

Universities have traditionally considered their primary tasks to be the education of full-time on-campus students and the research to produce new knowledge. A number of engineering schools participate in a variety of continuing education programs, but there has been no systematic effort of sufficient magnitude to develop the methodology for providing educational services to practicing engineers on a continuing basis. The closer ties between the academic and the industrial engineering communities may result in a stronger effort to provide such services.

*Future directions in graduate engineering education*

The direct interrelation between the health of the engineering education system and the strength of the nation's technological enterprise is increasingly recognized. Industrial and governmental decisionmakers have shown greater concern about the problems facing the engineering education system. Some progress is being made in the problem areas discussed in this paper, but their chronic nature is also becoming more evident.

If the engineering schools are not able to attract or to retain first-rate U.S. faculty members and U.S. graduate students, their

6. Edward B. Fiske, "Engineers to Get Course by Satellite" *New York Times,* February 5, 1985.

7. The National Research Council has under way a major study on the "Education and Utilization of the Engineer." As part of this study a report by a panel chaired by Morris A. Steinberg, of the Lockheed Corporation, has collected the best available data on current participation by industrially employed engineers in continuing education programs, whether provided by schools of engineering or in house.

knowledge-generation function may in the long term atrophy. The U.S. system might then become closer to the French system of *grandes écoles* and the government-supported research laboratories of the Centre Nationale de la Recherche Scientifique (CNRS). Under such a system, engineering schools would focus on teaching, while research would become the responsibility of other organizations. This separation of teaching and research would weaken both enterprises. Some U.S. engineering schools will head in this direction if they continue to be unable to attract top U.S. graduate students or to find qualified U.S. Ph.D. recipients to accept faculty appointments.

The facilities and equipment problem will probably require multifaceted solutions. Regional facilities may be appropriate in some cases; in other cases special arrangements with industry may be preferable. Rough estimates of the funds required to bring the equipment and facilities of the nation's 300 engineering schools up to the state of the art are in the several-billion-dollar range. The engineering education system must find other ways to approach the problem. The facilities needed for engineering research in many fields already exist in industrial laboratories. University-industry cooperation could make industrial equipment and facilities accessible for educational purposes while not interfering with the productivity or with the proprietary concerns of the owning companies.

Some industrial facilities become accessible to students, primarily undergraduates, who are engaged in cooperative work-study programs. Cooperative work-study programs have been functioning in some engineering schools for many years, but only about 15 percent of all U.S. engineering undergraduates participate. Enlargement of such programs depends on the number of part-time jobs that industry is able to provide. Industry probably could not sustain a sixfold increase (to include 100 percent of engineering students).

The military services and other groups involved with large-scale personnel training have successfully resolved the facilities problem with computer simulation. A program for the systematic development of simulation packages for engineering education might be fruitful. The NSF would be an appropriate agency to undertake such an effort.

No single approach will solve the problem of lack of up-to-date facilities. Clearly schools undertaking engineering teaching and research require some in-house facilities, yet the financial resources available to most schools are inadequate. A comprehensive study of this problem and the identification of policy alternatives are overdue.

The industrial and university communities must also make a systematic effort to address the issue of continuing education for engineers, whether employed in industry, government, or universities. A recent MIT study noted that the main responsibility for such an effort belongs to the industrial and academic communities, but favorable government policies can accelerate progress.[8] Until more members of the academic community, together with their industrial colleagues, develop programs and undertake experimentation, it is unlikely that a great deal of progress will be made.

Development of educational programs in newly emerging technologies will probably not progress significantly until the federal government undertakes a more active role. Currently, the obvious need is for biochemical engineers who can undertake for the burgeoning biotechnology industry the counterpart of the role that chemical engineers play in the chemical process industry. Unless this engineering capability is rapidly developed, the scientific lead that U.S. research biologists have provided may not be translated into technological leadership.

New and emerging fields of technology present a great challenge. The engineering education community has not responded rapidly to such challenges, not because of lack of foresight or lack of knowledge of how to proceed but because of the lack of discretionary resources available to the academic community. The academic community requires external funding before it can take on new research initiatives or new instructional initiatives. Even fewer sources of external funding exist for instructional purposes. Among the federal agencies, the NSF is the most appropriate to undertake such support.

The U.S. engineering education community has the intellectual capability of responding rapidly to new educational opportunities and to new research opportunities. Ultimately, the capacity of the engineering schools to anticipate, to respond to, and to encourage the growth of new areas of teaching and research will shape the nation's competitive position in the world economy and will strengthen the technological foundation on which U.S. national security is based.

---

8. "Lifelong Cooperative Education," a report of a faculty committee of the Department of Electrical Engineering and Computer Science, Massachusetts Institute of Technology, Cambridge, Mass., chaired by R. M. Fano, October 2, 1982.

# The Computer Revolution and Graduate Education

JAMES W. JOHNSON

IN A 1982 talk, Nobel Laureate Herbert A. Simon observed, "Nobody really needs convincing these days that the computer is an innovation of more than ordinary magnitude, a one-in-several-centuries innovation and not a one-in-a-century innovation or one of these instant revolutions that are announced every day in the papers or on television. It really is an event of major magnitude."[1]

American graduate education has not avoided the effect of this one-in-several-centuries innovation. As tools for augmenting our ability to process information, computers and related technologies have an increasingly important effect on science and engineering research and graduate education. Computing permeates every field of scientific endeavor, influencing the kinds of research and the methods of research conducted by countless scientists.

This paper explores the state of computing in science and engineering graduate education. Computing will be extended to include three elements in the information processing revolution: computing (the ability to manipulate data); electronic communications (the connection of people and machines that renders distance meaningless); and machine-stored data bases (data, text, indexes, or pictures that can be searched and displayed via computers). Related information technologies such as radio and television will not be included, because this paper's focus will be on the content and methods of graduate education, not on its delivery. Also absent will be a discussion of computer-assisted instruction and the issues surrounding it,[2] because computer-assisted instruction in a narrow sense can also be classified as delivery rather than as subject matter or research techniques.

---

1. Herbert A. Simon, "The Computer Age," in Alan M. Lesgold and Frederick Reif, *Computers in Education: Realizing the Potential* (Government Printing Office, 1983), p. 37. (The conference reported here was in 1982.)

2. See, for example, "Involvement in Learning: Realizing the Potential of American Higher Education," Report of the Study Group on the Condition of Excellence in American Higher Education, reprinted in *Chronicle of Higher Education*, vol. 29 (October 24, 1984), pp. 35–49.

In limiting this essay to science and engineering graduate education, I focus on disciplines categorized as physical science, biological science, environmental science, social science, mathematical (including computer) science, and engineering (including the numerous subfields of engineering such as aeronautical, chemical, civil, electrical, and mechanical). The arts and humanities and the legal, medical, education, and business professions are not considered, but any report on computer technology in graduate education would be remiss in not mentioning the astronomical growth in the use of computing in these fields during the past five years.

There have been many investigations of computing in higher education and a few investigations of computing in research. Two of the more comprehensive recent studies are *Computing and Higher Education: An Accidental Revolution* and "A National Computing Environment for Academic Research."[3] Reports on the status of undergraduate academic computing, such as *An Accidental Revolution*, are useful in exposing the breadth of the problem of providing a new resource—computing—for large numbers of students. Reports on the needs for research computing, such as "A National Computing Environment," explore the importance of specialized facilities in the academic research enterprise.

Neither orientation nor undergraduate education nor research directly addresses the needs of graduate education. The major purpose of graduate education is the development of talent necessary to extend our society's collection of knowledge and imagination. Talent is inexorably intertwined with the research enterprise. Excellence in academically based graduate education is impossible without first-rate faculty engaged in cutting-edge research, but graduate education goes beyond research. Facilities that are adequate for research may not be adequate in quantity for a large number of students or in quality for students who must be prepared to use tools that will be available in four or five years. By exploring computing in graduate science and engineering education, this paper charts a new course.

*Major issues*    The computer revolution has generated problems for graduate education that are neither unique nor difficult to identify: dealing with change, providing facilities, and picking a strategy. The

3. Robert Gillespie with Deborah Dicaro, *Computing and Higher Education: An Accidental Revolution* (Seattle: University of Washington, Department of Printing, 1981); Marcel Bardon and Kent K. Curtis, "A National Computing Environment for Academic Research," prepared for the National Science Foundation, Washington, D.C., July 1983.

computer revolution raises questions about how the graduate enterprise, in fact all of education, responds to changes in knowledge and skills needed by society. A casual observer might note that what is required is more perfect information about the state of the marketplace in five, ten, and twenty years. An appropriate plan is greater flexibility resulting from an emphasis on basic science. Of course, the casual observer has no obligation to explain how these goals are to be met.

In studying how graduate education responds to change, it would be helpful to study the emergence of computer science as an academic discipline over the past thirty years. Surely such a study would reveal the successes and failures of establishing a new discipline. Computer science may be "a discipline in crisis,"[4] but it is a childhood crisis, not a birth crisis or an aging crisis. Similarly, the biological revolution discussed by Martin Trow provides lessons on the effect of new technologies on the structure of existing disciplines.[5]

A study of how established disciplines nurture new fields would be most provocative. In 1979 about 3.5 times as many Ph.D.'s worked as computer professionals as had ever earned degrees in the discipline.[6] Today there is tremendous demand for scientists in artificial intelligence, although it was not long ago that the field was looked on with scorn. Graduates who are not founding start-up companies are commanding salaries approaching that of physicians. John Doyle, vice president of Hewlett-Packard, recently noted that the people working to develop expert systems and to design computers that are easier to use are recruited from pure mathematics and linguistics. Clearly the question of responding to change while maintaining diversity and basic science strength is a delicate one.

The computer revolution also raises familiar worries about facilities for graduate education and research. In some ways, computing is symbolic. Like buildings and laboratory instrumentation, it suffers from deficiencies caused by the financial constraints of the 1970s and early 1980s. It also is subject to questions about its contribution to educational and research productivity, its importance and cost relative to faculty and faculty salaries, and allocation of its costs and its use.

4. Peter J. Denning, "A Discipline in Crisis," *Communications of the ACM*, vol. 6 (June 1984), pp. 6ff.

5. See Martin A. Trow, "Reorganizing the Biological Sciences at Berkeley," *Change*, vol. 15 (November–December 1983).

6. National Science Foundation and Department of Education, *Science and Engineering Education for the 1980s and Beyond* (Government Printing Office, 1980), p. 73.

Computing, however, may be unlike other facilities in that it deals with the very substance of education and research—information. Information technology not only involves equipment used in every field of study; it is itself an area of study and an important research methodology. One observer passionately suggested, "Universities are faced with the unprecedented requirement of basic research in the very substance of their existence—information technology," and went on to say, "In the past, the existence or absence of the capacity for cutting-edge research in a particular field threatened only the survival of a particular department or discipline in the institution, rather than the institution itself."[7] This difference makes computing and communications a strategic issue rather than a facilities issue.

The key question about computing is whether its use is so critical to science and engineering that inadequate computing resources threaten the nation's ability to stay at the forefront of the world's ideas and markets. The question requires addressing what is done rather than how it is done.

Reasonable people may differ over the significance of computing and communications, but the weight of evidence indicates that the computer is a major intellectual invention. In a relatively short period of time computing has come to be used in every discipline, the arts and humanities as well as science and engineering. Today one would be surprised to find a laboratory without a computer. The pervasiveness of computing has resulted from the fact that academicians, who are reputedly not given to rapid change, have made independent decisions to embrace it to improve their effectiveness.

Computing also makes other technologies more useful. It works with communications networks to give scientists access to a broadening, worldwide data base. It helps investigators find patterns in data generated by devices such as nuclear magnetic resonance spectrometers. Like statisticians, computer scientists provide new techniques to be applied to other disciplines.

If computing is actually a modern equivalent of the printing press, a one-in-several-centuries innovation, it cannot be judged by the usual criteria. The wisdom of two scientists illustrates this point. In 1971 Herbert Simon observed that he advised several business firms not to acquire computers until they knew exactly how they were going to use them and pay for them. He stated,

7. Patricia Battin, "The Library: Center of the Restructured University," *Current Issues in Higher Education: Colleges Enter the Information Age*, no. 1 (Washington, D.C.: American Association for Higher Education, 1983–84), p. 30.

"I soon realized this was bad advice. Computers initially pay their way by educating large numbers of people about computers."[8]

In 1984 Lowell Steele, former General Electric staff executive for corporate technology planning, made a similar observation. He said that technological innovation was difficult because change is disruptive and because most innovations fail. He cited a study that found no correlation between corporate research and development expenditure and profitability. Studies do show, however, that companies that do not spend on research and development fail.[9]

If computer-based information technology changes the very substance of research and graduate education, what is at stake is not efficiency; what is at stake is survival. What is at issue is whether innovation in computer and information technology and its application is receiving adequate support.

*Adequacy of support*

The rest of this paper addresses the adequacy of computer support for graduate education by reviewing the history of academic computing, looking at the current situation, and projecting needs for the next few years. Computing will include computer networks and data bases.

### Historical Background

Electronic digital computer use in research and graduate education spans slightly more than three decades. This period can be divided into three stages. The first stage, running from the mid-1950s through the 1960s, was one of *start-up*; the second, beginning in the late 1960s and extending through the 1970s, was one of rapid *growth*; and the latest stage, beginning in the late 1970s, is one of *transformation*.

The start-up stage during the 1950s and 1960s saw most doctorate-granting universities gain access to new tools for computation, statistical analysis, and instrumentation. Computers were few (in the hundreds), did familiar tasks (albeit more quickly and accurately), and were used by relatively few scientists who were oriented toward computer use.

The major problem during the start-up period was to provide

8. Herbert Simon, "Designing Organizations for an Information-Rich World," in Martin Greenberger, ed., *Computers, Communications and the Public Interest* (Johns Hopkins Press, 1971), p. 51.

9. Speech to the First National Conference on Critical Issues in Strategic Planning, Policy Development, and Technology Management, Georgia State University, October 9, 1984.

scientists and engineers with access to large, scientific computers and to help fledgling computer science programs get started. Because a large computer in the early 1960s offered twenty times the speed at only five times the cost of a middle-sized system, access was limited to a centralized campus computer or to a few national laboratory computers.[10] Researchers readily gave up their obsolescent computing equipment to use more powerful, easier to use, centralized equipment. Data generated by laboratory instruments were recorded on paper or magnetic tape that was carried or transmitted to campus or national centers for data reduction and analysis. The centers developed staffs to provide scientific software and up-to-date programming techniques. The best-known software included IBM's Scientific Subroutine Package, UCLA's Biomedical Statistical Software, the International Mathematical and Statistical Library, and the Fortran programming language.[11]

Funds for million-dollar university computing centers were provided by federal grants and by the universities themselves; large vendor-provided discounts made acquisitions possible. Grants from the National Science Foundation (NSF) totaling $72 million in 1957–72 helped universities initiate and expand computing facilities for research and education.[12] National laboratories for a single discipline (or a group of related research activities), such as the NSF-supported National Center for Atmospheric Research, supplemented multipurpose campus centers. Other centers were supported by the U.S. Atomic Energy Commission and the National Institutes of Health.

By the late 1960s every large, major research university had access to computing. Further, with the acquisition of third-generation mainframe computers, such as the IBM 360, the CDC 6600, and the Univac 1108, university equipment was pretty much state of the art. The 1970s changed this picture dramatically.

Academic computing grew rapidly in the 1970s as scientists in most fields began using computers and as computer science and computer engineering became popular courses of study. Computers themselves were distributed throughout the academic community as they became smaller, interactive, and less expensive.

10. Vincent H. Swoyer, "Computer System Changes," in John W. Hamblen and Carolyn P. Landis, eds., *The Fourth Inventory of Computers in Higher Education: An Interpretive Report* (Boulder, Colo.: Westview Press, 1980), p. 45.

11. Peter K. Lykos, "Changes in Research Computing in Higher Education," in ibid., p. 139.

12. The total resulting expenditure was $250 million. Gillespie with Dicaro, *Computing and Higher Education*, p. 17.

Scientists, engineers, and computer specialists collaborated to produce new techniques and tools that became essential to research and development laboratories.

Total expenditures for computing in higher education grew from an estimated $220 million in 1966–67 to almost $1 billion in 1976–77 according to the *Fourth Inventory of Computers in Higher Education*.[13] The estimated number of computers grew from 700 in 1965 to more than 5,000 in 1977.[14] Both estimates were probably low because of the difficulty of accounting for facilities hidden in laboratories.

By the early 1970s project teams were producing well-documented software that allowed relative novices to use powerful computational tools. The best known and most widely used software was the Statistical Package for the Social Sciences (SPSS), which combined many existing routines in an easy-to-use wrapper.[15] Together with a growing number of machine-readable data bases, such as the 1970 census, SPSS became the essential tool for social scientists. Computer specialists also produced test processors (crude precursors of today's word processors) and interactive, simplified programming languages. The most widely accepted was a language called Basic.

New and expanding computer science departments supplied talent to fuel new developments in scientific computing such as image processing, numeric simulation, and instrument control. Degree programs in computer science and related fields increased at the baccalaureate level from 83 in 1966–67 to 506 in 1976–77; from 87 to 198 at the master's level; and from 52 to 101 at the Ph.D. level.[16] These programs provided scientists with collaborators and assistants for their computational work, but they also created additional demand on computer facilities.

Increased use of computing could not have come at a worse time. Financially constrained universities found themselves having to upgrade aging mainframe computers that were originally acquired with federal grant assistance. The NSF computer acquisition grant program, having accomplished its mission to provide access, was discontinued in 1972. Large discounts provided by computer vendors, once as high as 60 percent, fell to 10 percent.

13. John W. Hamblen and Thomas B. Baird, eds., *Fourth Inventory of Computers in Higher Education, 1976–77* (Princeton: Educom, 1979), p. III-5.

14. Ibid., p. II-2.

15. Norman Nie and others, *Statistical Package for the Social Sciences* (McGraw-Hill, 1970).

16. Bruce K. Alcorn, "Institutional Resources for Computing," in Hamblen and Landis, eds., *Fourth Inventory of Computers: An Interpretive Report*, p. 7.

The portion of research computing that was externally funded fell from about 40 percent in 1969–70 to less than 30 percent in 1976–77. More dramatically, at major universities the portion of federal funds covering total expenditures for computing was 10 percent in 1976–77, in contrast to 34 percent in 1966–67.[17] Rapid growth combined with fiscal constraints created the treadmill effect of running faster and faster but never catching up.

The combination of crowded university facilities, NSF funding of individual investigators, and a newer technology resulted in the growth of departmental and laboratory computing facilities. By 1976–77 a typical large university had two or more large computer systems and thirty to fifty departmental minicomputers.[18]

Reliance on departmental computers had several results. Computing became more accessible and better tailored to a single discipline's needs, but the computing power available to the average researcher was not much greater than it was in 1970. Departmental computing created a gap between haves and have-nots. This gap was often filled by campus-wide computing facilities, which moved further and further away from meeting the needs of graduate education in science and engineering.

Universities lost their position in state-of-the-art research computing in the 1970s. A 1983 NSF report pointed out that during the 1970s "academic facilities fell behind industrial laboratories in computing resources for research including minicomputers, workstations, graphics, etc., as well as supercomputers."[19] It also observed that while some universities in the early 1970s had the supercomputers of their day, by the mid-1970s there were no supercomputers in universities. The consequences of falling behind in computing became serious in the 1980s.

Transformation as a stage of technological development implies moving beyond doing old things in new ways or even doing new things in new ways. Transformation means that it is difficult to imagine doing things without the new technology. Life styles or inquiry styles are changed. Two observations from the 1983 NSF academic computing environment report illustrate transformation in scientific computing.

The attitude toward computers for research marks a generation gap in the community of scientists. Older scientists may use, or have

17. Ibid., p. 10.
18. Derived from reports from representative universities in Hamblen and Baird, eds., *Fourth Inventory of Computers.*
19. Bardon and Curtis, "A National Computing Environment," pp. 4–5.

their graduate students use, computers for a variety of measurement and analysis tasks but consider the role and importance of computers to be limited. Younger scientists, who grew up with computers as part of their culture, view them quite differently.[20]

Science has passed a watershed in using computers for research. Computers are no longer just tools for measurement and analysis but large computers, in particular, have become the means of making new discoveries.[21]

Daniel Bell, among others, recognized in the 1960s that computing would be a transforming technology.[22] Yet even the most ardent converts to this position were amazed by the rapidity of developments in the late 1970s and early 1980s. Computers moved from the hands of an elite few to millions of ordinary citizens. Personal computers offered the power of the full-sized computers of the late 1960s in inexpensive, small packages, while professional computers offered the power of super minicomputers such as the Digital Equipment Company's Vax. Scientists began thinking of a modern version of a chicken in every pot—a computer on every desk.

Word processing, image processing, graphics, computer-aided design and manufacturing, and automated bibliographic and data base searches became recognized as superior technologies; after using these tools, people would not return to traditional ways of doing things. As a result, word processing and graphics have attracted scholars in the arts and humanities. While these fields provide essential insight and new creative uses of computing that are helpful to science, they also compete with scientists and engineers for scarce university resources.

The power of computers is fairly well understood these days; two important and related developments, networking and data base services, are less well accepted. For this reason more detail is needed about these services, which will be transforming technologies in the mid- to late 1980s.

Networking connects computers and communications facilities to other machines and their users. Networks may connect departmental, campus-wide, or national computers. Networks are valuable to scientists and engineers because they have many functions. Electronic mail is used to send messages through a

20. Ibid., p. 1.
21. Ibid., p. 2.
22. See, in particular, Daniel Bell, *The Coming of Post Industrial Society: A Venture in Social Forecasting* (Basic Books, 1976).

network from one scientist to another or to a group of scientists. Remote terminal connections make special computing services accessible to a wide audience. File transfer allows for sharing of data in many different forms.

Networks are pivotal resources because they allow for specialization and improve communication. But without an easily used, easily accessed network that makes the location of resources known to the user, meaningful specialization makes little sense. Communication allows for rapid sharing of ideas such as preprints, it eliminates needless duplication, and it helps build a worldwide community of scientists and engineers.

A significant step in network development was the establishment of Arpanet in 1966; it was operated by the Department of Defense, which pioneered many technical innovations in networking technology. The network connected university and industrial computers used by people who were part of the Office of Advanced Research Projects Agency research program in computer science.[23] Arpanet's success surprised its developers. They expected the network to be used for computer-to-computer communication and resource sharing; instead its major use was for electronic mail.[24] Kenneth Wilson of Cornell University sees Arpanet as providing a "remarkable achievement," because users ask for help when they need it by using electronic mail and bulletin boards.[25]

Networks are growing at a rapid, undisciplined rate. Electronic mail is provided commercially by services such as GTE's Telemail and Western Union's Easylink. More versatile networks include CSnet, a computer science network supported by the National Science Foundation, and Bitnet, an evolving network of universities, with more than sixty-six universities now connected and the number growing at a rate of three or four per month.[26] The NSF is planning a network to join governmental, industrial, and academic scientists and engineers who have an interest in large-scale computer use.[27]

23. The network consists of 88 nodes connecting 185 host computers.

24. Allen Newell and Robert F. Sproull, "Computer Networks for Scientists," *Science*, vol. 215 (February 12, 1982), p. 846.

25. Kenneth G. Wilson, "The State of U.S. Science—1982," *Views on Science Policy of the Nobel Laureates for 1982*, Hearings before the House Committee on Science and Technology, 98 Cong. 1 sess. (GPO, 1983), p. 2.

26. John W. McCredie, "BITNET's Changing Role in Higher Education," *Educom Bulletin*, vol. 19 (Summer 1984), p. 2.

27. National Science Foundation, Office of Advanced Scientific Computing, "Access to ͡ ͡rcomputers," June 1984, p. 3.

Data base services provide selective access via computers to information banks. Most data banks contain bibliographic, numerical, or textual data. A few, such as the legal data base LEXIS,[28] contain complete documents, while others provide graphics or pictures.

Automated indexing and abstracting services first operated in the late 1960s and early 1970s, with nationwide services offered by the National Library of Medicine, Chemical Abstract Services, National Technical Information Service, and dozens of other companies. These services spawned commercial data base services, including those from Systems Development Corporation, based on work with the National Library of Medicine in developing Medline; Lockheed Information System, based on contract work with the National Aeronautics and Space Administration (NASA); and Bibliographic Retrieval Services, based on a package developed by IBM for internal information dissemination.[29] Today there are about 1,600 commercially available data retrieval services offering bibliographic, reference, or source record information.[30]

The campus equivalent of bibliographic data bases is the automated library catalog, which provides enhanced searching and remote access. Meaningful library catalog automation began when the contents of the familiar three-by-five-inch cards were produced in a computer-readable form. Catalog automation was aided in the late 1960s, when the Library of Congress began distributing to libraries magnetic tapes of bibliographic entries. The tapes, called Marc tapes, for "machine-readable cataloging," set a standard for catalog information.[31] The process of generating catalog cards and ultimately machine-readable records has been further aided by the Ohio College Library Center (OCLC) and more recently by the Research Libraries Information Network (RLIN). Together these services offer information on 24 million entries for books, monographs, manuscripts, periodicals, and so on.

While libraries are not primary resources for much of engineering and the sciences, they are important resources for most of the university community. Further, libraries provide scholars with bibliographic control and access to programs that turn raw

28. LEXIS, Mead Data Central, Dayton, Ohio.

29. R. M. Hayes, "Information Resources: Technical Issues," in James C. Emery, ed., *Closing the Gap Between Technology and Application* (Boulder, Colo.: Westview Press, 1978), p. 171.

30. "Online Business Information Sources" (Bryn Mawr, Pa. Newsnet, May 1983).

31. Hayes, "Information Resources," p. 173.

data into usable information. Patricia Battin of Columbia University has said that one of our "best kept secrets" is a national system of indexing that can retrieve a specific item from among more than 250 million volumes housed in the nation's research libraries.[32]

Computer facilities at universities for graduate education and research are formidable. Total university expenditures for computing approximate total expenditures for libraries, and a significant portion is devoted to research computing. Many departments have computers dedicated to research, and several disciplines have developed facilities for resource sharing and networking. On-line bibliographic data base services are available via packet-switched networks such as Tymnet, Telenet, and Arpanet. Universities lead in using technologies such as computer architecture, artificial intelligence, and image processing. In some cases, entire industries have been born based on these research efforts.

Yet amid apparent progress, even excitement, several troubling situations exist. These range from obsolete equipment to lack of appropriate technical assistance. Graduate students do not have universal access to state-of-the-art equipment. While a graduate student or faculty member could be assured of access to the latest computing facilities in 1970, the same cannot be guaranteed today. University computing facilities lag behind those available to industry and those existing in universities in other countries.[33] For example, Kenneth Wiberg, a chemist at Yale, has reported that no U.S. university can match the computing power available to Japanese chemists.[34] Some progress is now being made in providing access to supercomputers, but clearly identified supercomputer demand greatly exceeds supply.[35] Also, access is difficult, often requiring travel to the computer site, which requires that computing be done in a crash program of sleepless nights with little time for reflection. Further, students need access to artificial intelligence machines, image processing equipment, robotic devices, and computer-aided design facilities as well as supercomputers. State-of-the-art equipment is particularly crucial in com-

32. Patricia Battin, "The Electronic Library—A Vision for the Future," *Educom Bulletin*, vol. 19 (Summer 1984), p. 13.

33. See Bardon and Curtis, "A National Computing Environment"; NSF and DOE, *Science and Engineering Education*, p. 81.

34. Kenneth B. Wiberg, letter to Dr. Richard Nicholson, National Science Foundation, May 26, 1982, included as appendix AIII-17 to "Report of the Panel on Large Scale Computing in Science and Engineering," sponsored by the Department of Defense and the NSF in cooperation with the DOE and NASA, December 26, 1982.

35. NSF, "Access to Supercomputers," p. 2.

puting because what is high-powered and scarce today will be commonplace when students go to work in laboratories.

Effective networks for resource sharing are rare, with a few impressive exceptions, such as Arpanet. National networks are often difficult to tap into and use. Serious questions remain about organizing networks and controlling access. Yet without easy-to-use, fast, accessible, and compatible networks, little can be done to offer specialized, shared resources. Practices that discourage use of off-campus facilities also inhibit use of national networks. At most universities, for example, the individual bears the cost of using information resources such as on-line Chem Abstracts, while the institution bears the cost of a printed version. University-based networks for sharing local facilities face enormous problems in connecting a diverse community of incompatible equipment, but they suffer more from lack of useful, specialized resources, such as artificial intelligence machines, array processors, and expertise, than from lack of communications.

A serious shortage of skilled personnel inhibits effective use of computing and communications technologies. Using computing for research often involves collaboration among computer scientists and other scientists and engineers to develop new techniques. It also involves support personnel such as programmers and electronics engineers. Currently computer science and computing engineering personnel are in short supply because of heavy demand for them in all sectors of the economy. The decline in graduate students in computer sciences and electrical engineering limits the pool available to work in university labs, a problem exacerbated by the need to have graduate students teach in undergraduate programs with exploding demands. The well-publicized problems of computer science and engineering education are problems for all sciences because of the pervasiveness and power of computer-based techniques.[36]

Existing departmental computing facilities are limited and underfunded. The emergence of departmental computing facilities was a healthy development; it placed computer facilities near the work. As the dominant approach to providing academic computing, however, it has some flaws. One is the attempt to fit problems on departmental or laboratory computers regardless of their adequacy. This limits the types of research that are done. In most scientific laboratories, for instance, computing is limited to the kind of computing that a Digital Equipment Company's Vax

36. Denning, "A Discipline in Crisis"; NSF and DOE, *Science and Engineering Education.*

does, because few universities know of or use alternative methods such as parallel processing or special purpose equipment. The benefits from cross-pollination of the different intellectual backgrounds among scientists with common computing interests are also lost. [37]

Underfunding results from focusing on hardware acquisition and expenditures and forgetting about ongoing costs such as programming, maintenance, software, and equipment upgrading. At well-supported scientific computing facilities, hardware costs represent about one-third to one-half of total operating costs.[38] Most departmental facilities are hard pressed to cover maintenance costs, let alone prepare for replacement of obsolete equipment. The results are out-of-date, out-of-service equipment, home-built software, and heavy implicit costs as scientists and engineers perform tasks more appropriately performed by support personnel. Research libraries are lagging in putting their catalogs in machine-readable form. The cost of indexing the 200 million volumes in our libraries is enormous. Columbia University estimates about five years and $8 million will be needed to convert its 2.5 million records.[39] Currently libraries are barely indexing fast enough to keep up with new materials. Added to this burden are demands that libraries index and archive machine-readable data bases, audio tapes, and videodiscs. Computer systems for storing the library data base are either out of date or nonexistent. Older systems are not easy to use, do not integrate various library operations such as acquisitions and circulation, and are not accessible from remote sites. Currently available systems do not address the relationship between library data and scholars' workstations used for manipulating the data.

Against the current setting, several trends will shape the next several years. Students will be arriving for graduate education with considerable computing experience. Today most college freshmen have had some computing in high school; those in science and engineering are more apt to have had computing at an early age. As many as 20 percent of these students have computers in their homes, and all are familiar with arcade games, which do more to shape attitudes toward computing than most people believe.

Many colleges and universities are planning computer-intensive

---

37. See Bardon and Curtis, "A National Computing Environment," p. 23.

38. See Charles H. Warlick, ed., *Directory of Computing Facilities in Higher Education, 1983–84* (University of Texas at Austin Computation Center, 1984).

39. Battin, "The Electronic Library," p. 15.

environments, where undergraduates have their own computers or have access to ten hours of high-quality computing per week. Brown University, the Massachusetts Institute of Technology, and Carnegie-Mellon University have received the most recognition in this area, but other schools such as Clarkson, Stevens Institute of Technology, Drexel, Drew, the Polytechnic Institute of New York, and the Virginia Polytechnic Institute Engineering College are now requiring their students to purchase computers. At Stanford, more than 2,000 students purchased computers in the two weeks following the announcement of a student purchase program.[40] These students will join younger faculty who view computers as an indispensable tool. They will assist their mentors in using computers, but they will also demand high-quality computing resources as a matter of course. The computers they purchase for undergraduate work are not likely to be adequate for their graduate studies.

The computing and communications industry will continue to grow, becoming the nation's largest industry. It will be an area of increasing international competition—high-quality research and development requiring state-of-the-art equipment will determine a nation's productivity and place in the economic marketplace. The industry will produce better tools for research and development on one hand, and require that scientists and engineers know how to use them on the other. Links between universities and industry will become closer as universities seek access to the latest facilities and industry seeks new talent.

Costs of computing and communications equipment will continue to fall. One result will be the continued substitution of computers for more expensive resources. A second will be the use of greater cost performance to enhance graphics, to increase complexity of models, and to improve ease of use. Both factors will increase the use of computing and increase the total cost of computers as a portion of a university's budget. Continued improvements in computer design will reduce costs, but they will also make existing equipment obsolete. State-of-the-art equipment, such as supercomputers, will be obsolete every two to four years.

Institutional arrangements for computing will change. Many distinctions between service groups in universities will disappear with the merger of computers, communications, and data retrieval technologies. Computing and communications resources will

40. Private discussion with Michael Carter, director of Microcomputer Project at Stanford.

become more specialized, requiring a hierarchy of services. Supercomputers, artificial intelligence machines, image processors, and data-base handlers will supplement general purpose computing. Effective use of these resources will require networks, management, and standardized protocols for access and use.

Personnel shortages in computer science and electrical engineering will continue, and they will continue to make it difficult to retain faculty. All projections show that the numbers of graduates in computer science and electrical engineering will fall far short of demands over the next five years.[41] These areas will be joined by others required for artificial intelligence work, such as linguistics, pure mathematics, and cognitive psychology.

In short, the problems now evident in providing computing and communications resources for graduate education will not abate; they will worsen. During a period of little growth or of modest decline, universities will find it very difficult to meet growing computational demands. An equal or greater challenge will be the need to develop new structures and methods to cope with socioeconomic and technology changes.

### Projecting Needs

Estimating the needed computer facilities and associated support for science and engineering graduate education is a difficult but fruitful business. It is difficult because it is hard to separate wants from needs and because new techniques are constantly being developed that create new requirements. It is fruitful because it sets forth roughly the magnitude of the problem of keeping graduate education up to date with computing gear.

Computer demands are perhaps best approached by dividing requirements into base-level services, which are available to all researchers and graduate students, and specialized services, which are required for specific research areas that are awarded on a competitive basis. This division simplifies projection because base-level services can be determined by estimating the level of service needed by an individual and then multiplying that number by the number of individuals in that category. Specialized services are more difficult to project; the most common methods are estimates based on surveys of scientists and engineers or the judgments of panels of esteemed scientists and engineers. Those two methods will be used here, with a third method: projection of the past used as a check on the reasonableness of the estimates.

---

41. NSF and DOE, *Science and Engineering Education.*

Estimates of specialized computing needs for graduate science and engineering education are provided by the 1983 study mentioned earlier, "A National Computing Environment for Academic Research." This study, known as the Bardon-Curtis report, suggested a systematic, comprehensive plan to improve the nation's computing services for academic research. The report covered local facilities, supercomputer capacity, national networks, and advanced computer systems research and computational mathematics. The report developed the following total funding program (in millions of dollars):[42]

|  | FY 1984 | FY 1985 | FY 1986 |
|---|---|---|---|
| Local facilities | 45.5 | 90.8 | 106.7 |
| Supercomputers | 14.4 | 70.0 | 110.0 |
| Networks | 2.1 | 7.3 | 11.5 |
| Advanced computer systems research and computational mathematics | 8.0 | 20.0 | 33.0 |
| Total | 70.0 | 188.1 | 261.2 |

Assuming that the Bardon-Curtis report accurately estimates the need for specialized facilities for research, the need for base-level services can now be added. These include computer equipment for graduate students and faculty, funds for data-base access, and support for library automation. The estimated base-level computer equipment needed for graduate students in 1986 is a powerful workstation, connected to a departmental network, and graphics, computation, and data storage. This equipment would be used for tasks ranging from word processing to moderately complex mathematical simulations. Such a workstation should cost about $4,000 and have a life of four years, for an equipment cost of $1,000 a year. Yearly equipment cost should be matched by funds for maintenance, software, and personnel assistance, making the total $2,000 annually. A conservative estimate is that one such station will be required for every two graduate students in 1986. Estimating about 350,000 students in science and engineering graduate education, the total annual cost would be $350 million.

Base-level services for faculty must be more substantial. A workstation for connecting to the network will need to be more powerful to support several associates' development projects and complex software such as computer-aided design analysis. A low-

---

42. Bardon and Curtis, "A National Computing Environment," p. 23.

end cost would be $20,000 for equipment lasting four years, or $5,000 annually. Matching the $5,000 with an equal amount for support and providing one workstation for each doctoral faculty member in graduate science and engineering (estimated to be 40,000) would result in an annual expenditure of $400 million. The total of student and faculty base-level computing needs equals $750 million per year.

The cost of accessing off-campus data-base services such as Dialog and Chem Abstracts is more difficult to estimate. If each graduate student were provided with $100 per year (which would cover the cost of about three full-scale searches) and each doctoral faculty member, $250, the total cost would be about $45 million annually.

Library automation also demands attention. The total cost of automating the major research libraries in the United States will approximate $250 million over the next several years. Coverage for automating the portion of the collection of greatest importance to scientists and engineers will cost about $20 million a year for the next several years.

Combining these base-level requirements with those predicted by the NSF and dedicating NSF local facilities support to extraordinary grant-related requirements over the above base-level support produce the following requirements for 1986, with 1984 amounts shown for comparison (in millions of dollars):

|  | 1984 | 1986 |
|---|---|---|
| Base-level computing | 300 | 750 |
| Data-base access | . . . | 45 |
| Serials conversion | . . . | 20 |
| Local facilities | 46 | 107 |
| Supercomputer | 14 | 110 |
| Networks | 2 | 12 |
| Advanced computer systems | 8 | 33 |
| Total | 370 | 1,077 |

The result is an annual expenditure of $1,077 million a year for an intensive computer environment comparable to that of industrial laboratories.

Are these figures reasonable? As a check, current expenditures for research and graduate education, estimated at $300 million for local facilities,[43] can be projected. Using survey data, the Bardon-

43. Derived from Gillespie with Dicaro, *Computing and Higher Education*, p. 18; Warlick, *Directory of Computing Facilities*, p. A-4.

Curtis report projected an increase of NSF local facilities support from $45.5 million in 1984 to $106.7 million in 1986, a ratio of 2.33 to 1. Applying that ratio to current estimates of local research and graduate education expenditures of $300 million yields about $700 million, close to the projection above.

Are the overall figures reasonable? If current trends hold, such expenditures may be necessary to keep graduate education competitive with industry and universities in other countries. Consider that the $4,000 workstation provided in base-level support is approximately the type of facility projected for Carnegie-Mellon University undergraduates at a rate of one per student. Consider as well that the yearly cost to society of a student in graduate education probably exceeds $30,000 and that some preliminary estimates of the effectiveness of computer-based techniques show that the material covered in a computer science course can be doubled and that the material covered in a computer-aided design course can be increased fifty times.[44] Finally, consider that many clerks and secretaries are regularly provided with $5,000 to $10,000 word processors at an annual cost of from $2,000 to $4,000.

These projections are not all-inclusive, nor are they intended to set standards. If they err as guideposts, they err by underestimating needs and failing to include the enormous problem of bringing existing faculty and staff up to date with new technologies. Additional problems that are difficult to estimate relate to starting new fields of study and cutting back in others—a result of the increasing degree of specialization and the greater rapidity of change.

Nevertheless, these projections set the size of the problem graduate education faces in providing appropriate computing and communications technology. They suggest that current expenditures will more than triple over the next few years. By that time, according to some measures, information technology will represent about 20 percent of the total science, engineering, and medical science research and development budget in higher education.

*Conclusion: issues and questions*

This report has covered one aspect of the computer revolution, that of providing adequate support for graduate education in science and engineering. The problem of adequate support is large, current, and compelling. But other effects of the computer

44. Discussion with Maurice Glicksman, provost, Brown University; Gillespie with Dicaro, *Computing and Higher Education*, p. 34.

revolution, such as the need for continuing education and changes in the location and methods of education, may have greater long-term impact.

Several issues arise in attempts to provide adequate support: what resources are needed, in what quantity those resources are needed, who pays for them, and how they are distributed.

There is amazing agreement in the academic community about what computing should be provided for science and engineering graduate education and research. (1) There must be a hierarchy of computing: starting with a personal workstation with high computational, graphics, and data storage capacity, sharing local resources such as programs and plotters, and accessing campus or departmental specialized facilities and national or regional resources such as supercomputers. (2) A high-speed national data network is needed so that scientists in university, industry, and government laboratories can communicate with each other and have access to special data bases and computer resources. (3) Disciplines underlying information technology, such as computer science and information engineering, must be strengthened so that adequate personnel are available to collaborate with scientists and engineers in developing new techniques and tools. (4) Access to data bases, including bibliographic services, the local research library, and stored images such as molecular structures, must be enhanced, and services themselves must be developed. (5) Research and development efforts are needed to explore alternative computer designs suited for scientific purposes. Also, research in numerical techniques and computational mathematics is necessary.

While there is agreement that all of the these elements are needed, there is understandable disagreement on how much should be spent on each area, particularly how much should be spent relative to other demands for resources.

The question of how much to spend on information technology for graduate education and research is complicated. One approach to simplifying the problem is to divide resources into base-level and specialized categories. Presumably base-level resources promise returns so far in excess of cost that their value is not in question. To attempt to define a base level, more information is required:

—What is the current level of computing use among students in graduate science and engineering by area?

—What tools are judged essential to scientific and engineering research by discipline?

—What gains are recorded by computer-intensive environments such as Brown University?

—How much are data-base services used, and how much would they be used if subsidized?

—What are the benefits of communication networks for students, for faculty?

Answers to these questions should be used to focus on an appropriate base-level resource for all of the graduate science and engineering community. First steps in improving the base level need not await the answers, however.

Providing specialized resources requires reviewing specific projects and research areas and identifying their needs. This task is not easy when people are unaware of new tools and techniques and when resources needed are of such a scale that they cannot be provided on a case-by-case basis. Both the university level and the national level lack a mechanism for identifying critical shared resource requirements on something other than a crisis basis.

There is agreement that providing adequate resources will require contributions by all who have a stake in graduate education: federal government, state governments, industry, private donors, universities, and students. Beyond this, questions are many but familiar. What is the responsibility of the federal government? What are the dangers and opportunities of industry-university cooperation? What is the state's role? How much should the universities put up via internal reallocation? And how much should students pay? Reiterating the arguments here would be fruitless.[45] Two issues, however, deserve mention. One is the need for sustained support, be it from government or industry. A worry expressed by Feigenbaum and McCorduck applies to government as well as industry: "that industry's emphasis on the short term, whether profits, product improvement, or proprietary information, is the functional equivalent of a one night stand, whereas university computer science needs a well-dowered marriage."[46]

The second issue relates to a growing trend of having students pay for resources through special fees or required purchases. For example, the University of Michigan now assesses engineering students a fee of $100 per term to pay for improved computer facilities. Higher fees, while workable for undergraduate engineering students and medical students, would seem to present special difficulties for graduate science and engineering education,

45. For an excellent discussion of various responsibilities for funding, see "The Federal Role in Higher Education. Facilities Funding: The Case Study of the University of California," in *Discussion Issues 1984; Academic Science and Engineering: Physical Infrastructure*, vol. 2: *Background Material*, NSB84-160 (National Science Board, 1984).

46. Edward A. Feigenbaum and Pamela McCorduck, *The Fifth Generation* (Reading, Mass.: Addison-Wesley, 1983), p. 206.

where there are already economic disincentives for continued study. Students probably should not have to pay for new resources in greater proportion than they now pay for the total cost of their education, which, according to this paper's projections, is about $200 per year, approximately Michigan's fee.

The core issue in resource allocation is who makes decisions about how resources are used. Federal funding for computing shifted from institutional awards in the 1960s, when universities decided use, to individual investigation awards in the 1970s. Neither method proved entirely satisfactory. What may be needed is a combined approach of block grants and individual awards. The difficulty then becomes determining the appropriate proportion of funds toward each. For example, to match the 1957–72 level of support for institutional computing, the NSF would have to award about $200 million annually, a total greater than the sum of current individual awards.

Some questions most directly related to computing resource allocations include:

—Should allocations be on a disciplinary, general research area, or institutional basis? Should they be mission-directed or basic science–oriented?

—What is the effect of indirect federal assistance to industry, such as tax incentives, on the type of research and the quality of graduate education?

—Should emphasis be on increasing the base quality of science and engineering graduate education or on aiding the most productive programs?

—If mixes of funds are provided—for example, supercomputer access awards to individuals and to institutions—does the dual system operate according to Gresham's law?

—What is the overall effect of matching awards on quality and access?

These are not unique questions, but some thought to them is necessary if the nation mounts a large-scale effort to encourage universities to improve computing resources for graduate education.

The computer revolution raises many questions and creates many issues for American graduate education. The most basic question is whether computing is special and deserves special attention or whether it should be included with other capital needs. The position taken here is that it is special, that it is a transforming technology for a new generation of scientists and engineers. As an intelligence amplifier, it can be compared to few other resources.

If indeed computing and related technology are special, decisions must be made about the appropriate national, state, and university strategies for computing and communications. If the strategies are wise, details will not matter much. For, as stated earlier, if computer-based information technology changes the very substance of research and graduate education, what is at stake is not efficiency. What is at stake is survival.

# The Capital Facilities Dilemma in the American Graduate School

LINDA S. WILSON

UNIVERSITIES conduct more than half of the nation's fundamental research and about one-quarter of its total research. They are an integral part of the search for solutions to problems in national security, health care, energy, productivity, education, and the environment. They are the principal providers of the training of future generations of scientists, engineers, teachers, and professionals. The health and strength of these institutions are therefore matters of national interest.

The general state of the physical plant of America's higher education institutions has recently been diagnosed in dismal terms: "The halls of academe are crumbling. Buildings, grounds, and utilities . . . are in a dilapidated condition, endangering life and property. The vitality of the higher education enterprise is in jeopardy."[1] One-half of higher education's physical plant is more than twenty-five years old; one-quarter was built before World War II. The aging physical plant needs renewal, realignment, and replacement. The cost of needed renewal and replacement is estimated at a staggering $30 billion.[2] During the 1950s and 1960s the nation expanded its facilities for instruction and basic research. It failed, however, to provide adequately for their renewal and replacement.

The focus of this paper is on the universities' physical facilities for graduate education and research in science and engineering. Other aspects of higher education's infrastructure will be considered only as they share features or trends with the physical facilities for graduate education and research.

Several conditions create additional demands for renewal and

The author gratefully acknowledges the valuable assistance of Karen Arnold, Ph.D. candidate in higher education administration at the University of Illinois, and helpful discussions with many colleagues in government, universities and university associations, industry, and private foundations.

1. Harvey H. Kaiser, *Crumbling Academe: Solving the Capital Renewal and Replacement Dilemma* (Washington, D.C.: Association of Governing Boards of Universities and Colleges, 1984), p. vi.

2. Ibid., p. 13.

modernization of the universities' physical facilities. In the post-industrial, knowledge-based society, national imperatives for economic progress require enhanced investments in human capital and more effective communication of knowledge and technology. Acceleration of the rate of technical change and of international competition in science and technology places new emphasis on the role of graduate education and research. Emerging scientific and technological opportunities change the research and generate requirements for higher-quality laboratories. Work with smaller dimensions and greater measurement sensitivities requires cleaner environments, which are difficult to achieve in old facilities. Technical advances in instrumentation and communication technology profoundly affect methods of research, exchange of ideas, and patterns of work of scientists and engineers.

*The role of facilities in graduate education and research*

The prolonged period of fiscal constraint has taken a heavy toll on the capital assets of higher education. The magnitude of renewal costs strains the nation's capacity for response, especially when there are many pressing needs on the national agenda. As one considers the renewal problem one must first specify how outdated facilities affect the quality and productivity of graduate education and research. Some good work has been done in spite of abominable facilities. Excellent facilities cannot in themselves ensure high-quality graduate education and research.

Three principal features of the U.S. science support system are concentration of basic research in the universities, integration of advanced research and graduate instruction, and emphasis on support of research projects rather than support of institutions. The U.S. experiment with concentrating basic science research in its universities has facilitated a wide range of contacts among scholars, researchers, and students, and it has encouraged independent research at all levels.[3]

Integration of advanced research and graduate instruction is a hallmark of the U.S. system. It has encouraged students to participate in original research, in which they learn new and creative techniques, they learn to question, and they learn responsibility. It has also helped maintain the vitality of the research faculty.[4]

---

3. Carnegie Foundation for the Advancement of Teaching, Carnegie Council on Policy Studies in Higher Education, *Three Thousand Futures: The Next Twenty Years for Higher Education* (San Francisco: Jossey-Bass, 1980), p. 112.

4. Wolfgang K. H. Panofsky, "Big Science and Graduate Education," in Harold Orlans, ed., *Science Policy and the University* (Brookings, 1968), pp. 192–93.

Integrating graduate education and research is considered effective, but it has not been rigorously tested. Because of formidable methodological obstacles, the cause-and-effect linkage will probably never be proved. International comparisons of scientific leadership and productivity, however, lend credibility to the view that this U.S. design is very advantageous.

The emphasis on project support in the U.S. science system has many advantages, but it has some disadvantages in ensuring adequate infrastructure for research. As the project system now operates, firm commitments of support are rarely given for longer than one year, and planned commitments are often given for only three years, rarely for more than five years. The system requires accountability by discrete project. Neither of these features ideally ensures adequate infrastructure. Both approaches encourage narrow focus and short-term effectiveness; infrastructure requirements are usually broad and long term.

*Effects of facilities limitations*

Empirical data on the relationship between the quantity and state of facilities on the one hand and graduate education and research on the other are limited. That there is a strong connection, however, seems obvious. The National Science Board's study on graduate education in 1969 identified the amount of physical plant available for graduate education as an important potential indicator of quality of graduate programs, but it acknowledged that insufficient information was available for satisfactory analysis.[5] None of the subsequent national assessments of quality of graduate programs, however, has used facilities other than library resources as an indicator of quality, presumably because of the difficulties in obtaining the necessary data. A more recent multinational study of the factors that affect scientific productivity in research groups suggested that there is a minimum threshold of necessary resources (including both funding and facilities). Above that threshold, productivity is related more to the researchers' perception of the reasonableness of the share of resources available to them than to the actual amount of resources available.[6]

A recent effort to develop a methodology for assessing basic research compared the scientific progress at the major high-energy physics laboratories in the world. This work clearly demonstrated the critical role played by the age and design of the accelerator

5. National Science Board, *Graduate Education—Parameters for Public Policy* (Government Printing Office, 1969).
6. Frank M. Andrews, ed., *Scientific Productivity: The Effectiveness of Research Groups in Six Countries* (Cambridge University Press/UNESCO, 1979).

facilities in the quality and effect of the work produced.[7] The influence of the physical environment on the learning process has been studied more than its influence on research and graduate education.[8] In the absence of further empirical evidence, one must draw on general wisdom to suggest ways in which the physical plant affects graduate education and research. The actual measurement of these effects is more difficult.

Since it influences most human endeavors, the notion of what is possible influences the development of research ideas and plans. Overcrowding, inflexibility of space, and inadequacy of environmental controls can stifle the imagination of students and faculty, especially if they perceive little or no opportunity for improvement. In the physical sciences there are reports of an increasing trend for graduate students to choose doctoral research in theoretical rather than experimental topics.[9] Several factors may be involved, including the intellectual attraction of theory; the availability of computer simulation as a substitute for experimentation; and the advances in equipment, which have increased the rate of progress in experimental research. The frustrations resulting from inadequate equipment and facilities may also be a significant and growing cause of the shift. The importance of well-trained experimentalists for industry suggests that more careful analysis of the trends is in order.

The ability to take advantage of new directions in research is also limited by facilities. Scientists specializing in the mechanisms of photosynthesis may recognize the potential for important applications through extension of their studies to aquatic plants. Without extensively modified facilities, however, they cannot pursue this line of investigation. The exploitation of the scientific opportunity depends on the availability of funds for realignment of laboratory space.

Limitations on facilities can also lead to conservative science. Those whose experimental efforts are limited to what can be accomplished at shared regional and national facilities worry that

7. Ben R. Martin and John Irvine, "CERN: Past Performance and Future Prospects," *Research Policy*, forthcoming; "Assessing Basic Research: Some Partial Indicators of Scientific Progress in Radio Astronomy," *Research Policy*, vol. 12 (April 1983), pp. 61–90.

8. J. King and R. W. Marans, *The Physical Environment and the Learning Process: A Survey of Recent Research* (Ann Arbor: University of Michigan, Survey Research Center, Institute for Social Research, and Architectural Research Laboratory, College of Architecture and Urban Planning, for UNESCO, 1979).

9. William A. Fowler, Testimony before the House Subcommittee on Science, Research, and Technology, 97 Cong. 2 sess., March 4, 1982, in *Revitalizing Laboratory Instrumentation* (Washington, D.C.: National Academy Press, 1983), appendix C, pp. 68–69; personal communication from Herman Fishbach, Massachusetts Institute of Technology.

the processes used to determine access will discourage lines of inquiry that have a high payoff but are speculative.

Although there have been efforts to ascertain what specific research problems are not being addressed because of limitations in equipment or facilities, the attempts have not been extensive or systematic.[10] The evidence is largely anecdotal. The difficulty of the judgments at issue hampers the design of methods to assess the effect of stifling research. The more creative the ideas, the less predictable they would be and the less noticeable their absence would be in the short term. More thorough methods for assessing the effects of facilities on the choice of research problems are needed if we are to act with confidence in investing scarce resources in facilities or in denying such investments.

The degree of collaboration and interaction among scientists and students is affected by physical facilities. Close proximity of personnel is important for effective scientific communication. The sharing of instrumentation and laboratory facilities can stimulate and facilitate the development of collaborative scientific efforts. The growing need to share major research instrumentation may encourage the development of new disciplines at the interfaces of traditional disciplines.

When individual research groups are dispersed because contiguous space is not available, interaction is reduced, and the quality of research supervision and training may be undermined as well. The new communications technologies may overcome some of these difficulties, but face-to-face interaction still plays a key role in the stimulation and development of ideas among scientists. Face-to-face interaction is perhaps even more important for the socialization of students within their professions.[11]

Physical facilities also affect university responsiveness to regional and national interest in the transfer of knowledge and technology to industry. University-industry cooperative research in many cases represents an expansion, or at least a shift in emphasis, in the universities' scope of activities. Much of the university-industry cooperative work will require additional facilities or at least modification of existing space. This is especially true for the cooperative efforts designed to respond to the needs of new high-technology enterprises and other small businesses. Few of these organizations have their own internal research facilities. They

---

10. Association of American Universities, *The Nation's Deteriorating University Research Facilities* (Washington, D.C.: AAU, 1981).

11. A. W. Chickering, ed., *The Modern American College* (San Francisco: Jossey-Bass, 1981).

must, therefore, rely on university facilities to house collaboration. Cooperative research arrangements may be of short duration, so the design of the research facilities must remain flexible.

Perhaps the most serious effect of inadequate facilities is on the recruiting and retention of the most productive faculty members. The erosion of academic facilities is seriously limiting the attractiveness of the academic profession for some of the best and brightest of both new and senior scientists. Failure to overcome such disincentives will seriously affect the universities' role as a major research performer and as the primary provider of advanced training.

Clearly, research facilities have an effect on the validity of research results. Inadequacies in environmental control limit the quality of data. Crowding limits the access to research facilities and reduces the number of experiments that are undertaken. Physical deterioration and overload lead to downtime, which seriously affects productivity. A recent survey of a sample of NSF-funded investigators found that 60 percent reported having lost some time in the past year because of facilities-related failures.[12] Scientific areas that rely on computerized data acquisition require air conditioning. Inadequate provision for air conditioning yields downtime on the order of 50 percent during the summer months in some parts of the country. Deferred maintenance and aging of buildings cause leaks, which ruin instrumentation and experiments and cause extended interruptions in work. Probably all professionals lose some time every year to facility-related difficulties. The issues are the severity and duration of such difficulties and the cost imposed by them.

Old buildings accommodate current scientific purposes with difficulty. Their systems for distributing utilities and services cannot satisfy current scientific demands. Their construction is rarely adequate for experiments that are sensitive to vibration or that demand a dust-free environment. They have only limited flexibility for rearrangement to locate related groups of scientists near each other. Productivity diminishes as students and faculty spend time traveling among laboratories and gaining access to needed instrumentation.

The ability of each graduate student to develop as an independent investigator is affected by the facilities and the instrumentation

12. National Science Foundation, Division of Policy Research and Analysis, "University Research Facilities: Report on a Survey among National Science Foundation Grantees," in *Discussion Issues 1984, Academic Science and Engineering: Physical Infrastructure*, vol. 2: *Background Material*, section C (Washington, D.C.: GPO, 1984).

available. The development of team approaches for complex problems and the need to share major instrumentation limit independent work. The ability of the physical plant to accommodate state-of-the-art instrumentation profoundly affects the training of graduate students. Deteriorating physical plants and obsolete equipment have already put many programs, especially in engineering, far behind current professional practice. To the extent that universities lag rather than lead in state-of-the-art practice, they do not meet the needs of industry and government for highly trained personnel.

Limitations in instrumentation and physical facilities also affect the extent to which undergraduates are able to participate in research. In some institutions space more than anything else limits undergraduate participation in research.[13] If this problem spreads, it will impair the recruitment of undergraduates into graduate study and the quality of their preparation for graduate study.

The inability to take all the precautions needed to ensure safety in the laboratory and to comply with environmental standards is a matter of growing concern. As the frontiers of science have advanced, new potential hazards have emerged and must be addressed. Difficult compromises must be made when resources are not available to make the necessary major renovations in old buildings. Safety education, extraordinary laboratory "housekeeping," and careful segregation of risks can only partially compensate for inadequacies in facilities design. The long-term loss in productivity and the cost of such compromises indicate the need for more fundamental solutions.

The openness of the facilities and the involvement of all levels of students in the university setting intensify the need for careful attention to safety. Universities also have a responsibility to train the next generation of scientists in safe practices. The nature and use of university laboratories, however, require different safety standards and management from those designed for industrial plants. Application of regulations that ignore or overlook these differences can cause an unnecessary drain on scarce resources for facilities renewal.

Specific examples of the consequences of deficiencies in facilities include diminished international competitiveness of U.S. industry, especially with European industry and Japanese industry; diminished knowledge for the development of new processes and products; decelerating innovation and delay in achievement of

13. Personal communications from Jiri Jonas, Samuel Kaplan, and Emanuel Donchin, University of Illinois.

national objectives; and inability to provide critical technical assistance in emergencies.[14] The capacity for renewal and replacement of capital assets is essential for any enterprise. For science, the essence of which is change, the consequences of failure to ensure capital renewal and replacement may be especially severe.

*Evolution of the research facilities problem*
A recent background paper developed for the National Science Board's discussion of physical structure problems in academic science and engineering summarized the evolution of the research facilities problem.[15] The sources of support for the physical plant of America's research universities have changed over the past century. Before World War II most support for facilities and equipment for academic science came from the private sector (including industry), from state appropriations, and in some areas from federal land grants and formula appropriations. After World War II the federal government was the major source of support for academic research programs, but not for facilities. The period from 1950 to 1970 saw a boom in construction of instructional facilities and housing to accommodate a rapid expansion of enrollments. At the same time the demand for research space increased because of expansion of faculty and because of changes in faculty workloads. The demands for resources to expand exceeded the capacity of philanthropic organizations and industry to respond. The successful Soviet orbiting of Sputnik stimulated federal support. The government saw that facilities construction was needed to ensure the nation's research capacity.

The peak of the science facilities construction boom occurred in the early 1960s. At that time the federal contribution to construction of academic R&D facilities was about 35 percent of the total. The balance was met by state governments, endowments, philanthropic and corporate contributions, and special building fundraising drives. By the early 1970s the rapid growth in academia began to subside. Federal programs to stimulate expansion of research and training capacity were phased down; most, in fact, were eliminated. Today almost no federal programs fund academic research facilities other than those that house very specialized research instrumentation, such as accelerators. Table 1 describes the various federal facility programs.

University budgeting and planning for facilities have encoun-

---

14. Association of American Universities, *Nation's Deteriorating University Research Facilities*, p. 4 and appendixes.

15. National Science Foundation, "University Research Facilities," in *Discussion Issues 1984*, vol. 1: *Issues and Options*, pp. 1–2.

Table 1. *Federal Facility Funding Programs*

| Date | Funding source | Purpose | Amount of funding |
|---|---|---|---|
| 1948–50 | National Cancer Institute 1948 Construction Authority | Cancer research facilities construction | $16.3 million |
| 1950 | National Heart Act | Heart disease research facilities construction | $6.059 million |
| 1956–68 | Health Research Facilities Act of 1956 | Nonfederal health sciences research facilities construction | $438.76 million |
| 1956–70 | Academic Computational Facilities and Operations Program, National Science Foundation (NSF) | Purchase, rental, and operation of electronic computers and related equipment for university and college science programs | $71.2 million to 184 institutions |
| 1959 | Ford Foundation Special ("Challenge") Program in Education | Development of selected institutions to become regional and national centers of excellence | $349 million; total grants and matching funds: $1.3 billion |
| 1960–70 | Graduate Science Facilities Program (NSF) | University laboratory space construction and general purpose equipment for such space | $188.16 million to 977 grantees |
| 1960–62 | National Heart Institute Primate Research Center Program | Primate research center facilities construction | $9.396 million |
| 1961–72 | Institutional Grants for Science (NSF) | Sustaining and improving academic science in existing high-quality institutions | $120 million to 939 institutions |
| 1961–72 | Interdisciplinary Laboratories for Materials Research (Advanced Research Projects Agency of Department of Defense; transferred to NSF in 1972) | Development of manpower and interdisciplinary approaches to materials research problems; construction of major central research facilities | $158 million (currently funded by NSF at $13.9 million a year) |
| 1962–71 | Sustaining University Programs, National Aeronautics and Space Administration (NASA) | Graduate training in space-related sciences, including facilities construction | $224.8 million |
| 1963–65 | Higher Education Facilities Act of 1963 (Office of Education) | Undergraduate and graduate academic facilities construction, reconstruction, and renovation; wider distribution of graduate schools | Not available |
| 1963– | Health Manpower Training Facilities Program, National Institutes of Health (NIH) | Teaching and multipurpose facilities construction for health profession students | Not available |
| 1964–67 | Mental Retardation Facilities and Community Mental Health Centers Construction Act of 1964 | Facilities construction for research on mental retardation | $65.561 million |
| 1964–72 | University and Department Science Development Programs (NSF) | Broad-scale program development to upgrade science and engineering research | $22.3 million to 140 institutions |

Table 1. *Federal Facility Funding Programs (continued)*

| Date | Funding source | Purpose | Amount of funding |
|------|----------------|---------|-------------------|
| 1965– | Higher Education Act of 1965 | Continued facilities construction authority of Higher Education Act of 1963 | Construction grants unfunded 1981–84; $28 million in 1985 |
| 1967–71 | Project THEMIS, Department of Defense (DOD) | Enhancement of academic capacity in science and technology; encouragement of increased numbers of institutions engaged in high-quality research; wider geographical distribution of research funds | $94.49 million |
| 1971–83 | National Cancer Act of 1971 | Cancer research facilities construction | $236.483 million |
| 1972 | National Heart, Blood Vessel, Lung, and Blood Act of 1972 | Hospital, clinic, and laboratory facilities construction | No funds appropriated under this authority |
| 1978– | Health Services Research and Health Care Technology Act | Public and nonprofit vision research facilities construction | $5 million |
| 1981 | National Agricultural Research, Extension, and Teaching Policy Act | Acquisition and improvement of research facilities in 1890 Land Grant institutions | Not available |
| Proposed | Construction of Animal Facilities Authority (Division of Research Resources, NIH) | Replacement of outmoded animal research facilities; improvement of existing NIH programs | Requested: $40 million for fiscal 1985 |
| Proposed | Research Facilities Rehabilitation Program (DOD) | Upgrading or replacement of selected university laboratories performing research essential to DOD's long-term mission | Requested: $100 million for fiscal 1985 |

tered a series of difficulties. During the 1960s and early 1970s expansion efforts strained the budgets and planning capacities of the universities. Then several major changes intensified the difficulties: inflation, government regulation, technological advance, and sources and terms of financing.[16] At the same time research facilities obsolesced as the frontiers of science and technology advanced. The structure of the U.S. academic science support system, by focusing principally on short-term, individual transactions, has obscured the broader needs of the research system as a whole. The universities have not been able to compensate for this flaw.

**The magnitude of the problem**

How serious is the facilities problem? What trends need to be taken into account? What are the responsibilities of the various actors in the process? Table 2 summarizes the major published

16. Lawrence L. Landry and Rodney Mebane, "Capital Crisis in Higher Education," *Business Officer*, February 1982, pp. 20–22.

Table 2. *Studies of Academic Facilities*

| Study | Description of study | Findings |
|---|---|---|
| "Health Related Research Facilities in the U.S. in the Nonprofit Nonfederal Sector," conducted by Westat Corporation for National Institutes of Health (NIH), 1969 | Survey gathered data on the amount, age, and ownership of space in 1968; the amount of space under or scheduled for construction; and the estimated space needed to eliminate overcrowding by 1980 | —10 million of 42 million square feet in unsatisfactory condition<br>—Over 50 percent available space in poor condition<br>—Additional 55 million square feet of space needed by 1980, with 17 million square feet requiring remodeling |
| "Higher Education General Information Survey" (HEGIS), conducted by the National Center for Education Statistics (NCES), 1974 | Survey of 3,200 colleges and universities, including data to estimate facilities needs | —20 percent of facilities at surveyed institutions in need of replacement (2.3 billion square feet)<br>—$2 billion needed just for remodeling of facilities |
| "Health Research Facilities: A Survey of Doctorate-Granting Institutions," conducted by the American Council on Education (ACE) with funding from the National Science Foundation (NSF) and NIH, 1976 | Survey of 155 Ph.D.-granting institutions gathered data on status of academic health research facilities, new construction in progress, and plans for expansion in succeeding five-year period | —29 percent of academic facilities for health research in need of renovation or replacement (23 million square feet)<br>—Cost estimates to meet needs: $547 million for 1975, $560 million for each of succeeding five years |
| "National Survey of Laboratory Animal Facilities and Resources," conducted by the National Academy of Sciences (NAS), NIH Publication 80-2091 (1978) | Survey of 922 nonprofit NIH-eligible institutions gathered data to estimate facilities needs | —16 percent of institutions reported need for replacement of facilities<br>—38 percent reported need for remodeling of facilities<br>—47 percent reported need for additional space |
| Report of Research Facilities Branch of National Cancer Institute on survey of facilities needs in cancer research, conducted at request of National Cancer Advisory Board, 1979 | Survey of 106 institutions receiving National Cancer Institute support gathered data to evaluate current and future needs to upgrade cancer research facilities | —$149 million for 1980–85 estimated for cancer research facilities |
| "A Program for Renewed Partnership," prepared by the Sloan Commission on Higher Education, 1980 | Commission report on federal government–university relations (no data collected) | —Recommendations for competitive program for facilities research grants: $50 million annually for five years, to be allocated by NSF and NIH, to upgrade research laboratories and equipment |
| "The Nation's Deteriorating Research Facilities: A Survey of Recent Expenditures and Projected Needs in Fifteen Universities," conducted by the Association of American Universities (AAU), 1981 | Survey of 15 leading universities gathered data on expenditures for research facilities and major equipment and estimates of funding needs for faculty research only for succeeding three-year period | —Surveyed institutions spent $400 million for facilities construction, repair, and renovation in 1972–82<br>—$765 million needed for facilities and equipment over succeeding three-year period just to sustain faculty research activities |

Table 2. *Studies of Academic Facilities (continued)*

| Study | Description of study | Findings |
|---|---|---|
| Report on academic facilities survey (in 1980–81 Comparative Cost and Staffing Report), conducted by the Association of Physical Plant Administrators (APPA), 1981 | Survey of 226 institutions with 454 million square feet of academic space gathered data on facilities conditions and projected needs | —$1.85–$2.00 per square foot required to eliminate most pressing needs<br>—Deferred maintenance need per institution of $9.5 million at universities, $1.1 million at four-year colleges, $0.4 million at two-year colleges |
| "Strengthening the Government–University Partnership in Science," conducted by the Ad Hoc Committee of NAS, National Academy of Engineering and Institute of Medicine, 1983 | Committee report on federal government–university relations (no data gathered) | —Critical, growing need for replacement of academic science facilities and equipment<br>—Recommended comprehensive program for facilities construction and for development, acquisition, maintenance, and operation of modern equipment |
| Report of Department of Defense (DOD) Working Group on Engineering and Science Education, prepared by the DOD–University Forum, 1983 | Working group report on condition and needs of academic science and engineering | —Deficiencies in research facilities and equipment acute in most universities |
| "Report on NIH Experience with Extramural Construction Authority," prepared by the Office of Program Planning and Evaluation, NIH, 1983 | Historical comparison of legislative authorities for construction of health research facilities analyzing past facilities funding experiences | —Funding authorities mainly for special, not general, use<br>—Almost all funds made available under grant mechanisms<br>—Recent authorities fail to separate funds for construction and research<br>—None of funding authorities based on systematic analysis of need |
| "Adequacy of Academic Research Facilities," conducted by the Ad Hoc Interagency Steering Committee on Academic Research Facilities, NSF, April 1984 | Pilot study of 25 major research institutions, with major study planned to gather data for detailed analysis of the condition of facilities used for science and engineering and medical research. Estimated future needs for construction, remodeling, and refurbishment of academic research facilities | —Over succeeding five-year period all colleges and universities require about $1.3 billion a year for research facilities alone (Note: Present level of capital facilities expenditures for academic research, development, *and* instruction is $1 billion a year) |
| "University Research Facilities: Report on a Survey Among National Science Foundation Grantees," conducted by the Division of Policy Research and Analysis, NSF, for Infrastructure Task Group of National Science Board (NSB), June 1984 | Survey of 1983 NSF grant for principal investigators (248 randomly sampled) to determine condition of existing facilities and impact of facilities on research | —70 percent of facilities had been renovated in last ten years using 7 percent federal dollars<br>—50 percent of facilities slated for renovation in next three years<br>—80 percent of PIs rated safety of facilities as excellent |

Table 2. *Studies of Academic Facilities (continued)*

| Study | Description of study | Findings |
|---|---|---|
| | | —60 percent of PIs reported having lost some research time in past year because of facilities-related failures; 40 percent reported graduate students had spent three or more days fixing problems created by facilities over past year |
| Proposed study of cancer research facilities, conducted by the President's Cancer Panel and the National Cancer Institute | Proposed survey study to gather data to inventory the quality and quantity of current research facilities in cancer research | In progress |
| Study of facilities needs in chemical science and engineering, conducted under the aegis of the Board on Chemical Science and Technology, National Research Council (in progress) | Survey to ascertain specific facilities data for research and teaching in chemistry, biochemistry, and chemical engineering academic departments | In progress |

studies that address facilities problems from 1969 to 1984. The definitions, assumptions, and criteria for recommending replacement or remodeling vary among reports. While the studies support an overall conclusion that renewal and replacement of facilities are needed, they leave unanswered some questions that are important in the design of effective remedial action.

To assess the magnitude of the need, past expenditure levels and current short-range plans can be compared with available funding. Using this approach, a recent preliminary analysis revealed the following picture. The current level of capital facilities expenditures for academic research, development, and instruction is roughly $1 billion a year. The federal government contributes approximately 15 percent of this amount. (Similarly, federal obligations for capital expenditures for federally funded research and development centers run about 15 percent of their total R&D expenditures.) The universities' level of capital expenditure for science and engineering was relatively constant during 1968–81 in current dollars, but decreased 60 percent in constant dollars. The federal share of that amount declined by a factor of two over that period. Federal obligations to universities for R&D plant peaked in the 1960s, declined sharply until 1973, and remained relatively constant in current dollars between 1973 and 1983. In constant dollars, however, from 1966 to 1983 federal obligations to universities for R&D plant decreased by 90 percent.[17] Univer-

17. National Science Foundation, "University Research Facilities," in *Discussion Issues 1984*, vol. 1: *Issues and Options*, pp. 5–7.

sities' planned academic capital expenditures for R&D facilities (excluding instruction) are estimated at approximately $1.3 billion annually from 1983 to 1988, an expenditure rate approximately double that of the past five years.[18]

Past expenditure levels and current plans for the future are inadequate as measures of the need for future expenditures. Institutional plans are heavily guided by pragmatic assessments of the amount of capital funds expected from public and private sources. Recently, such plans have grossly underestimated actual need.[19] Furthermore, the institutions' objectives may or may not coincide with national objectives. To address the differences between these objectives, data must be disaggregated to distinguish between fields of science and to distinguish research and graduate education from all academic science.

Another approach to assessing need is to consider the total area of the academic R&D physical plant, the age of the facilities, the cost of replacing existing facilities, and the cost of renovation as a fraction of replacement cost. Estimates of the frequency of need for renovation as well as the relative costs of various types of space permit development of rough guidelines for determining the need for capital funds. Based on the 1974 Higher Education General Information Survey of all facilities in institutions of higher education, and projection to 1981 levels, for example, the total replacement value for buildings was estimated at $143 billion and building renewal and remodeling needs were projected at $30 billion. For an average university, the combined renewal and replacement needs were estimated at $70.4 million.[20] (For a research university the needs would obviously be much higher, perhaps three or four times higher.) Note that current capital requirements are roughly similar to the total expenditures of all higher education in one year; they are at least three times the current value of all college and university endowments in the United States.

The Interagency Steering Committee on Academic Research Facilities has planned to study academic research facilities in depth. This study will survey the amount of R&D space in use; the condition of the space; the additional construction, modernization, and repair required to carry out innovative research; and institutional and disciplinary perceptions of the priorities for future needs

18. Ibid.

19. Personal communications from Steve Rugg, Anthony Graziano, and Harlan Bareither, University of Illinois, and Barbara Hansen, University of Southern Illinois.

20. National Center for Education Statistics, *Inventory of Facilities in Higher Education* (Washington, D.C.: GPO, 1974).

in facilities. The survey will also address past and future funding for facilities, the cost of the R&D, and the number of persons using the space.[21]

A third approach to assessing need is to develop estimates of the capitalization required per researcher, as was done in the Snowbird Report on the Computing Resource Needs of Faculty in Computer Science.[22] Unfortunately, the NSF data on capital expenditures for academic R&D do not distinguish between facilities expenditures and equipment expenditures.[23] Furthermore, the capitalization requirements may be far more difficult to determine in fields that use a broader array of equipment and facilities than is required in computer science.

All efforts to assess the magnitude of the academic R&D facilities problem are complicated by the absence of a common definition of need. Need may be defined as it affects the capacity to respond to specific national objectives, as it affects each institution's own interests, and as it affects the orderly development of science. Although these three aspects of need are related, they do not coincide. Common standards for determining the level and the urgency of the need are missing. Within the broad categories of "compelling need" and "calculated risk," the institutions establish priorities based on the need to protect occupants, buildings, built-in equipment, and other facilities, in that order. Once these needs are met, programmatic concerns can be addressed.[24]

Those who support academic R&D require information that will permit choices among competing claims. They need information on the potential of emerging scientific opportunities. A study of recent experience with strategic research forecasting in France, in West Germany, in Japan, and in the United States concluded that governments or research funding agencies will have little success in predicting radical breakthroughs generated by basic research. Longer-term forecasting activities in emerging areas of strategic research, however, can be helpful, especially if the forecasting of government, funding agencies, and industry can be integrated.[25]

21. Personal communication from Carlos Kruytbosch, National Science Foundation.

22. Peter J. Denning and others, "The Snowbird Report: A Discipline in Crisis," *Communications of the Association for Computing Machinery*, vol. 24 (June 1981), pp. 370–74.

23. National Science Foundation, "Federal Support to Universities, Colleges, and Selected Non-Profit Institutions, Fiscal Year 1982," Surveys of Science Resources Series (Washington, D.C.: GPO, 1984), pp. 84–315.

24. Kaiser, *Crumbling Academe*, p. 24.

25. John Irvine and Ben R. Martin, *Foresight in Science: Picking the Winners* (London and Dover, N.H.: Frances Pinter, 1984), p. 150.

The needs for equipment and facilities in the leading research universities (identified on the basis of their level of R&D expenditures) differ from those in other graduate higher education institutions. The institutions themselves differ in the extent of research activities, in the emphasis on doctoral studies, in the emphasis on particular disciplines, and in size.[26] The leading research universities on the average conducted 20 times as much sponsored research as other graduate institutions and 1,000 times as much as was conducted by all other institutions. These differences vary by field. The leading research universities enroll at least five times as many graduate students as other graduate institutions, they grant twelve times as many doctoral degrees, and they are more than twice as large in overall enrollment. Public research universities enroll almost twice as many students as the leading private research universities.

The facilities renewal problem is large, it is complex, and its consequences will vary in time and among scientific fields. Concerted efforts are needed to arrest the decay and to enable the facilities to take advantage of technological opportunities. The problem must be delineated so that the most critical needs can be addressed first.

Renewal of capital facilities, of course, is not the only financial issue. Aged, worn-out, and obsolescent equipment is also a very serious problem; table 3 summarizes some recent reports on the nature and extent of the equipment problem. Faculty salaries need upgrading to rectify a 20 percent loss in purchasing power over the last decade.[27] In fields subject to high demand, efforts to recruit and to maintain faculty are straining both institutional budgets and collegial relationships.[28] Financial support for graduate students is still a significant problem, especially as demographic changes occur and as the competition for highly talented students increases within academia and between industry and academia.

Future developments that will influence institutional needs for facilities include the projected enrollment declines, demographic

26. Marilyn McCoy, Jack Krackower, and David Makowski, *Financing at the Leading 100 Research Universities: An Executive Overview* (Boulder, Colo.: National Center for Higher Education Management Systems, 1981).

27. Richard E. Anderson, "Higher Education in the 1970's: Preliminary Technical Report for Participating Institutions" (New York: Columbia University, Teachers College, Institute of Higher Education, 1983), reported in Ann E. Austin and Zelda F. Gamson, *Academic Workplace: New Demands, Heightened Tension*, ASHE-ERIC Higher Education Research Report 10 (Washington, D.C.: Association for the Study of Higher Education, 1983).

28. William Prokasy, "The Dilemma Colleges Face on Pay Scales," *Chronicle of Higher Education*, vol. 29, no. 7 (1984), p. 80.

Table 3. *Studies of Academic Research Instrumentation*

| Study | Description of study | Findings |
|---|---|---|
| "Survey of Research Equipment Needs in Ten Academic Disciplines," conducted by the National Academy of Science, 1971 | Survey of 8 science and engineering departments in 10 major disciplines to evaluate equipment needs of research universities | —Identifies deteriorating research equipment situation and estimates need to be "well over $200 million" <br> —Recommends ongoing effort to monitor and assess instrumentation needs |
| "Research Equipment Assistance Programs: A National Science Foundation Research Management Improvement Project Research Report," prepared by Iowa State University, 1976 | Report of project to develop cost-effective rapid response system for faculty sharing of scientific equipment | —Describes model for equipment sharing |
| "Equipment Needs and Utilization," prepared by Task Group of the NSF Advisory Council, 1978 | Report of task group documenting research equipment needs and discussing role of federal funding in alleviating instrumentation needs | Descriptive report |
| "Report of the 1979 Instrumentation Subcommittee of the Department of Energy (DOE)/ NSF Nuclear Science Advisory Committee," prepared by DOE/ NSF Nuclear Science Advisory Committee, 1979 | Committee report evaluating status of instrumentation in nuclear science, including current use of instrumentation, identification of state-of-the-art equipment, and determination of future needs | —Identifies serious problem in present instrumentation resources in nuclear physics |
| "Shared Use of Scientific Equipment at Colleges and Universities," Higher Education Panel Report #44, American Council on Education (ACE), 1979 | Survey of 676 institutions gathering data on formal and informal procedures of universities and colleges to facilitate sharing scientific equipment | —Over 25 percent of surveyed institutions had systems to facilitate equipment sharing <br> —An additional 18 percent of institutions planned such programs |
| "Expenditures for Scientific Research Equipment at Ph.D. Granting Institutions, FY 1978," Higher Education Panel Report #47, ACE (1980) | Survey of Ph.D.-granting institutions gathering data on level of institutional expenditures on research equipment, federal contribution to equipment, and the share of funds spent on high-cost items | —$280 million used for research equipment in fiscal 1978 at surveyed institutions <br> —50 percent of funds for life sciences, 19 percent for engineering, and 16 percent for physical sciences equipment <br> —65 percent of cost met with federal funding <br> —9 percent of equipment cost over $50,000 |
| "Studies of U.S. Universities' Research Equipment Needs Inclusive," prepared by the General Accounting Office, 1984 | Literature review and analysis of completed studies on equipment needs in academic research | —Current studies cannot be used to determine equipment needs and are not comparable <br> —Westat study (in progress) will provide more data but lacks thorough development of need indicators |

Table 3. *Studies of Academic Research Instrumentation (continued)*

| Study | Description of study | Findings |
|---|---|---|
| "Instrumentation Needs of Academic Departments of Chemistry," conducted by the American Chemical Society, 1984 | Survey of major chemistry and chemical engineering departments to determine state of instrumentation and needs for instrumentation in university and college chemistry and chemical engineering programs | —Average age of instruments between eight and nine years<br>—Needs of smaller and major institutions vary<br>—15 percent of instruments not fully operational at smaller institutions, 9 percent at major institutions |
| "The Nationwide Study of University Research Equipment," currently being conducted by the Westat Corporation for NSF, as mandated in P.L. 96-44 (to be completed in 1985) | Three-year survey of 43 institutions in 4 science and engineering disciplines to develop statistically reliable indicators of need for major research equipment and to document trends in instrumentation cost, use, and condition | In progress |

change, the increasing demand for part-time and continuing professional education, and maturation of the renewed relationship between industry and universities. The institutions heavily involved in federally sponsored research will probably be shielded from major enrollment declines, but some of them, especially those in metropolitan areas and within easy reach of high-technology industries, will experience an increase in the demand for part-time and nondegree instruction. Aggregate projections of these variables cannot be easily translated into forecasts for facilities.

**Roles of the various sectors in graduate education support**

Multiple factors determine how well the state and federal governments and the universities themselves will respond to the capital needs for graduate education and research. Is there any consensus about the roles various sectors will play in providing support, particularly support for facilities?

Constitutionally and historically, the states have had primary responsibility for public higher education.[29] The federal government has supported basic research and has augmented other sources of support for higher education to ensure that national needs are met. The federal government played an important role in development of the national capacity for research and graduate education after World War II. The state and federal roles, however, have

29. Lawrence E. Gladieux and Janet S. Hansen with Charles R. Byce, *The Federal Government, the States, and Higher Education: Issues for the 1980's* (New York: College Entrance Examination Board, 1981); Task Force on Graduate Education, *The States and Graduate Education*, Report 59 (Denver: Education Commission of the States, 1975).

never been articulated, and coordination has been limited. The argument for, and the design of, a national policy for graduate education was well stated in the National Science Board's 1969 report,[30] but subsequent decisions to provide federal support to individuals, not to institutions, aborted its implementation. The consequences of the lack of coordination of federal and state roles become all too clear as the expansion of higher education ends and fiscal pressures persist.

The response of state governments to the physical facility problems will depend partly on the projections for undergraduate enrollments and partly on how much the states accept the responsibility to ensure the continuing development of disciplines of study at the graduate level. The Carnegie Council has projected undergraduate enrollment trends into the 1990s[31] and analyzed the variations by state. In the East and the Midwest, enrollment will decrease by about 10 percent. In the South it will increase by about 5 percent and in the Southwest by about 10 percent. Competing needs in the states, the general economic climate, and the nature of the institutions (public or private) will determine whether reduced enrollment permits improvements in quality of resources per student or triggers retrenchment. Careful analysis of higher education financing in the fifty states may permit more specific conclusions about the capacity of states to respond.[32] For both the federal and state governments, a key factor will be whether graduate students and university research programs are required to meet state and federal objectives and responsibilities. The increasingly close relationship of research and advanced training to the economic development of the states and of the nation as a whole will certainly have an important influence.

The universities' ability to allocate any of their operating budget to capital renewal costs will influence the capacity of the higher education institutions themselves to place higher priority on addressing capital needs. For many public institutions state governments determine the apportionment between capital and operating costs. Even when universities have the flexibility to make such choices, the problems of reallocation from operating support to capital support are extremely severe, without major increases

---

30. National Science Board, *Toward a Public Policy for Graduate Education in the Sciences* (GPO, 1969).

31. Carnegie Council, *Three Thousand Futures*, p. 66.

32. Marilyn McCoy and D. Kent Halstead, *Higher Education Financing in Fifty States: Interstate Comparisons, Fiscal Year 1981* (Boulder, Colo.: National Center for Higher Education Management Systems and National Institute of Education, 1984).

in the total funding of the institutions. For one major university, for example, the cost of major remodeling and renovation needs approaches $30 million a year. This amount equals about 10 percent of the salary base.

The capacity of universities to respond will also depend on their planning and management. They need comprehensive audits of the condition of their physical facilities and effective mechanisms for setting priorities for the assignment of space and the selection of renovation and renewal projects.

**Broad strategies**

The facilities renewal problem can be addressed by three primary strategies: by assessing user charges, by increasing the investment in capital renewal and replacement, and by modifying or redefining need.

The responsibility for facilities costs could be realigned to provide a more realistic capital recovery mechanism. Most institutions currently assess the cost of facilities used in sponsored projects through a use charge built into the indirect cost rate. The use charge is limited to 2 percent of the original building cost, and it substantially underestimates the cost of providing adequate facilities. The cost of interest on money borrowed by institutions for acquisition, for major reconstruction, or for remodeling of buildings only recently became an allowable cost in federally sponsored agreements with educational institutions. More realistic charges for external use of university research facilities could be assessed as an indirect cost, or some more direct charging mechanism (such as rent) could be developed. The cost recovery could be handled on a project-by-project basis or on an aggregate basis. Combining capital recovery mechanisms with the existing project-support system could produce a system of cost allocations that is both proportional to use and responsive to scientific merit and priority decisions. Full application of systems of user charges will probably increase the cost to sponsors, including the federal government, for research undertaken by universities, but it would better reflect reality.

Adjustments in tax policy and legislative authority are strategies that might increase investment in facilities by increasing the capacity of the various sectors to respond to academic needs. The health of institutions of higher learning, public as well as private, depends on their ability to attract private support. The level of private support is quite sensitive to changes in tax policy such as changes in the marginal tax rate and limits on deductions of charitable contributions and of gifts of appreciated property.

Economic studies of the sensitivity of charitable giving to its price suggest that charitable giving decreases between 1.2 and 1.3 percent for every 1 percent increase in its price.

The predominant form of individual giving to colleges and universities for capital purposes is appreciated property, which composes 60 percent of individual gifts for capital purposes and 40 percent of all gifts.[33] The Economic Recovery Tax Act of 1981 permits investment tax credits that may be useful in designing support for capital renewal projects, but proposals for tax reform include disincentives for charitable giving. Any foreseeable benefits of an improved economic picture will not outweigh these disincentives.[34] The tax reform proposals are a matter of concern because of the significant role that private giving has played in capital support of universities.

Federal legislative authority for programs to finance science and engineering facilities is limited at this time. Almost all the federal programs that helped finance the building of U.S. academic research capacity have been eliminated and not replaced (see table 1). This constriction is partially responsible for the recent intensive lobbying efforts of some individual institutions, which have resulted in congressional authorization or appropriation of $130 million during fiscal 1983 through 1985 for fifteen major academic facilities. Considerable controversy surrounds these awards because they were made without competition and without the review procedures assumed by many to be an important element in such decisions. The controversy is stimulating debate about fundamental issues such as criteria for judging proposed facilities; mechanisms for balancing the various needs for scientific facilities; the proper roles of competition, technical review, and pertinent social, political, and economic factors; and the responsibilities of applicants, Congress, and the federal agencies. Restoration of funding authority to federal agencies and appropriation of funds would permit more effective distribution of capital support.

Several institutions are addressing the capital renewal problem through the use of industrial development bonds, land development, divestiture of assets, and lease-back arrangements with tax-depreciation benefits. Removal of the obstacles to responsible debt financing for higher education research facilities in several states could open another avenue of funding for capital renewal and

33. Derek Bok, William G. Bowen, and Robert M. Rosenzweig, "Analysis of Treasury Department's Tax Proposals," December 13, 1984 (informal communication).
34. Ibid., specific attachment entitled "A Comparison of the Costs and Potential Economic Benefits of the Treasury Proposal on Charitable Giving," December 11, 1984.

replacement, but responsible use of this method demands realistic ways to amortize the costs. Indeed, there is some concern within the financial community about the rising level of university debt. More vigorous fund-raising efforts among alumni and friends of higher education will also have to occur.

Some of the solutions may be useful on an ongoing basis, but some are necessarily nonrenewable. The long-term strategy for assurance of adequate investment in capital renewal and replacement will need to include recurring resources as part of the operating budgets. General economic recovery is perhaps the most critical element in the capacity of the various sectors to respond to the capital renewal and replacement needs in academic R&D.

In the search for solutions, ways to change the magnitude of the need for capital renewal and replacement should be examined. Careful attention should be given to the institution's criteria and mechanisms for assigning space among competing needs. Is existing space being used effectively? Can rearrangements provide substantial improvement without much cost? Many universities have already thoroughly explored this avenue. Most realignments within the existing space involve significant costs in remodeling and in dislocation and disruption of the activities affected.

Another avenue to be explored is the availability and accessibility of underused capacity in neighboring institutions and other organizations that have mutual interests. Cooperative arrangements with business and industry can make available needed facilities and equipment and at the same time stimulate intellectual exchange, especially in applied science and engineering. The logistical problems and costs of such solutions have to be recognized.

The new communication technologies offer major improvements in accessibility to shared facilities when data acquisition can be automated. The computing, astronomy, and high-energy physics communities are exploring these technologies and capitalizing on the opportunities they present. For many areas of science and engineering, however, telecommunication links and data transmission networks do not address the facilities problems faced.

Federal and state regulatory policy on environmental standards, on occupational health and safety, on access for the handicapped, and on laboratory animal welfare add to the need for capital renewal. Regulatory reforms might reduce the cost of filling these needs.

Specialization and stratification can reduce some needs. Perhaps the simplest example is the establishment of central instrumentation facilities, such as mass spectrophotometry centers, electron microscopy laboratories, and machine shops. The efficiency of such arrangements, however, depends on the nature and extent of the individual user's needs: some users will press the instruments to their limits, while some will use them more routinely.

Constraints on resources in the past fifteen years, and probably in the future as well, suggest that consolidation and stratification may have to provide part of the solution. The U.S. system of higher education is already partly stratified, as indicated by the concentration of most doctoral production and research activity in a few institutions. Institutions may have to cooperate and differentiate further if the United States is to continue to work at the frontiers in every field.

As a last resort we may need to reconsider the fundamental design features of our system. We may need to reexamine our adherence to some of its basic tenets, such as broad geographical dispersion, access to advanced education for a large portion of the population, and concentration of basic research in universities. The benefits of these design features have served this nation as well. Any major design would need genuinely favorable trade-offs for both the short and the long term.

As we search for solutions we need to keep in mind the incentives that operate in a university setting, especially the need for individual flexibility and for organizational autonomy. We need to bear in mind the political realities of an annual budget cycle, a biannual election cycle, and dispersed responsibility for science within the federal government. Sustained support for long-term needs, such as capital renewal, has been difficult to achieve within this system. The present economic and demographic realities may provide the impetus for finding more effective ways to work with this system or for making some adjustment in it.

*Policy issues related to capital needs*

One fundamental question in the capital facilities debate is whether this country will try to sustain its leadership in science and technology, particularly in every field. Choices about capital renewal will affect the nation's capacity to meet these leadership objectives.

A second fundamental issue is the distribution of responsibility for supplying capital for basic research among the sectors that have contributed in the past—the universities, foundations and other philanthropic groups, state governments, and the federal government.

A third major issue is whether our current pluralistic system can provide adequate planning for the academic science on which the nation must depend. The system seems to provide inadequately for certain aspects of academic science, particularly renewal of facilities and equipment, training of new scholars, and incubation of new directions and new ventures. Over the long haul, a responsibly managed enterprise must make adequate provision for such needs. The key question is whether the structure of our particular system, which was designed to expand and improve capacity for graduate education and research, can be adjusted to provide for its sustenance and renewal. In whom shall we vest the principal responsibility for planning? How can we ensure the introduction of the necessary expertise and breadth of vision into the planning processes?

The values underlying the resolution of these policy issues need to be acknowledged, especially the commitment to excellence, the commitment to broad participation in education, the value placed on wide geographic distribution, and the commitment to government by the people, that is, widespread participation in decisionmaking processes.

Another category of issues involves the mechanisms for distribution of resources for capital renewal and the selection of criteria for setting priorities. One critical question is whether capital renewal resources should be treated separately from operating support at the appropriation level and the budget level. Construction authority has traditionally been separate from operating budget authority. Such a separation may be necessary to prevent shortsighted diversion of capital funds to operating uses to avoid programmatic reduction in periods of no growth or retrenchment. The present capital crisis has partly resulted from prolonged fiscal constraint. Institutions have repeatedly deferred maintenance and renovation in the hope that the fiscal constraints were only temporary. The existing construction authority for some of the National Institutes of Health (National Cancer Institute, National Heart, Lung, and Blood Institute, and National Eye Institute) has been used little or not at all, perhaps because construction authority and the operating budget authority are combined.[35] Research projects compete with capital projects for a pool of funds that is not commensurate with the scientific opportunities and the human resources available.

The peer review issue has emerged as critical for capital facilities for two reasons. One is the recent rash of intensive lobbying by

35. Kurt Habel, "NIH Experience with Extramural Construction Authority," report prepared for Director of National Institutes of Health, Office of Associate Director for Program Planning and Evaluation (Washington, D.C.: National Institutes of Health, 1983).

individual institutions to obtain appropriations earmarked for facilities for their own institutions. The pork-barrel characteristics of this approach undermine the long-established commitment to allocate funds for science primarily in open competition among scientists and institutions and to include in the decision process the results of merit reviews made by professionals who are competent to judge. This commitment to fairness and to scientific merit is often cited as a major part of the productivity and vitality of American science.

The second reason for the importance of peer review in the capital facilities debate is the recurring controversy over indirect costs. When a federally sponsored R&D project uses university facilities, the government reimburses its share of the institution's indirect costs. Scientists are deeply concerned about the extent to which reimbursement of indirect costs reduces the amount of funds available for research projects under their direct control. Federal rules on the apportionment of indirect costs to research projects allow the recovery of part of the costs of buildings and equipment. The recovery rate through this mechanism, however, is far below what is needed for renewal and replacement of scientific equipment and facilities. The building use rate is based on a long life cycle (fifty years) and makes no provision for renewal and replacement of capital items purchased with federal funds. Considerable resistance within the institutions to the use of more accelerated depreciation rates results from the concern that indirect costs are already "too high." The concern arises because indirect costs are not subject to the same kind of peer review given to the direct costs of research projects.

Another set of issues involves how we will guide the evolution of graduate education itself. As the frontiers of science advance, the complexity, sophistication, and cost of the instrumentation and facilities increase. In some fields, it is already infeasible to provide the research facilities at the local level. In astronomy and high-energy physics, for example, most of the experimental work must now be done at national or even international facilities. Development in some other fields is also proceeding in this direction.

The implications of these trends for graduate education include earlier specialization by graduate students, less opportunity for interaction with persons in other fields or with students at the undergraduate level, and strain on the collegiality within the campus community. Faculty will share with nonfaculty profes-sionals the responsibility for the development of the graduate student. The risks and benefits of that sharing need to be examined. The move to team supervision and team research is driven in part by internal scientific needs, but also in part by economics. The sharing of facilities, which brings together experimentalists from more than one discipline, may strengthen graduate education and contribute to the evolution of new disciplines. In a period of limited hiring of new faculty, such sharing may provide a useful mechanism for stimulating new ideas. The long-term effect of these developments on the quality of graduate education and on its benefits for undergraduate education must be considered.

Finally, stratification and specialization of institutions should be considered if sufficient resources cannot be garnered to allow the necessary capital renewal for all the institutions engaged in graduate education and research. There are obvious limits to what government can do in "targeting" assistance to research universities. Just as "picking winners" in industrial policy is impossible within the U.S. system, programs to support only selected institutions are problematic. Unless the benefits are broadly distributed, support for a program is difficult to mobilize. Although peer review has sustained the scientific enterprise in the United States, the siting of large-scale facilities involves more than judgments of scientific merit. The solutions for the universities' facilities problems will require a combination of strategies involving the institutions' own resources, their access to financial markets, and the support of industry and both the state and federal governments.

*Data needed*   A comprehensive inventory of needs for academic R&D capital renewal and replacement and a delineation of priorities should be agreed upon early as we look for solutions to the capital renewal dilemma. Such an inventory should be collaboratively designed by the academic institutions, industry, philanthropic organizations, and state and federal government. It should be designed with mutual understanding of the terminology and the criteria used in assessing the need. It should be differentiated by type of institution, by geographic location, and by field of science, and it should include information on the number of scientists and engineers the facilities would serve and on the cost and space utilization standards used to estimate need. The survey recently planned by the Interagency Steering Committee for Academic Research Facilities would provide some of those data.

In addition, we need to develop data on three aspects of the university research environment: trends in operating expenditures per research worker, trends in level of support staff per research worker, and trends in capital expenditures per research worker. The overall patterns of support could be plotted by using these trends for the United States by field of science and in total. Together with information about the rate of inflation for scientific expenditures, these data would show how well human and physical resources balance. Comparison of these patterns with those of other industrially developed countries will be important. Although some of the data needed to follow these trends are available, some are not. The present NSF data on R&D expenditures, for example, do not distinguish between facilities expenditures and equipment expenditures.

The space allocation standards widely used in academic institutions were developed many years ago. Since that time new disciplines have developed and old disciplines have changed. The current validity of the space standards needs to be examined, both to ensure wise decisions and to foster credibility for the fairness of the choices that will have to be made. We also need to take advantage of computer-assisted decision support systems to model changing facilities needs and to project realistic assessments of the capital investment requirements, at both the national and the institutional levels.

Trade-offs will occur between optimal arrangements designed for traditional behavior patterns and less expensive arrangements requiring changed work patterns. An analysis of the effect of changes in work patterns on scientific productivity could begin with a study of the use of regionally and nationally shared facilities. Such a study would focus on the numbers of research scientists and engineers dependent on the national and regional facilities as their principal source of data and on the trends in R&D expenditures at these facilities for university-based research scientists and engineers. Comparison of these data with data on total scientific manpower and R&D expenditures would permit monitoring of the shift of the principal research location away from the university campuses.

Better information is also needed about the incentives that operate in the academic setting and the factors that influence productive work patterns. When the means to realize career goals and the capacity to act in accordance with professional values are limited, the classical characteristics of anomie develop. An aging faculty and deteriorating facilities, together with the above limitations, may so seriously affect morale that a substantial number of the best and brightest minds will turn away from the satisfactions of science toward other pursuits.

Longer-term data needs include improved information on the effect of graduate education and research on economic growth and measures of the effect of technological changes on scientific productivity, graduate education quality, and faculty needs for capital equipment and facilities. Most existing information is qualitative and anecdotal. Research on correlations and causality is extremely difficult to do. Some investment in methodological research to develop indicators or surrogates for indicators would sharpen decisionmaking.

*Conclusion*

The pace and direction of science are affected by our capacity for ideas and insights, our understanding of the goals and needs to be served, and our human, physical, and financial resources. The continuing challenge is to find an acceptable balance among these factors. The capital renewal problem is a symptom of serious imbalance in our system.

The capital renewal problem presents a challenging dilemma. Although the academic R&D facilities renewal problem is large, its dimensions and its distribution among scientific fields and institutions remain undefined. Academic research is a significant element in maintaining the nation's technological and economic competitiveness, but the specific cause-and-effect links of the relationship have not been rigorously analyzed. The solutions to the facilities renewal problem will require multiple sources of support, but we have inadequate mechanisms for marshaling that collaborative support. Incentives and "market factors" guide investment in facilities, but these factors operate with a long lead time and are poorly understood.

The gap between the quality of industrial facilities and the quality of academic facilities (in which future industrial scientists are trained) contributes to the erosion of academic training. The consequences of this gap will grow.

The present uncertainties about the nature, the magnitude, and the consequences of the facilities renewal problem can be reduced. Efforts should certainly be expended toward reducing these uncertainties, but there are limits on our ability to understand deeply in a reasonable length of time or with reasonable cost. The strategy must be to converge toward solution, to reconcile the desire for detailed understanding with the limits on knowing, and to balance the risks of proceeding with inadequate information against the risks of delay.

What seems called for at the present crossroads is the following: interim strategies to limit the general decay of academic R&D

facilities and to solve critical needs in high-priority areas; a comprehensive inventory of academic R&D facilities; indicators to monitor the status of facilities to target continuing investment in renewal and replacement; and collaborative efforts by the stakeholders (universities, governments, and industry) to develop a set of mechanisms to ensure that the infrastructure of American universities will support the academic enterprise that the nation needs.

# Minority Students
# in Graduate Education

JOHN C. VAUGHN

THIS PAPER describes the problem of underrepresentation of minority students in graduate education, discusses factors contributing to that underrepresentation, and identifies some promising approaches for increasing minority participation. The paper focuses on doctoral education in science and engineering. The analysis is conducted from the perspective of graduate education policy; it therefore emphasizes near-term strategies for increasing the size of the pool of minority college graduates and the proportion of that pool that enrolls in and successfully completes doctoral programs. Any long-term solution to the problem, however, must involve concerted efforts at every level of the educational hierarchy.

*Nature and magnitude of the problem*

The participation of minority groups in graduate education in science and engineering has increased significantly over the past several decades. The number of minority students earning Ph.D.'s in science and engineering between 1970 and 1980 was more than twice the number earning Ph.D.'s between 1960 and 1970. The number of blacks in this category increased most dramatically, from 700 Ph.D.'s earned between 1960 and 1969 to 3,200 earned between 1970 and 1980 (table 1).

Underrepresentation of minorities in doctoral education remains a serious problem, however, in almost all fields. Minorities constitute more than 20 percent of the nation's population, but in 1983 they received only 10.9 percent of doctoral degrees. Blacks constitute 12.1 percent of the population, but they receive only 4 percent of doctorates. Hispanics constitute 6.7 percent of the population, but they receive 2.4 percent of doctorates. Native Americans constitute 0.6 percent of the population, and they receive 0.3 percent of doctorates. In contrast, although Asian-

I am grateful to Arthur Hauptman, who compiled the data used in tables 2 through 6 as part of an Association of American Universities project on graduate and professional education funded by the Ford Foundation.

151

Table 1. *1981 Population of Science and Engineering Ph.D.'s by Race and Year of Earned Doctorate*[a]

| Racial or ethnic group | Total, 1938–80 | Year of doctorate | | | |
|---|---|---|---|---|---|
| | | 1938–49 | 1950–59 | 1960–69 | 1970–80 |
| All | 358,600 | 20,500 | 51,300 | 101,100 | 185,700 |
| | (100.0) | (5.7) | (14.3) | (28.2) | (51.8) |
| White | 313,800 | 19,200 | 47,900 | 88,800 | 157,600 |
| | (100.0) | (6.2) | (15.2) | (28.3) | (50.2) |
| All minorities | 39,300 | 600 | 2,700 | 10,300 | 25,700 |
| | (100.0) | (1.5) | (6.8) | (26.2) | (65.6) |
| Hispanic | 4,900 | 100 | 400 | 1,100 | 3,300 |
| | (100.0) | (2.2) | (7.8) | (23.4) | (66.6) |
| Black | 4,500 | 100 | 500 | 700 | 3,200 |
| | (100.0) | (2.9) | (9.8) | (16.4) | (70.8) |
| Asian and | 27,700 | 300 | 1,500 | 7,800 | 18,100 |
| Pacific Islander | (100.0) | (0.9) | (5.5) | (28.1) | (65.5) |
| Native American | 2,200 | 100 | 300 | 600 | 1,200 |
| | (100.0) | (3.2) | (14.5) | (28.4) | (54.0) |
| No report | 5,500 | 400 | 700 | 2,000 | 2,400 |
| | (100.0) | (7.0) | (13.0) | (36.8) | (43.2) |

Source: National Research Council, *Departing the Ivy Halls: Changing Employment Situations for Recent Ph.D.s,* Survey of Doctorate Recipients (Washington, D.C.: National Academy Press, 1983).

a. The numbers in parentheses are percentages.

Americans constitute only 1.5 percent of the population, they receive 4.2 percent of doctorates (table 2).

Progress since 1975 in increasing minority participation in graduate education has been uneven. Overall results are encouraging: although the number of whites receiving doctoral degrees decreased 10 percent from 1975 to 1983, the number of minorities receiving doctorates increased 7 percent. This increase was not uniform across fields, however. While minority doctorates in social science and psychology increased 34 percent, those in the life sciences increased 9 percent and those in engineering only 1 percent; in the physical sciences minority doctorates decreased 10 percent.

Furthermore, results have varied considerably among groups. From 1975 to 1983 the number of doctoral degrees received by blacks declined 4 percent, from 1,047 to 1,000. Over that same period Hispanic doctorates increased 81 percent (from 334 to 604), Asian-American doctorates increased 2 percent (from 1,024 to 1,040), and Native American doctorates declined 44 percent (from 143 to 80). (See table 3.)

More important, perhaps, are the striking differences among minority groups in their representation by field. Fifty-seven percent of total doctorates are granted in the sciences and engineering. Seventy-eight percent of doctorates earned by Asian-Americans but only 33 percent of doctorates earned by blacks are

Table 2. *Minority Groups as a Percentage of Population, Enrollments, and Degrees Received*

| Item | Black | Hispanic | Asian | Native American | All minorities |
|---|---|---|---|---|---|
| Population, 1980 | 12.1 | 6.7 | 1.5 | 0.6 | 20.9 |
| Full-time undergraduate enrollment, 1982 | 9.7 | 6.0 | 2.8 | 0.7 | 19.2 |
| Bachelors' degrees received, 1981 | 6.7 | 2.4 | 2.1 | 0.3 | 11.4 |
| Full-time enrollment for advanced degrees, 1982 | 5.5 | 2.6 | 2.6 | 0.4 | 11.1 |
| Doctorates received, 1983 | 4.0 | 2.4 | 4.2 | 0.3 | 10.9 |
| Professional degrees received, 1981 | 4.1 | 2.2 | 2.1 | 0.3 | 8.7 |

Sources: U.S. Bureau of the Census, *Statistical Abstract of the United States, 1984* (Government Printing Office, 1984); National Research Council, *Summary Report, 1981* and *1983: Survey of Doctorate Recipients from United States Universities* (Washington, D.C.: National Academy Press, 1982, 1984); National Center for Education Statistics, *Digest of Education Statistics, 1983–84* (GPO, 1984), pp. 122–23, 126–27.

in science and engineering fields. Looking at the distribution of black doctorates differently, of the 1,000 doctorates received by blacks in 1983, 715 were in education and social science and psychology; only 32 were in the physical sciences.

Hispanics are somewhat more evenly distributed across disciplines, but they are still comparatively underrepresented in the sciences and engineering; 47 percent of their doctorates were granted in these fields. The numbers of Native American doctorates are too low to permit meaningful generalizations about their distribution across fields; suffice it to note that forty-four of the eighty doctorates granted to Native Americans in 1983 were in the single field of education (table 3).

The proportion of minorities in the population will continue to increase into the twenty-first century as the majority population ages at a faster rate than the minority population. Minorities now constitute a majority of the school enrollments in twenty-three of the nation's twenty-five largest cities. By the year 2000, minority groups will constitute the majority population in fifty-three major cities.[1]

As the minority population expands, its continued underrepresentation in graduate education will have a progressively more serious effect on the American educational system's capacity to meet the national need for scientists and engineers. Thus, a condition that raises serious social concerns about equal oppor-

1. Ian McNett, *Demographic Imperatives: Implications for Educational Policy*, Report of the June 8, 1983, Forum on the Demographics of Changing Ethnic Populations and Their Implications for Elementary-Secondary and Postsecondary Educational Policy, sponsored by the American Council on Education, Forum of Educational Organization Leaders, and the Institute for Educational Leadership, September 1983.

Table 3. *Minority and White Students Receiving Doctoral Degrees in 1975 and 1983*

| Group and year | Physical sciences | Life sciences | Engineering | Social science and psychology | Arts and humanities | Education | Professional fields and other | Total |
|---|---|---|---|---|---|---|---|---|
| | | | | Number of students (thousands) | | | | |
| **All** | | | | | | | | |
| 1975 | 0.3 | 0.3 | 0.3 | 0.4 | 0.3 | 0.8 | 0.1 | 2.5 |
| 1983 | 0.3 | 0.4 | 0.3 | 0.5 | 0.2 | 0.9 | 0.2 | 2.7 |
| Percent change | −10 | 9 | 1 | 34 | −12 | 3 | 62 | 7 |
| **White** | | | | | | | | |
| 1975 | 3.4 | 3.7 | 1.6 | 5.0 | 4.2 | 5.9 | 1.1 | 24.8 |
| 1983 | 2.9 | 4.1 | 1.1 | 4.6 | 2.8 | 5.4 | 1.2 | 22.2 |
| Percent change | −13 | 11 | −30 | −7 | −34 | −8 | 10 | −10 |
| **All minorities** | | | | | | | | |
| 1975 | 3.7 | 4.1 | 2.0 | 5.3 | 4.5 | 6.7 | 1.2 | 27.3 |
| 1983 | 3.2 | 4.5 | 1.4 | 5.1 | 3.0 | 6.3 | 1.4 | 25.0 |
| Percent change | −12 | 11 | −25 | −4 | −32 | −6 | 14 | −9 |
| | | | | Number of doctoral degrees by minority group | | | | |
| **Black** | | | | | | | | |
| 1975 | 41 | 61 | 16 | 178 | 94 | 617 | 40 | 1,047 |
| 1983 | 32 | 74 | 29 | 199 | 79 | 516 | 71 | 1,000 |
| Percent change | −22 | 21 | 81 | 12 | −16 | −16 | 78 | −4 |
| **Hispanic** | | | | | | | | |
| 1975 | 31 | 42 | 15 | 60 | 78 | 97 | 11 | 334 |
| 1983 | 44 | 59 | 29 | 150 | 113 | 185 | 24 | 604 |
| Percent change | 42 | 40 | 93 | 150 | 45 | 91 | 118 | 81 |
| **Asian** | | | | | | | | |
| 1975 | 249 | 230 | 267 | 90 | 69 | 73 | 46 | 1,024 |
| 1983 | 216 | 239 | 247 | 109 | 47 | 118 | 64 | 1,040 |
| Percent change | −13 | 4 | −7 | 21 | −32 | 62 | 39 | 2 |
| **Native American** | | | | | | | | |
| 1975 | 14 | 15 | 5 | 23 | 36 | 48 | 2 | 143 |
| 1983 | 9 | 7 | 1 | 12 | 6 | 44 | 1 | 80 |
| Percent change | −36 | −53 | −80 | −48 | −83 | −8 | −50 | −44 |

Source: National Research Council, *Summary Report, 1975* and *1983*. Percentages are derived from unrounded figures.

tunity will increasingly have practical consequences as well. Public policy should not have as its objective exact proportional representation of all groups in graduate education, but substantial underrepresentation should concern everyone responsible for and dependent on graduate education.

***Factors limiting minority participation in graduate education***

Policies for increasing the participation of underrepresented minorities in graduate education will succeed if they accurately identify and find solutions to the problems that cause the underrepresentation. Minority underrepresentation has its roots in the socioeconomic disadvantages that still characterize disproportionate numbers of minorities in this society. Poverty, unemployment, poor neighborhoods, single-parent families, and other factors combine to produce a poor learning environment that from the beginning of the educational process militates against the successful completion of advanced education.

Since each higher level of education builds on what was mastered at the preceding level, early deficits grow more severe at each succeeding level. More often than whites, minorities receive a poor-quality elementary and secondary education, with a lower proportion of students completing high school. Fewer minority students completing high school have taken college-preparatory courses than is the norm among high school students in general. These factors compound each other, reducing the numbers of minorities eligible for college. Of those enrolling, minority students are less likely than white students to complete college. Blacks, Hispanics, and Native Americans are thus more underrepresented at each higher level of our educational system.

Education is often regarded as a mechanism for escaping from poverty and from its consequences, which make poverty self-perpetuating. The unfortunate irony is that the actual education acquired by the children of low-income families—in which minorities are represented at a disproportionately high level—is likely to be inferior to that received by the children of middle- and upper-income families. Inferior education is more likely to perpetuate than to eliminate poverty because it places students at a competitive disadvantage.

Despite the handicaps that confront many of them, thousands of minority students receive bachelors' degrees each year. What considerations govern their decisions about whether to pursue a graduate education? What factors affect the probability that those enrolling will successfully complete their graduate programs?

### Size of the Undergraduate Pool

Although minority students earned 104,500 bachelors' degrees in 1981, these constituted only 11.5 percent of the total of 909,000 bachelors' degrees granted in that year. Thus the pool of college graduates from which minority graduate students are recruited is approximately half what it should be to maintain proportionality with minority representation in the general population. The pool of minority college graduates with majors in science and engineering fields is slightly more constricted: minorities received 18,100, or 10.1 percent, of the 179,600 bachelors' degrees with science or engineering majors (table 4).

Not only is the pool of minority college graduates small, but the proportion of that pool that earns a doctoral degree is less

Table 4. *Students Receiving Bachelors' Degrees, 1976 and 1981*
Numbers in thousands

| Group and year | Science and engineering | Other fields | All degrees |
|---|---|---|---|
| *All* | | | |
| 1976 | 157.5 | 754.3 | 911.8 |
| 1981 | 179.6 | 729.4 | 909.0 |
| Percent change | 14 | −3 | −0.31 |
| *White* | | | |
| 1976 | 144.3 | 667.3 | 811.6 |
| 1981 | 161.5 | 643.0 | 804.5 |
| Percent change | 12 | −4 | −1 |
| *All minorities* | | | |
| 1976 | 13.2 | 87.0 | 100.2 |
| 1981 | 18.1 | 86.4 | 104.5 |
| Percent change | 37 | −1 | 4 |
| *Asian* | | | |
| 1976 | 3.1 | 8.2 | 11.3 |
| 1981 | 6.6 | 12.1 | 18.7 |
| Percent change | 113 | 48 | 65 |
| *Black* | | | |
| 1976 | 5.7 | 53.5 | 59.1 |
| 1981 | 7.4 | 53.1 | 60.5 |
| Percent change | 30 | −1 | 2 |
| *Hispanic* | | | |
| 1976 | 3.8 | 22.4 | 26.2 |
| 1981 | 3.6 | 18.1 | 21.7 |
| Percent change | −5 | −19 | −17 |
| *Native American* | | | |
| 1976 | 0.6 | 2.9 | 3.5 |
| 1981 | 0.5 | 3.1 | 3.6 |
| Percent change | −16 | 7 | 3 |

Sources: National Center for Education Statistics, *Digest of Education Statistics, 1983–84*; U.S. Department of Health, Education, and Welfare, Office of Civil Rights, *Racial, Ethnic, and Sex Data from Institutions of Higher Education, Fall 1976* (GPO, 1976). Percentages are derived from unrounded figures.

than that of white college graduates. This proportion can be estimated by comparing the number of bachelors' degrees received with the number of doctoral degrees received at some later date (table 5).[2]

Which factor contributes more heavily to underrepresentation in number of doctorates earned by a given minority group, the small size of the pool of college graduates or the lesser proportion of those graduates that enroll in graduate programs and earn doctoral degrees? This question is important to answer because increasing the size of the pool of college graduates calls for different policies than those needed to increase the proportion of college graduates who successfully pursue a doctoral education.

2. Comparing bachelors' to doctoral degrees directly incorporates differences in both rate of enrollment and retention in doctoral programs. Enrollment and retention cannot be separated because available data do not disaggregate masters' and doctoral enrollments.

Table 5. *Doctorates Received in 1983 as a Percentage of Bachelors' Degrees Received in 1976*

| Group | Bachelors' 1976 | Doctorates 1983 | 1983 doctorates as percent of 1976 bachelors' |
|---|---|---|---|
| All | 911,700 | 25,000 | 2.7 |
| White | 811,600 | 22,200 | 2.7 |
| All minorities | 100,100 | 2,724 | 2.7 |
| Asian | 11,300 | 1,040 | 9.2 |
| Black | 59,100 | 1,000 | 1.7 |
| Hispanic | 26,200 | 604 | 2.3 |
| Native American | 3,500 | 80 | 2.3 |

Sources: National Research Council, *Summary Report, 1983*; National Center for Education Statistics, *Digest of Education Statistics, 1976*; HEW, *Racial, Ethnic, and Sex Data, Fall 1976*.

An assessment of the differential effect of these two factors suggests that the small size of the pool of college graduates has more effect on underrepresentation than does the proportion of bachelors' recipients earning doctoral degrees.[3] Increasing the number of underrepresented minorities who receive college degrees should therefore be a major component of any plan for increasing the number of minority doctorate recipients.

Although the number of minority students receiving bachelors' degrees is disproportionately low, the trends are generally encouraging. Table 4 shows that minority students receiving bachelors' degrees increased 4 percent from 1976 to 1981; the number of those degrees with science or engineering majors increased 37 percent. Generalizations once again mask significant differences among groups, however. The number of Hispanics receiving bachelors' degrees decreased 17 percent over this period,[4] and the number of Native Americans receiving bachelors' degrees with science or engineering majors dropped 16 percent.

## Academic Preparation

Although it is a sensitive topic, the quality of the pool of minority college graduates is an important aspect of increased

3. To estimate the differential effect of the two factors, consider the data for blacks. In 1983 blacks earned 1,000 doctoral degrees, 1.7 percent of the 59,100 bachelors' degrees earned by blacks in 1976. If their percentage of 1983 doctorates to 1976 bachelors' degrees had been 2.7 percent—the overall percentage—they would have earned 1,596 doctorates. However, if the percentage of black bachelors' recipients earning doctoral degrees remained at 1.7 percent but the pool of bachelors' degrees had been proportional to the percentage of blacks in the overall population—12.1 percent rather that 6.5 percent—blacks would have earned 106,732 bachelors' degrees and 1,814 doctoral degrees.

4. This decrease presages a reversal of the substantial gains in Hispanic doctorates documented in table 3.

minority participation in graduate education. Beginning with the pool of students enrolling in college, minorities fall below whites in academic preparation as measured by standardized tests. Blacks, Hispanics, and Native Americans all score below the national average on the Scholastic Aptitude Test (SAT). If scores of high school seniors on the SAT are categorized on the basis of anticipated college major, students with the highest SAT scores anticipate majors in the physical sciences and mathematics, while those with the lowest scores anticipate majors in education. Minorities are least likely to major in those fields with high SAT scores and most likely to major in those fields with low SAT scores.[5]

This pattern is carried forward in graduate education. Under-represented minorities score below whites on the Graduate Record Examination (GRE), and their distribution of earned doctorates is similar to their distribution of college majors, concentrating in those fields associated with lower GRE scores.[6]

A long-standing debate about the validity of standardized test scores centers on whether the tests are systematically biased against minorities. Data can be cited on both sides of this unresolved question. Some observations by Clifford Adelman are apposite: "The products and services of the testing industry may not be ideal, but are of generally high quality. Certainly we have been flooded with enough studies of reliability and validity to convince us that the products and services are worth what we pay for them. . . . [Yet if] test scores decline, we blame everything but the quality of student learning. If the scores go up, any commentary is complimentary to schools, colleges and students."[7]

The testing community has stated unequivocally that test scores should not be used in isolation to select or to reject a candidate, but should serve as one component of a set of variables used to predict future performance; that caveat applies to the use of test data to form judgments about academic potential generally. Meanwhile educators continue to try to establish within-group predictors of graduate school performance that will permit better identification of promising minority candidates.

The distinction between academic preparation and academic potential is important. Available evidence suggests that the un-

5. Alexander W. Astin, *Minorities in American Higher Education* (San Francisco: Jossey-Bass, 1982).

6. *Professional Women and Minorities: A Manpower Data Resource Service*, 5th ed. (Washington, D.C.: Scientific Manpower Commission, August 1984).

7. Clifford Adelman, *The Standardized Test Scores of College Graduates, 1964–1982*, prepared for the Study Group on the Conditions of Excellence in American Higher Education (Washington, D.C.: Educational Resources Information Center, 1984).

derrepresentation of minorities in graduate education in part reflects inadequate academic preparation. Inadequate preparation manifests itself in inappropriate undergraduate course selection, reduced graduate enrollments, skewed enrollments, and reduced graduate student retention. The challenge for educational policymakers is to intervene effectively to overcome the academic deficiencies of minority students who have the potential for successful graduate study. Given the interdependent, progressive nature of the educational system, the earlier the intervention, the more effective it is likely to be. Nonetheless, programs now in place, which intervene at the undergraduate and graduate levels, show considerable promise for increasing graduate enrollments, beginning to restore a balanced distribution across fields, and increasing graduate student retention. Some of these programs will be described later.

### Financial Aid

The effect of financial aid is difficult to analyze. At the graduate level, financial aid is available in a variety of forms from federal, state, private, and institutional sources. The nature and the amount of financial aid vary considerably by discipline and have changed markedly over time. These variations are superimposed on the steadily rising cost of attending graduate school.

Flamer, Horch, and Davis conducted a study of college graduates who applied for need-based financial aid to attend graduate and professional schools.[8] Their results indicated that "nonpersisters"—those students who applied for need-based aid and then declined to enroll in a graduate or professional program—frequently cited inadequate financial aid among reasons for electing not to attend. The study did not, however, show any significant differences between minority and white respondents on this basis.

Minority and white students do differ in other ways that relate to financial aid. Minority students are generally more reluctant to depend on loans to finance their education. On average, minority graduate students are also older than white graduate students and are therefore more likely to have additional family financial responsibilities.

Statistics on the population of students applying for need-based aid omit a substantial portion of graduate students who receive

8. Herbert J. Flamer, Dwight H. Horch, and Susan Davis, *Talented and Needy Graduate and Professional Students: A National Survey of People Who Applied for Need-Based Financial Aid to Attend Graduate or Professional Schools in 1980–81* (Princeton: Educational Testing Service, 1982).

teaching and research assistantships, fellowships, and traineeships. Fellowships and assistantships are available to both minority and nonminority graduate students, and several minority fellowship and traineeship programs have recently been established. Inadequate financial aid is unlikely to be a deterrent to graduate education for competitive minority students who are awarded such support.

According to the report of the Graduate Education Subcommittee of the National Commission on Student Financial Assistance, the number of graduate students supported on federally funded fellowships and traineeships fell from a peak of approximately 60,000 in 1970 to 12,800 in 1981.[9] Over that same period the number of students supported on research assistantships rose from approximately 20,000 to an estimated 27,600, an increase that falls far short of compensating for the decline in fellowships and traineeships. Furthermore, minority graduate students are less likely than are white students to be supported as research assistants.

One interpretation of the low level of research assistantship support provided to minority students is that principal investigators are less willing to support minority students than they are to support white students on their research project grants. But underrepresented minorities enroll predominantly in such fields as the social sciences and education, in which less research assistantship support is available for all students. Asian-Americans, in contrast, enroll primarily in physical science and engineering fields, and they receive a higher proportion of research assistantship support than white students do.[10] Data are not available to show whether minorities receive proportionately fewer research assistantships than white students within fields.

The Council of Graduate Schools conducted a national survey in 1982 of institutional programs supporting minority graduate students.[11] The results of that survey indicated that, although federal support for graduate education had decreased overall, support for minority students remained approximately level. Presumably, institutions managed to find other funds to replace the federal funds that had previously supported minority students. (The survey report appropriately noted that such an institutional response cannot be relied on in the event of further reductions in federal funds.)

9. National Commission on Student Financial Assistance, *Signs of Erosion: A Report on Graduate Education in America* (Washington, D.C.: NCSFA, December 1983).

10. National Research Council, *Summary Report, 1983: Doctorate Recipients from United States Universities* (Washington, D.C.: National Academy Press, 1984).

11. Council of Graduate Schools in the United States, Committee on Minority Graduate Education, "Survey of Minority Graduate Education," Washington, D.C., 1983.

Financial aid is available for minority graduate students through a variety of programs providing loans, fellowships, and assistantships. A critical question is whether promising minority students are aware of such programs and are dissuaded from attending graduate school by the actual lack of adequate financial aid or by the perceived lack of aid. Even talented minority undergraduates are often poorly integrated into the informal academic networks of undergraduate college life and are therefore less aware than white students of the nature of graduate education and the ways by which it can be financed.

### Perceived Labor Market Conditions

Total annual doctorate production declined by 9 percent from 1975 to 1983. Undoubtedly perceived labor market conditions contributed significantly to this reduction. The greatest decrease in earned doctorates was in the arts and humanities. The total labor market for doctorate recipients in these fields extends little beyond the academic, and the academic market is tight. The second largest decrease in earned doctorates was in engineering, where strong nonacademic markets are drawing potential students away from doctoral studies.[12]

The labor market has thus been generally unfavorable for doctorate recipients. In that context the 7 percent increase in minority doctorate recipients from 1975 to 1983 is encouraging. Trends for individual minority groups differ considerably, however: the 7 percent increase for all minorities contrasts with an 81 percent increase for Hispanics and a 4 percent decline for blacks (table 3).

Labor market conditions certainly interact with alternatives in career choices. Minorities are underrepresented in the corporate and professional sectors as well as in the academic community. It has frequently been asserted, but not verified, that a preponderance of the talented minority college graduates who form the recruitment pool for graduate programs select professional programs, such as law and medicine, that offer career options more attractive to them.

The competition from professional programs for minority participation in graduate education raises two separate issues for analysis. One is whether the most talented minority college graduates choose alternatives to graduate education independent of labor market conditions. Clearly, professional programs com-

---

12. Ernest May and Dorothy Blaney, *Careers for Humanists* (Academic Press, 1981); Michael S. McPherson's paper in this volume.

pete with graduate programs for talented students from both majority and minority baccalaureate populations. Some anecdotal evidence, however, suggests that the most talented minority students are more likely than similarly categorized white students to enroll in professional programs.

The second issue is whether, to a greater degree than white students, minorities pursuing postbaccalaureate education have shifted their preference from graduate to professional programs because of the generally declining labor market for Ph.D.'s. The data presented in table 6 indicate that this is not happening. From 1976 to 1981 the number of both minority and white students earning professional degrees increased 15 percent. Over the same period, however, the number of minority students receiving doctoral degrees increased 6 percent, while the number of white students receiving doctoral degrees decreased 9 percent.

The lack of role models has been cited as a factor in the persistence of minority underrepresentation in graduate education. Certainly there are few minority members on the faculties of the major research universities to serve as role models for minority undergraduates at those institutions. A higher proportion of minority undergraduates than of white undergraduates, however, express an intention to pursue an advanced degree. Further, with the exception of Native Americans, doctorate recipients from underrepresented minorities tend to earn their undergraduate degrees from nonresearch universities in states where their groups are clustered.[13] Many of these institutions, such as the historically black colleges and universities, have substantial numbers of minority faculty members.

Role models may be less a factor in deciding to attend graduate school than in taking the steps to implement that decision, such as choosing a field of study and choosing appropriate courses in preparation for graduate school. An undergraduate relationship with a faculty member actively involved in research may influence these choices. In graduate school, role models can play an important part in the success with which minority graduate students are able to integrate themselves into the informal extracurricular networks of students and faculty, where much professional development occurs.[14]

13. Dorothy M. Guilford and Joan Snyder, *Women and Minority Ph.D.s in the 1970's: A Data Book* (Washington, D.C.: National Academy of Sciences, 1977); Boone, Young and Associates, *Minority Enrollment in Graduate and Professional Schools* (Government Printing Office, June 1984).

14. Walter N. Allen, Angela Haddad, and Mary Kirkland, "Preliminary Report, 1982 Graduate Professional Survey, National Study of Black College Students" (Ann Arbor:

Table 6. *Doctorates and Professional Degrees, 1976 and 1981*

| | Doctorates | | | Professional degrees | | |
|---|---|---|---|---|---|---|
| Group | 1976 | 1981 | Percent change | 1976 | 1981 | Percent change |
| Black | 1,139 | 1,104 | −3 | 2,693 | 2,931 | 9 |
| Hispanic | 361 | 525 | 45 | 1,469 | 1,541 | 5 |
| Asian | 984 | 1,062 | 8 | 962 | 1,456 | 51 |
| Native American | 148 | 89 | −40 | 205 | 192 | −6 |
| All minorities | 2,632 | 2,780 | 6 | 5,329 | 6,120 | 15 |
| White | 24,722 | 22,400 | −9 | 56,307 | 64,551 | 15 |

Sources: National Research Council, *Summary Report, 1981;* National Center for Education Statistics, *Digest of Education Statistics, 1983–84.*

*Increasing minority participation in graduate education*

A variety of programs have been developed to increase recruitment and retention of minority graduate students. These programs generally fall into one of three categories: interaction with the undergraduate recruitment pool; graduate fellowship programs; and advising or mentoring programs for minority graduate students.

Name exchange programs assist institutions in identifying undergraduate minority students who may be eligible for graduate study. The most effective of these programs circulates to participating institutions the names of undergraduate minority students, accompanied by information on students' academic performance and areas of interest. Institutions are then able to contact eligible students with information about their graduate programs. Thus name exchanges also function as an information service for minority students.

Early intervention programs provide enhanced educational programs for talented minority undergraduates to increase their interest in and competitive preparation for graduate education. Key characteristics of these programs are early research experience, usually in the form of summer research internships, and financial support for those who successfully complete the undergraduate program and enroll in graduate school.

The Minority Access to Research Careers (MARC) Program conducted by the National Institutes of Health is a major multilevel research training support program designed to increase the numbers and capabilities of minority scientists engaged in biomedical research. Approximately 70 percent of MARC funds are used for an early intervention program, the Undergraduate Honors Pro-

University of Michigan, Center for Afro-American and African Studies, November 1984); Jaime E. Rodriguez and others, "Faculty Mentoring of Minority Graduate and Professional Students: The Irvine Experiment," Working Paper (University of California at Irvine, Division of Graduate Studies and Research, January 1984).

gram, which awards grants to institutions with substantial minority populations. Institutions receiving grants select able students for enhanced training. A major component of their training is an external summer research internship at a major research university. The program provides up to five years of fellowship support to distinguished graduates of the undergraduate program who are admitted to doctoral programs in biomedical science. Informal evaluations of the undergraduate grant program indicate that it has been successful in producing a competitive pool of minority graduate students.[15]

Individual universities and corporations, including Carnegie-Mellon University, the University of California at Santa Barbara, the National Action Council for Minorities in Engineering, and Bell Laboratories, support similar early intervention programs.

A large number of graduate fellowship programs, funded by federal, state, and private sources, provide support specifically to minorities for postbaccalaureate study in virtually all graduate and professional fields.[16] These programs focus on identifying and recruiting promising minority students. There are two general types of fellowship program. Individual "portable" fellowships are awarded directly to students, usually on the basis of the academic promise of students as judged by review panels. Institutional or departmental traineeships are grants to institutions or to individual departments or programs, which then select students to support with grant funds. Typically traineeships are also awarded competitively on the basis of review panel judgments, in this case, on the quality of graduate programs.

The federal government currently provides funds for both kinds of program. The National Science Foundation Minority Graduate Fellowship Program awards three-year fellowships to beginning graduate students from underrepresented minorities for graduate study in the mathematical, physical, biological, engineering, and social sciences, and in the history and philosophy of science. The Graduate and Professional Opportunities Program (GPOP), administered by the Department of Education, provides grants to institutions for the support of minorities and women in a wide

15. Personal communication, Elward Bynum, program director, MARC Program, National Institute of General Medical Sciences, National Institutes of Health.

16. Most of these programs are identified in a guide produced periodically by the Department of Education. See Linda Byrd-Johnson and Carol J. Smith, *Higher Education Opportunities for Minorities and Women . . . Annotated Selections* (GPO, 1983). *Directory of Special Programs for Minority Group Members: Career Information Services, Employment Skills Banks, Financial Aid Sources,* 3d ed. (Garrett Park, Md.: Garrett Park Press, 1980) also includes a large number of programs offered through individual universities.

variety of graduate and professional fields approved by the secretary of education.

Philanthropic foundations have been especially active in support of minority graduate education. Through the Committee on Institutional Cooperation (CIC), comprising the universities of the Big Ten plus the University of Chicago, the Lilly Foundation provides funds for graduate study in the social sciences; the Mellon Foundation, for graduate study in the humanities; and the Exxon Educational Foundation, for graduate study in the sciences and engineering. Through the Dorothy Danforth Compton Fellowship program, the Danforth Foundation has provided funds to each of ten universities—Brown, Chicago, Columbia, Howard, Stanford, the University of Texas at Austin, UCLA, Vanderbilt, the University of Washington, and Yale—to award fellowships to minority students who want to become college teachers. The Ford Foundation has recently announced the establishment of a new program of individual portable fellowships for minority graduate students.

Several corporations support minority fellowship programs, and a number of universities allocate substantial funds from their own resources for minority fellowships.

Another type of program focuses on increasing the retention rate of minority graduate students once enrolled. These programs range from counseling and advising services to highly structured faculty-student mentoring relationships. The University of California at Irvine has recently developed perhaps the most systematic mentoring program. The program awards funds to faculty-student pairs for both student support and research support, contingent on approval of a research proposal. Student and faculty participants must operate under a set of flexible guidelines that specify criteria for participation and responsibilities of the participants. The program explicitly identifies and monitors goals to be accomplished during the year.

Preliminary evaluations of this program are strongly positive. Student participants become involved early in substantive research, which usually leads directly into their dissertation research. Faculty report higher expectations of quality and sophistication of research that minorities are capable of performing. Several elements of the program appear to contribute to its success. The systematic structure built into the program ensures a match of research interests, a clear specification of program goals developed by each student-faculty pair, and a high level of interaction in the mentoring relationship. Students have financial support as research assistants, which ensures early substantive involvement in research and the concomitant opportunity to sharpen writing and analytical skills. Faculty incentives to participate include additional research assistants at no cost and funds to offset additional research support costs.[17]

**Conclusion**      Viewed against the declining baseline of overall doctoral degree production, encouraging progress is being made in increasing the participation of underrepresented minorities in doctoral programs. Blacks, Hispanics, and Native Americans remain substantially underrepresented, however. Their distribution across disciplines is sharply skewed, with more acute underrepresentation in science and engineering fields than in graduate education overall. Although the most effective long-term solutions to underrepresentation will focus on what happens in precollege education, much progress can be made now with programs designed to increase the number of minority college students enrolling in and successfully completing doctoral programs.

The two most effective approaches seem to be early intervention programs for undergraduates and graduate student mentoring programs. Through research internships and related educational activities, early intervention programs allow talented minority undergraduates direct involvement in those aspects of graduate education that they are least likely to encounter yet that are perhaps the most central to success in graduate school. These programs also make contact with students who are committed to postbaccalaureate education but would most likely not have chosen to enter a doctoral program without early exposure to research. Properly designed, an early intervention program can be responsive to each of the factors that affect minority participation in graduate education: increasing the size of the undergraduate pool, enhancing academic preparation, providing predictable financial aid, developing career prospects that successfully compete with alternatives, and providing role models.

The key to the success of faculty-student mentoring programs appears to be a faculty-student relationship that ensures early, intensive, closely monitored involvement in research. This involvement improves the skills and self-confidence of the student and raises the expectations of the faculty about the capabilities of minority graduate students.

Fellowship programs are the most frequently used mechanism for targeting support on minority graduate students. The most

17. Rodriguez and others, "Faculty Mentoring" and personal communication.

effective programs select recipients based on demonstrated achievement and future promise and provide long-term financial support. Fellowship programs are likely to be most helpful if they are incorporated into a larger systematic strategy involving intervention with minority undergraduates and assimilation of minority graduate students into all aspects of the graduate program, particularly research and teaching.

To improve existing programs and to develop new approaches for increasing minority participation in graduate education, many factors need explanation. What causes the different rates of participation by different minority groups? How do the availability and nature of financial aid affect the decision to attend graduate school? What are the best predictors of success for minority students in graduate education? What procedures increase the likelihood of success in graduate education? When and in what ways do role models affect behavior? How are postbaccalaureate decisions affected by perceived labor market conditions? Do minority and white students differ in these perceptions?

Some of these questions can be answered only by thorough studies. A carefully constructed survey of minority college seniors, however, could quickly produce a considerable amount of useful information. Regular systematic evaluation of existing programs can also generate valuable information. Such evaluations not only would provide information for refining those programs, but also would produce fundamental knowledge concerning minority participation in graduate education.

The major responsibility of the federal and state governments is to improve the condition of minority education at the elementary and secondary levels. Equal education at these levels will do more to equalize minority postbaccalaureate opportunities than any other efforts. The federal government should assist in providing the necessary funds for research on factors affecting minority graduate education, as well as assist in supporting minority graduate education programs themselves. To be operated effectively, programs such as early intervention and graduate mentoring are unavoidably costly, and universities cannot underwrite the costs for such programs on the scale that is needed.

Foundations can be especially helpful in working with universities to develop innovative approaches to increasing minority participation and to filling gaps not met by existing programs. Corporations, singly and in consortia, can effectively target resources on minority graduate education in fields of importance to them.

The universities must assume a major responsibility for increasing minority participation in graduate education. The ultimate success of early intervention and graduate mentoring programs will depend on concerted university efforts to identify and recruit promising minority students, on faculty commitment to minority students and their education, and on administrative procedures that will encourage and support faculty involvement in minority graduate education and in outreach programs for minority undergraduates.

The increasing attrition of blacks, Hispanics, and Native Americans at each higher level of the educational system raises serious social concerns about the causes of such systematically differential outcomes. Demographic projections raise an additional pragmatic concern for the future capacity of this nation to produce sufficient numbers of teachers, researchers, and scholars. The available evidence indicates that progress is being made and can be accelerated through a concentrated effort in research and program development carried out jointly by universities, federal and state governments, foundations, and corporations.

# Change and Transition in Graduate Education

## MICHAEL J. PELCZAR, JR.

THE CONCERN of the public about the condition of education has focused largely on the nation's elementary and secondary schools, but higher education has not been overlooked. Indeed, this end of the spectrum of education, including graduate education, is receiving increasing attention. With evidence gathered from across the graduate community, the National Commission on Student Financial Assistance (NCSFA) prepared a comprehensive report. Although the report focuses primarily on graduate education in the arts and sciences, the commission's concern is the condition of the entire graduate enterprise, particularly the interdependence between graduate education and research. The commission acknowledges the great diversity that characterizes American graduate education.[1]

The NCSFA report concludes that a strong national security program, a healthy, growing economy, and prospects for improvement in the quality of life all depend on a system of vigorous, high-quality graduate education. This relationship is more important now than ever before. In the transition from an industrial society to an information society, knowledge has become the critical commodity. High technologies such as genetic engineering, silicon chips and microprocessors, telecomputers, fiber optics, and robotics are all making heavy demands for more and more knowledge. But our need for new knowledge is not limited to science and technology. There are equally important needs for knowledge about and better understanding of world cultures, languages, arts and humanities, and other disciplines that contribute to human values and to the improvement of earth's environment. Kingman Brewster, former president of Yale University and erstwhile U.S. ambassador to the Court of St. James, summarized the importance of international education: "International education is education for survival."

1. National Commission on Student Financial Assistance, Subcommittee on Graduate Education, John Brademas, chairman, "Signs of Trouble and Erosion: A Report on Graduate Education in America" (Washington, D.C.: NCSFA, 1983).

The NCSFA report stressed this inherent relation between the condition of graduate education and the condition of our society at large. "Few of us comprehend," it declared, "that graduate education and research are the bedrock of every important area of our national life."[2] But as the title of the report suggests, the condition of graduate education is not robust; it is, in fact, undernourished.

Two other study panels have recently reported on the changing conditions and prospects of graduate education. The "Colloquium on Graduate Education in America," cosponsored by the Carnegie Foundation and the Institute for Advanced Study of Princeton University, considered the relation between graduate and undergraduate education.[3] The second study group, reporting to the secretary of education on "The Conditions of Excellence in American Higher Education," called for all graduate students "to present evidence of a broad liberal arts education" to balance the specialization of advanced studies.[4]

Steven Muller, president of Johns Hopkins University, has said, "We are . . . already in an environment for higher education that represents the most drastic change since the founding of the University of Paris and Bologna and the other great universities some eight or nine centuries ago." He asserted that universities will face dramatic changes in a number of important areas. In the decades to come the university will be serving a new clientele, delivering services in new ways, and reexamining what and how it teaches. Muller warned that within five years the faculty may not understand how their students are learning. "The most serious problem is the post-Gutenberg university with a pre-Gutenberg faculty."[5]

New options are needed in our programs of graduate education, programs that will attract highly qualified students and will prepare them for productive performance both inside and outside the academic halls, by means of broader, more flexible curricula. To accomplish these goals, the universities need new resources. In many instances the universities also need some modifications in

2. Ibid., p. 13.

3. Carnegie Foundation for the Advancement of Teaching and the Institute for Advanced Study, "Colloquium on Graduate Education in America" (Princeton, N.J.: CFAT, 1983).

4. National Institute of Education, Study Group on the Conditions of Excellence in American Higher Education, "Involvement in Learning: Realizing the Potential of American Higher Education," Final Report (U.S. Department of Education, 1984), p. 64.

5. Steven Muller, "The Post-Gutenberg University," *Current Issues in Higher Education,* no. 1 (1983–84), pp. 32, 38.

faculty attitudes. Eric Ashby has said that our universities need faculty members who are willing to "reconcile, somehow, the intellectual detachment essential for good scholarship with the social concern essential for the good life."[6]

What are some of the changes now occurring or being contemplated that will affect planning for the next decade of graduate education? In 1983 the Council of Graduate Schools (CGS) in the United States made some forecasts for graduate education in the next ten years. Total enrollment in graduate programs will show a small annual increase during the decade. Enrollments will become more differentiated by institution (location and function) and by subject area and curriculum. Enrollment of regular-age students in the arts and sciences programs will decline, and enrollment in professional or career-oriented masters' programs will continue to increase across student-age groups. Professional school enrollments in law and medicine will stabilize (or decrease slightly). Midcareer students will return in increasing numbers to do additional graduate work part time. The number of women in graduate study will continue to increase. Black and Hispanic enrollments will increase slightly, if at all, in the first half of the decade, but these enrollments will accelerate slightly, notably among Hispanics, in the second half. The enrollment of foreign students will level off, in part because of the high cost of education in the United States for persons from developing countries. The elite research universities will show little change in overall enrollment, although the subject area changes within the institutions may be large. The changes that do occur will be largely self-induced. The number of these elite universities will shrink during the decade. Enrollment will be strongest in universities that provide quality programs for part-time, career-oriented students with technological interests.[7]

The CGS report predicts that financial resources will remain tight for the next decade, and this will be one of the universities' major impediments in adapting to new needs. Federal support for graduate education (mainly channeled through student aid) will remain essentially level, with slight increases in the first half of the decade and additional increases in the second half. The combination of loans and fellowship funds, in some balance, will remain. Federal research support, particularly in applied areas,

6. Eric Ashby, *Adapting Universities to a Technological Society* (San Francisco: Jossey-Bass, 1974), p. 85.

7. Paul A. Albrecht, "The Next Decade," Council of Graduate Schools in the United States, internal communication, December 1983.

will increase. State support will probably not keep pace with inflation in many cases. Tuition in both public and private universities, but notably in the latter, will continue to rise sharply. A tuition increase could affect enrollments and could even cause some movement from private to public institutions. Philanthropy will continue to provide increased support for education, but it will not assume a significantly greater portion of education costs.

The continued shift of emphasis in graduate education from the traditional arts and sciences to more career-oriented, techno-logical, and applied programs will cause change. The distinction between "academic" and "professional" education, already blurred, will continue to recede. Industry-university collaboration in re-search and education will increase slowly. As this collaboration increases, the relation of graduate education to its patrons and clients will increase in importance. The case for graduate endeavors will have to be presented in more differentiated, focused, and supported ways. A new level of social responsibility for graduate education may emerge. The report also notes the present strong interest in elementary and secondary education and describes its effect on graduate education as an "important potential trend." Computers, telecommunications, and other technologies will also have a potentially significant effect on teaching, learning, research, and other dimensions of educational processes, such as delivery systems and interinstitutional coordination and cooperation.

John E. Corbally, president of the MacArthur Foundation, recently challenged universities to develop a comprehensive sup-port rationale. "Foundations hope to do significant things," he observed. "But foundations fund activities that meet their goals, not yours. And foundation goals rarely include the preservation of colleges and universities. The fate of university research is not in the hands of the private foundations of the nation. Society needs research. There are many ways in which this need can be met—one of them is university-based research. It is hardly possible to argue that there would be no research without the universities. Present existence is not sufficient to justify a continuing future."[8] This is a very sobering thought for higher education.

Other interesting developments are the university-industry partnerships that have been the subject of many recent national and regional conferences. University-industry partnership is not a new phenomenon, but it has been receiving a high level of attention in all quarters—the academic community, the industrial

8. John E. Corbally, "Private Funding of University Research" (Athens: University of Georgia, National Conference on the Future of University Research, 1984).

community, and local, state, and federal governments. Scores of actual partnership arrangements have occurred. These partnerships are viewed as a potentially significant opportunity for exploiting technological innovations to enhance economic growth and to expand the pool of resources available to universities.

University-industry cooperative arrangements are not free from potential problems. Problems may arise from differences between universities and industries in practices and in objectives. Industries may want results in months, whereas the typical M.S. and Ph.D. research programs span two to five years. Furthermore, industries may not fully appreciate scholarship or broad education and schooling, favoring instead narrow, subject-intensive training. An additional problem centers on competition. An area of research frequently includes several independent researchers. Involving one faculty member in a research agreement does not prevent another faculty member from working in a closely related area with another company. Finally, universities and industries frequently have an equipment difference: university equipment may be outmoded, whereas industries typically have state-of-the-art equipment.

Universities must maintain a traditional balance of program objectives. Popular subjects need to be made part of the curricula, but not at the expense of the more traditional—but perhaps currently less attractive—academic subject areas. A smaller university must be careful not to exceed its level of useful energy, time, and funds for engaging in these programs. Further, no institution of any size can afford to let new industrial partnerships transform teaching responsibilities. The practice of allowing senior faculty members to concentrate on industry-supported research should be weighed against the potential loss of a superb teacher and the effect of that loss on the quality of education at the institution.

There is a danger that industrial support will concentrate on certain leading institutions to the detriment of university departments that are on the rise. This will be especially true if industrial support comes to be regarded erroneously as a substitute for basic governmental support.

Guidelines must be developed for university-industry cooperative arrangements. Caution should be taken to ensure that the appropriate faculty governing bodies are consulted at the negotiation stage and that these bodies have preestablished, widely accepted policies for handling these arrangements. Most of the relationships that have been publicized, notably those between major industries and major research universities, are not good models for all partnerships. What happens between Exxon or MIT and a university is not particularly relevant to the relationship between another university and the small engineering company that wants its development work done in a university laboratory.

The issue of patents, copyrights, and royalties is frequently troublesome to resolve. Industry may insist on full ownership of discoveries coming from contract research or on a royalty-free, nonexclusive, worldwide license with rights to sublicense the patent or the process. Consultancies with an industry that is also supporting research by the same faculty member can raise questions about the locus of discoveries.

Freedom and openness of information exchange, integral to the academic environment, must be preserved. The right to publish should be established in contract or grant provisions.

The university-industry partnership has much to offer. For industry, support of universities ensures flow of new staff in the future. For the university, these partnerships can yield additional resources (materials and equipment, money, human talent).

Limited resources, increased complexity and cost of research instruments, availability of new communications systems—these and other factors are encouraging universities to explore new synergistic coalitions. As the number of academic jobs stabilizes, institutions need to be sensitive to the fact that there are other marketplaces for their graduates. Industries offer one such source of employment, and the new partnerships aid in placing graduates. The university is provided with the possibility of using industry personnel in the classroom and in laboratories. Smaller universities have access to new equipment and technology. In general these relationships facilitate universities' fund-raising. They also benefit the universities by providing corporate assistance in lobbying efforts.

University-industry partnerships also enhance technology transfer. The most effective form of technology transfer is for industry to hire the people coming out of first-class university laboratories, since those people bring to their employer state-of-the-art experience in their particular field. It is, therefore, to the long-term advantage of any industry to participate in maintaining the quality of those institutions and those departments that educate and train individuals for industry.

University-industry partnerships can increase the opportunities for academic researchers and their discoveries to influence industry and economic development by improving performance and output. State-supported institutions in particular help stimulate local and state economic development. Improved university-industry partnerships can promote these economic development goals. Finally, university expertise can assist national, regional, and local economic development through research to improve use of national resources.

The benefits and problems associated with industry-supported research are distilled in the preamble of Harvard University's statement "Guidelines on Research Conducted with Industry":

> Harvard University welcomes industrially supported research agreements because they can stimulate its investigators, promote technological transfer, and provide the University with valuable support. At the same time, it recognizes the need to avoid arrangements that might compromise, or seem to compromise, its intellectual principles and purposes and the freedom of inquiry the members of its faculties enjoy.
>
> As an institution, the University benefits from public research funds and the public's trust, and it has an obligation to develop its research discoveries with concern for the public's interest.[9]

Despite the apparently substantial benefits to be derived from university-industry partnerships, various sectors of the academic community are apprehensive. The level of trust between the prospective partners needs to improve. Members of the academic community must have a greater concern for the promotion of the interests of the university as a community of scholars rather than as a community of independent, competitive entrepreneurs. Imaginative, forward-looking academics could establish networks for research and instruction that would lead the way for regional, national, and global coalitions whose existence will strengthen research and learning opportunities for students and faculties.[10]

Related to the consortia concept is that of centers for advanced study, notably in the humanities. O. B. Hardison, former director of the Folger Shakespeare Library, has referred to these centers as the "fifth layer" of American higher education (after primary and elementary, secondary, undergraduate, and graduate education). Such centers are practical and beneficial for advanced study in the humanities. They are the equivalent of laboratories in that they provide the infrastructure needed for research. They are "an

9. Harvard University, "Rules on Industry-related Research Adopted," *Harvard Gazette,* May 20, 1983, p. 4.

10. Frank E. Vandiver, "Universities: The Next Iteration," *Science,* vol. 220 (August 24, 1984).

example of the new connections that the humanities will have to establish if they are to remain vital during the coming decade."[11]

The knowledge explosion, new technologies and instrumentation, the fragmentation of subject material, and the need for interdisciplinary study of topics—these and other changes raise questions about the appropriateness of some existing degree programs and suggest the need for new programs. In a field like biology, the changes may include an increased emphasis on strong background in the hard sciences and an increased use of computers. There may be increased specialization, and as a consequence research may focus at the cellular and subcellular (molecular) level of life processes. This specialization may in turn call into question the traditional divisions of biology, zoology, and microbiology, with a subsequent decrease in interest in systematic biology and conventional ecology. Further changes may include trends toward "mission-oriented" research projects and accelerated transfer of results from basic research to practical applications. Existing departmental structures in some instances obstruct the flow of knowledge. High levels of specialization, which are regarded more as training than as education, also cause concern. The primary objective of the university is to educate and train the next generation of scholars and researchers, and it is for this reason that an excellent research program must be maintained.

Graduate programs need to attract a fair share of the nation's best and brightest students to ensure a continuous flow of scholars, researchers, and practitioners into society. To educate and train the best and brightest of students at the graduate level requires top-flight faculty, good physical facilities, including information resources and laboratories, and an environment supportive of the pursuit of knowledge.

The practical issue is how to assess quality. Great variations and uncertainties are associated with a definition of quality, but program quality must be assessed. Resources at all levels are shrinking. Funds must be allocated to programs in which quality exists or to programs in which there is assurance that quality will be improved. The considerable expansion in the last decade in the number and type of graduate programs has raised questions of duplication and quality. Agencies at many levels want to know if they are receiving their money's worth—quality education. Accrediting agencies likewise are being urged to make judgments on the quality of academic programs.

11. O. B. Hardison, "The Virtues of Necessity: New Connections for the Humanities," paper prepared for the twenty-third annual meeting of the Council of Graduate Schools in the U.S., Washington, D.C., 1983, p. 80.

National surveys of graduate programs for the purpose of making judgments on quality date from the early 1920s. Raymond Hughes conducted a survey in 1924 in which he included universities that awarded doctoral degrees. He ranked thirty-eight universities in twenty graduate disciplines by the number of top scholars employed.[12] This first attempt at assessment of the quality of graduate programs was followed by six similar but expanded surveys. All these surveys rated institutions (and their programs) and evaluated quality on the basis of a reputation and research-related characteristics (Ph.D. programs).

The Conference Board sponsored the most recent comprehensive assessment of quality of graduate programs (the Conference Board includes representatives of the American Council of Learned Societies, American Council on Education, National Research Council, and Social Science Research Council).[13] The survey used sixteen characteristics to evaluate individual research doctorate programs. The major categories included program size, characteristics of graduates, reputation (survey results), university library size, research support, and publication records.

The graduate community remains apprehensive about the present methodology for assessment of program quality. It fears that the program evaluations are likely to reflect bias toward institutions that are already generally esteemed (many departments may be given a high rating because of what is called the halo effect). The methodology of the assessment favors traditional offerings, thus tending to reinforce the status quo. Large, orthodox programs are rewarded with good ratings for concentration on research and scholarship, while quality of teaching and other program objectives are ignored. These assessments add little to self-knowledge about a program, so they make no contribution to efforts for improvement. Finally, the characteristics of program quality are multidimensional. All graduate programs do not have the same objectives, so a single set of criteria cannot determine the quality of all programs.

In 1984 the Association of Governing Boards of Universities and Colleges, with support from the Carnegie Corporation, issued a report on strengthening presidential leadership of universities.[14] One of the observations made in this report was that presidents

12. Raymond M. Hughes, *A Study of the Graduate Schools in America* (Oxford, Ohio: Miami University Press, 1925).

13. L. V. Jones, G. Lindzey, and P. E. Coggeshall, *An Assessment of Research Doctorate Programs in the United States* (Washington, D.C.: National Academy Press, 1982).

14. *Presidents Make a Difference,* Report of the Commission on Strengthening Presidential Leadership, Clark Kerr, director (Washington, D.C.: Association of Governing Boards of Universities and Colleges, 1984).

are too little engaged in making long-term plans and in preparing their institutions for the extended future. The diverse and urgent demands upon presidents make it difficult for them to devote enough time and effort to long-term planning.

In these times, campuses have a growing hunger for academic direction. Among the reasons for this demand are financial resources, demographic changes, the knowledge explosion, fragmentation of subject material, and the need for interdisciplinary programs. This avidity for leadership provides an opportunity and a responsibility for the graduate dean to assist the president in the development of new directions. The dean is usually better situated than any other officer within the management structure to be—or to become—aware of internal developments and external educational and social trends that affect those developments. The Council of Graduate Schools in the United States describes the role of the graduate school dean:

> The chief graduate school officer has institution-wide responsibilities to foster and facilitate interdisciplinary and inter-college graduate programs and research activities. This individual performs a major role in both academic and budgetary planning and in institutional organization. The chief graduate school officer should be a member of, or be represented on, councils or committees whose actions have an impact on graduate education (such as budget policy, library, computer resources, and research facilities).[15]

A national commitment for graduate education is essential. A strong graduate education program is vital to the continuing health of all of American society. The higher learning that it provides to individuals, the new knowledge that it discovers through research, and the services that it supplies are central to the health of the economy, to the well-being of our citizenry, and to the defense of the nation. Such an important enterprise needs a national commitment to flourish, a commitment that will guarantee a continuity of high-quality teaching, learning, and public service. A national commitment means a nationwide effort to acquaint the public with the vital position of graduate education in American society. The American people are, after all, graduate education's constituency. They must know what it does, what it stands for, and how it repays their support. A national commitment means maintaining the opportunity for the nation's most talented and capable students to go to graduate school so that they can, in

---

15. Council of Graduate Schools, *The Organization and Administration of Graduate Schools in the U.S.* (Washington, D.C.: CGS, 1981), p. 3.

turn, better serve society. Finally, a national commitment means action. We have heard the chorus of voices in the reports on the educational condition of the nation. We must begin now to implement the best and the most urgent of those ideas. In all these steps, the graduate school and its chief administrative officer need to work with other top university administrators to provide the leadership.

# The Outlook for Graduate Science and Engineering

HARVEY BROOKS

THE RAPID changes that have taken place over the past five years in disciplinary preferences among undergraduates have serious implications for university faculties. The dramatic growth of engineering enrollments and the shift among the engineering disciplines (from civil engineering to electrical engineering and computer science) pose a question whether the universities should play for time, with the expectation that the shifts in interest are temporary, or whether they should respond more urgently with more radical adaptations, including modifications of the tenure system itself. The current shifts in preference appear to be greater and more rapid than those of the 1960s. The rapid growth that favored the reconfiguring of faculties in the 1960s is absent in the 1980s, thus diminishing faculty resilience and intensifying the effects of shifts in disciplines.

*Issues arising out of current trends*

How necessary is it to maintain the flow of young faculty into the graduate education system? Is it necessary only for research, or is it equally essential for maintaining the vitality of teaching? The issue becomes more urgent because of new tools, such as computers and computerized data bases, and new ways of accessing, managing, and using information. How practical is it for universities to address this problem by bringing in temporary adjunct instructors from industry, armed with the latest techniques and not requiring long-term commitments from the university?

All levels of education seem to be on the threshold of becoming more capital intensive, with the long predicted but long delayed communications revolution now finally poised to take off. The implication that teaching will become less labor intensive is not so certain, especially at the most advanced levels. The same number of teachers may be needed to do different things. Until now planning for higher education has been anchored to the concept of the student-faculty ratio, yet there is almost no rationale other than tradition for the present ratio. Indeed student-faculty

181

ratios vary widely between certain professional schools and arts and sciences departments. Law schools give, perhaps, the most striking example, with medical schools at the opposite extreme.

The absence of a rationale for the student-faculty ratio does not necessarily mean that the present almost universal ratios are wrong or make no sense. The combination of available new technology, economic pressures, and the lack of a solid rationale, however, strongly suggests the need for much small-scale or pilot experimentation with more capital-intensive and less labor-intensive models of both undergraduate and graduate instruction, especially in the sciences and in engineering. Two challenges emerge for educators: how to design such experiments so that meaningful conclusions can be drawn from them within a reasonable time and how to develop evaluation criteria with enough credibility to lead to policy change.

The dramatic rise in the number of foreign students, especially students from so-called less-developed countries, is a focus of attention in the 1980s. Study of this problem requires more hard data and analysis on how the large and growing population of foreign students in U.S. graduate and professional schools benefits or harms U.S. society in general and American higher education in particular. Who are the winners and who are the losers in this situation? At present the foreign student population exists in the academic marketplace without serious consideration of either the positive or the negative consequences that may result. Should there be some kind of central national policy, or is the present decentralized system of decisions best in the long run? Can a central authority assimilate and interpret all the information necessary to formulate a coherent policy and predict its consequences?

Does the present de facto American policy, for example, contribute to the brain drain from third world nations, thus retarding the development and modernization of societies in the third world, especially the poorest societies? Does the American policy expand the opportunities and intellectual horizons of thousands of individuals who would otherwise be unproductive and frustrated within their own societies? Should U.S. graduate education devote greater resources and effort to bringing more of the underrepresented groups in American society into graduate and professional education than to training aliens? Would such a step use American advanced training capacity to educate people with less potential to contribute either to American society or to world social development? How do we balance enhancing social equity within the United States against maximizing the productivity of the U.S. research and engineering system?

Does our heavy involvement in the training of foreign nationals contribute to the export of American know-how to our potential commercial competitors or military rivals in the world, or does it enhance American capacity for innovation and experimentation? Are we generating future markets and political friends in the world among the students we train, or are we building up the enemies and competitors who will eventually bury us?

Science and engineering have a great potential demand for continuing education. The accelerating rate of technological change, the intensifying competition in world and domestic markets, and the ever-increasing complexity of managing technology will generate a need for lifelong learning at all levels of the work force. Which institutions will be in the best position to meet this greatly expanded need for educational services? Should the responsibility rest primarily in the current educational establishment or in new types of institutions? Should the need for lifelong learning be met by marketlike institutions that would capitalize on the new technologies available for this purpose? Is the nature of continuing education such that we cannot afford to depend only on market forces to develop and deliver the required services in the public interest? If we depend too much on the market, for example, is there a danger that the needs of small business will be neglected? Should industry and universities collaborate closely in continuing education? To what extent can the expanding market for continuing education be used to offset the adverse economic consequences for the universities of the declining college-age cohort? Finally, does educational technology have a different potential role in the field of continuing education? Would keeping continuing education within the university system provide an economic support base and a channel for the introduction of new educational technology into graduate education more generally?

During the expansion of the 1960s research support in the universities was sold to the public and to Congress on the basis that it was necessary to train the high-level technical manpower needed to meet the national commitments required by military-technological competition with the Soviet Union and the burgeoning requirements of our health care system. Today in some respects the situation may be reversed, with the public more sold on the need for and the economic benefits from basic and generic applied research than on the need for graduate education, especially Ph.D. education. The public, in other words, is now more skeptical that the universities are the best locale for basic and generic applied research, especially when that research is being justified for its benefits to the market economy rather than for its benefits to public sector responsibilities such as health or environmental protection. The idea that the universities are the principal locale for virtually all forms of research in the public domain needs restatement and updating.

The case for a large component of publicly sharable research also needs restatement. Proprietary research by itself will not meet the needs even of the private economy. At a certain level of generality, the knowledge needs of industry are better served by the wide sharing of research results and by the free flow of scientific and generic technological information than by additional proprietary research. This proposition is indirectly called into question by the control of scientific information flowing abroad, which is detrimental to free communication within our own scientific community; by wider general acceptance of the legitimacy of proprietary research in universities; by recent changes in patent and copyright law; and by the change from public to private of numerous services previously delivered exclusively by government or by the nonprofit sector. These developments are not necessarily bad, but they do reflect a political climate that could be detrimental to the unique role of universities as the leading repositories and generators of public knowledge. Even traditional free library services are being invaded by proprietary organizations and technology.

Since the boom of the 1960s, infrastructure generally has been steadily deteriorating. Deterioration has occurred in both buildings and equipment in the sciences and engineering, but the facilities situation is probably the worst. The prospects of meeting even a fraction of total infrastructure needs through traditional sources of public and charitable financing seem dim indeed. New modes of financing that do not depend so exclusively on government largesse, political decisionmaking, or the generosity of wealthy donors must be developed to resolve the problem. The outlook is darkened by the prospect of changes in the tax laws, which may severely curtail incentives for large private donations to universities.

One of the most disturbing secondary consequences of the reduction in budgeted federal funds for university facilities for science and engineering has been the success of a number of institutions in bypassing both the budgetary process in the executive branch and the peer review process of the scientific agencies.

These institutions have gone directly to Congress for special appropriations for particular projects. The appropriations are usually attached as riders to unrelated legislation. This practice has been publicly condemned by spokesmen of the scientific and academic communities, who, however, recognize that it is a symptom of government's abnegation of responsibility. The peer review process is most fair and effective when the stakes in any one decision are quite low, as is true of the typical project research grant. As the stakes become larger, even peer review becomes less effective. As the resources available become minuscule in relation to needs, the selection process, however well designed in theory, becomes more and more politicized, until eventually people begin to identify and to exploit the back channels to the public purse that are endemic to the American political system of checks and balances.

The universities may need to develop some kind of collective financing system for both student aid and facilities development. Individual state systems have initiated a form of collective financing through special bonding authority. One way of financing facilities and expensive equipment might involve the use of marketlike mechanisms, with recovery of capital costs through assessment of operating charges to research grants and instructional budgets. Small-scale pilot experiments, with careful evaluation conducted by independent assessors before embarking on across-the-board programs, are an arrangement universities and industry might emulate.

*Some broader philosophical issues and choices*

Should a primary goal of graduate education be regarded as the transfer of explicit specialized knowledge and skills to the next generation? Should another primary goal be to equip the individual for lifetime learning? How would these two purposes differ in their practical requirements for curriculum content and teaching modes? Do our present systems of graduate and professional education depend too much on memory of specific subject matter and too little on the development of skills in the use of new information technologies to formulate and solve problems? Our understanding of how adults actually learn and how they use what they learn in their professions is almost nonexistent.

The pace of technological progress demonstrates the futility of trying to keep large numbers of universities at the forefront of the state of the art in many different fields of knowledge at the same time, perhaps especially in engineering and technology. Two questions relate to this problem. How much access to state-of-the-art equipment is really necessary, especially if one adopts the lifelong-learning rather than the information-transfer model of advanced education? How much more could be achieved with shared resources, especially resources shared by universities and industry for both research and instruction?

Multipurpose tools of research and teaching, such as computers and data base accessing techniques, must be distinguished from special-purpose equipment whose usefulness is more restricted. Resource sharing may be more feasible with special-purpose equipment, but managing the arrangements is a challenge. One solution might encourage collaboration in both advanced research and advanced teaching equipment among universities in a region. Advanced instruction could be conducted in shared centers such as the proposed Microelectronics Center in Westborough, Massachusetts. Universities have learned how to do this effectively for graduate student and faculty research in expensive fields such as high-energy-particle physics and radioastronomy. A modest step further would use the same approach in advanced laboratory instruction. Collaboration with industry might be fruitful in some applied areas. Networks of regional centers, used for both research and instruction (including continuing education), could be shared by many institutions within reasonable geographical proximity.

Most academic planning today is done on the basis of predictions that are presumed to be free of surprises, with no changes in existing trends in federal budgets, in the economy, in student demographics, or in disciplinary preferences or career aspirations. Surprises, however, have been the rule rather than the exception in the past. Academic planning must somehow come to grips with the challenge of contingency planning without becoming paralyzed by the resulting caution. At the very least, planning should try to examine academic policies with respect to reasonably likely contingencies not included in the mainstream projections on which the policies are based.

One reason for the absence of contingency planning has been that, if a surprise is sufficiently disastrous for a large enough number of institutions, the government is likely to take action to forestall or to mitigate the disaster, and this becomes another component of the surprise. Rather than try to anticipate both the surprise and the countermeasures, planners have tended to ignore both. There may, however, be some virtue in having academic planners for the universities as a group think through in advance what countermeasures they would be prepared to advocate and what political strategy they should follow as a group should one of these contingencies actually arise. The planners should try to allow for surprises that seem to be in the realm of reasonable probability. These might include:

—a drastic scaling down of defense R&D spending because of the budget deficit and because of a decision to concentrate on force readiness in our defense posture;

—the increasing urgency of the federal deficit problem, which could change public and congressional attitudes toward appropriate responsibility of government in many areas hitherto considered untouchable;

—acceleration of the federal policy of exporting more responsibilities to the private sector or to state or local government;

—a return of double-digit inflation;

—leveling of growth in the information technology industry with reduced demand for scientists and engineers in that sector;

—regulation that drastically curtails access of foreign nationals to certain fields of graduate education and basic research;

—revival of the reaction of the late 1960s against technology and technical progress;

—tax reforms that reduce the incentive for private donations to educational institutions and possibly restrict the purposes for which such gifts can be used;

—increasing regulation of research; and

—legislation to mandate geographical distribution of all research funds spent by selected federal agencies in universities.

In the new environment of the 1980s pilot or experimental programs should test different mechanisms for stimulating or supporting advanced training and research. Possible examples include:

—more extensive use of career awards for researchers of demonstrated high originality and productivity, such as the MacArthur awards or Guggenheim fellowships in the private sector or the Waterman award of NSF;

—joint industry-university facilities, with capital financed by industry (with possible partial capital recovery from user charges) and joint operational financing by the users;

—grants that leave greater discretion to the local institution or laboratory, even at the expense of the agency project research budget;

—financing academic science or engineering projects through increased cost sharing with private industry or with state or local government;

—facilities sharing and cooperative research by universities and government laboratories, with extra financial incentives to the government laboratories; and

—extension of the use of the cooperative agreement instrument by government agencies and laboratories or universities.

*Data needs*      Universities are beginning to be much more active in the development of long-range academic plans, and many of these reports are being published. The universities could commission individual scholars to analyze these reports to elicit common and divergent themes and assumptions for the benefit of all institutions and government policymakers. Part of the analysis might include surveys by a university of the attitudes and career experiences of its own graduate students at various intervals after graduation, including, if possible, students who did not earn an advanced degree. The universities could incorporate some of these data into broader policy studies for higher education. Another part of the analysis might include data on mobility and career change, evaluated in such a way that various demographic and socioeconomic characteristics in the backgrounds of individuals could be correlated with the individuals' educational experience.

Any studies that could throw light on the net value to American society and the U.S. economy of the advanced training of foreign students in U.S. universities would contribute to a growing debate concerning the size and possible policy control over the population of such students in our graduate schools.

Admissions to graduate schools, especially in the sciences, are based on various quantitative measures of student quality such as high school ranking or grade point average, Scholastic Aptitude Test (SAT) scores, and Graduate Record Examination (GRE) scores. Some data already exist on the correlation between these measures and subsequent performance in graduate school, but more data are needed on graduate students' subsequent career experiences. Data in general should be differentiated by institution and by the background characteristics of the students.

# Conference Participants

*with their affiliation at the time of the conference*

Robert McC. Adams  *Smithsonian Institution*
Laurence Berlowitz  *Massachusetts Biotechnology Research Institute*
Sherman Beychok  *Columbia University*
Ilene Birkwood  *Hewlett-Packard Company*
William A. Blinn  *AT&T Bell Laboratories*
John O'M. Bockris  *Texas A&M University*
Harvey Brooks  *Harvard University*
John C. Crowley  *Association of American Universities*
Morton M. Denn  *University of California at Berkeley*
Humphrey Doermann  *Bush Foundation*
Alan Fechter  *National Research Council*
Penny D. Foster  *National Science Foundation*
A. Lee Fritschler  *Brookings Institution*
Albert J. Gelpi  *Stanford University*
Mary A. Golliday  *National Science Foundation*
James W. Johnson  *University of Iowa*
Carlos Kruytbosch  *National Science Foundation*
Jules LaPidus  *Council of Graduate Schools in the U.S.*
Michael S. McPherson  *Brookings Institution*
Michael J. Pelczar, Jr.  *Council of Graduate Schools in the U.S.*
William F. Raub  *National Institutes of Health*
Rustum Roy  *Pennsylvania State University*
F. James Rutherford  *American Association for the Advancement of Science*
Anne Scanley  *National Academy of Sciences*
Hedy E. Sladovich  *Meloy Laboratories*
Bruce L. R. Smith  *Brookings Institution*
Robert G. Snyder  *consultant, science and education policy*
Dwayne C. Spriestersbach  *University of Iowa*
Nam P. Suh  *National Science Foundation*

189

David Timothy  *U.S. Department of Agriculture*
Martin A. Trow  *University of California at Berkeley*
William Turner  *International Business Machines*
John C. Vaughn  *Association of American Universities*
Clarence L. Ver Steeg  *Northwestern University*
F. Karl Willenbrock  *Southern Methodist University*
Linda S. Wilson  *University of Illinois at Urbana-Champaign*

# Index